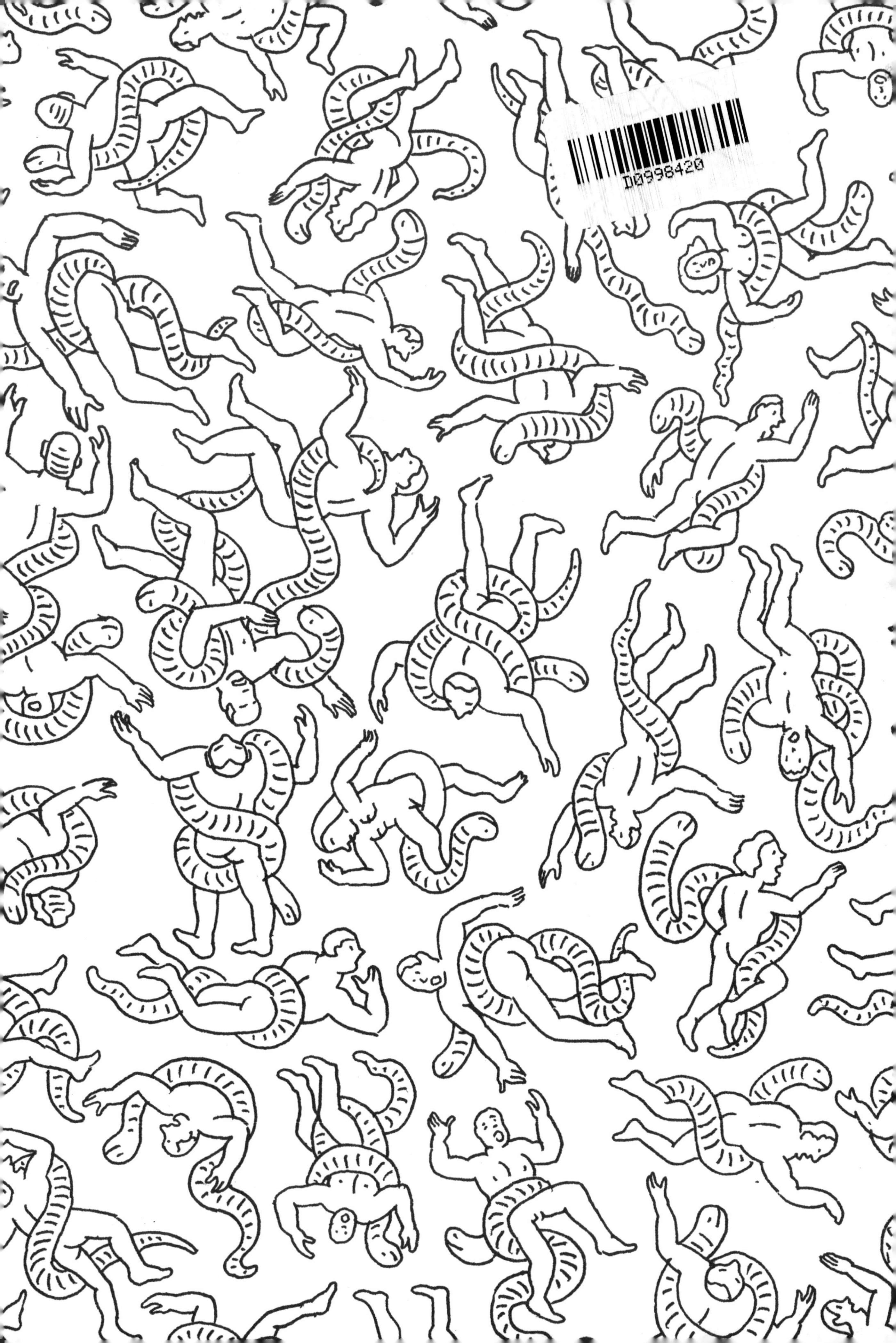

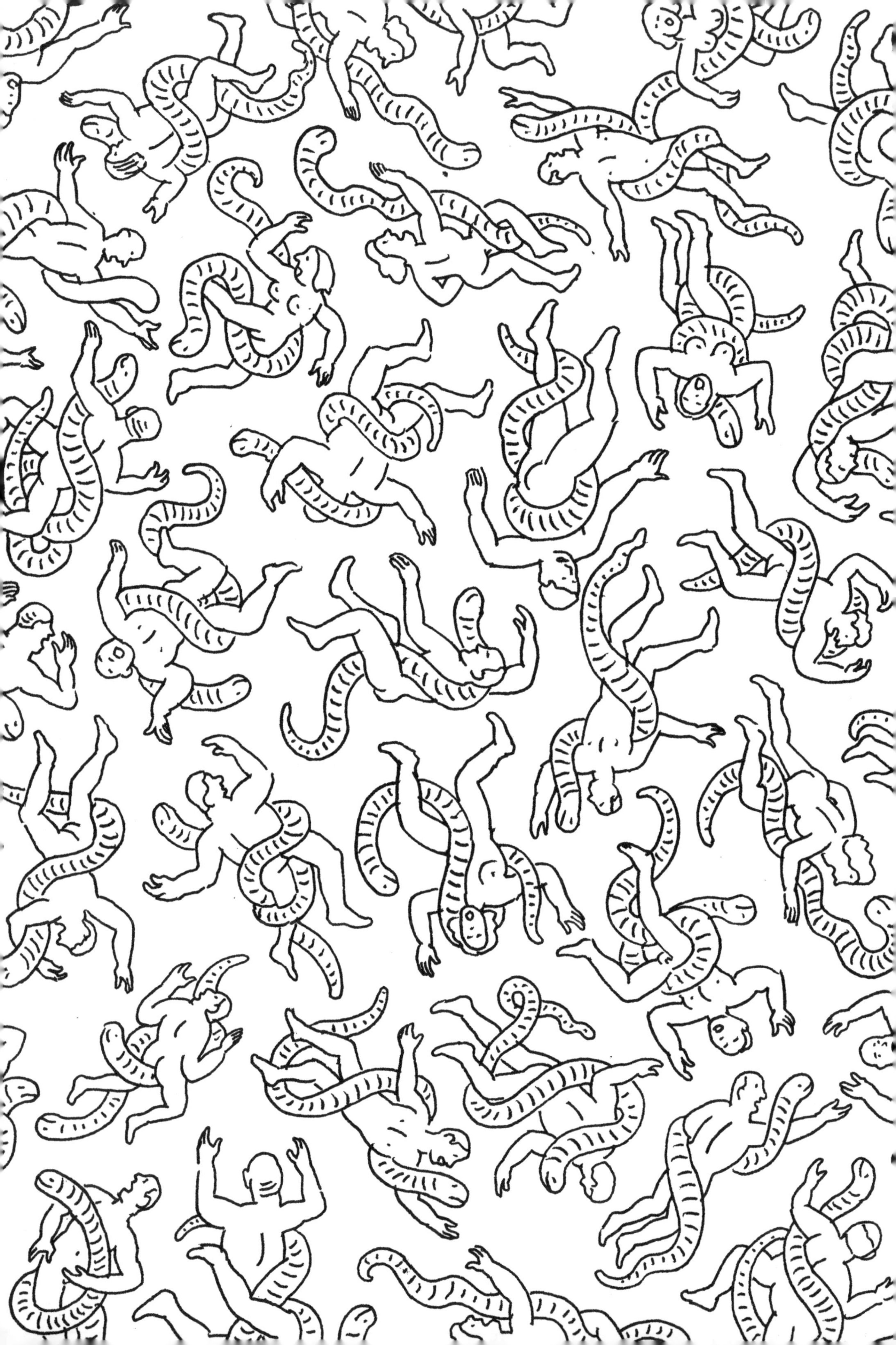

DANTE'S DIVINE COMEDY

BY THE SAME
AUTHOR

SEYMOUR: THE OBSESSIVE
IMAGES OF SEYMOUR CHWAST

MOONRIDE

THE 12 CIRCUS RINGS

THE ALPHABET PARADE

THE LEFT-HANDED DESIGNER

WITH STEVEN HELLER:

ILLUSTRATION:
A VISUAL HISTORY

GRAPHIC STYLE

DANTE'S DIVINE COMEDY

ADAPTED BY SEYMOUR CHWAST

BLOOMSBURY

NEW YORK BERLIN LONDON

FOR
BRIAN
JACOB
KYLE

THE ENGLISH TRANSLATION APPEARING AS THE LAST FOUR LINES ON PAGE 127 IS BY MARK MUSA

PUBLISHED BY BLOOMSBURY USA, NEW YORK

ALL PAPERS USED BY BLOOMSBURY USA ARE NATURAL, RECYCLABLE
PRODUCTS MADE FROM WOOD GROWN IN WELL-MANAGED
FORESTS. THE MANUFACTURING PROCESSES CONFORM TO THE
ENVIRONMENTAL REGULATIONS OF THE COUNTRY OF ORIGIN.

LIBRARY OF CONGRESS CATALOGING-IN-PUBLICATION DATA

CHWAST, SEYMOUR

DANTE'S DIVINE COMEDY / ADAPTED BY SEYMOUR CHWAST. -- 1st U.S. ed.

p. cm.

ISBN 978-1-60819-084-3

1. GRAPHIC NOVELS. I. DANTE ALIGHIERI, 1265-1321. DIVINA COMMEDIA. II. TITLE.

PN6727. C499 D 36 2010

741.5'973 -- dc22

2009044551

FIRST U.S. EDITION 2010

1 3 5 7 9 10 8 6 4 2

ART, DESIGN AND LETTERING BY SEYMOUR CHWAST
MEGHAN EPLETT, ASSOCIATE DESIGNER
PRINTED IN THE UNITED STATES OF AMERICA BY WORLDCOLOR Versailles

CONTENTS

❖ · INTRODUCTION · ❖

DANTE ALIGHIERI (1265-1321) WAS ARGUABLY THE GREATEST POET OF THE MIDDLE AGES, AND THE DIVINE COMEDY IS HIS MASTERPIECE. BORN IN FLORENCE TO A NOBLE FAMILY, HE WAS TWELVE YEARS OLD WHEN HIS FUTURE WIFE WAS CHOSEN FOR HIM. HIS LIFELONG LOVE, HOWEVER, WAS BEATRICE, HIS MUSE FOR A LIFE OF POETRY.

HE HELD SEVERAL OFFICES, INCLUDING AMBASSADOR TO ROME AND SUPERINTENDENT OF ROADS AND REPAIR. HE WAS INVOLVED IN THE POLITICAL LIFE OF FLORENCE, SIDING WITH THE WHITE GUELPH FACTION, WHICH OPPOSED THE BLACK GUELPHS. BOTH SIDES FAVORED THE POPE AND FOUGHT WITH THE GHIBELLINES, THE PARTY BACKED BY THE HOLY ROMAN EMPEROR. DANTE'S CRITICISM OF THE POPE'S INVOLVEMENT IN POLITICS AND ENSUING SCANDALS APPEARS IN DIFFERENT PARTS OF THE POEM. IN FACT, HE CONDEMNED THE CHURCH AND THE GOVERNMENT CORRUPTION THAT PLAGUED FLORENCE WHILE HE, IN TURN, WAS CHARGED WITH CORRUPTION AND WAS CONDEMNED. HE WAS ABLE TO ES-

CAPE A PUNISHMENT OF DEATH BY BURNING.

BETWEEN 1302 AND 1321 HE WAS IN EXILE, ROAMING FROM ONE ITALIAN TOWN TO ANOTHER. IT WAS DURING THIS TIME THAT HE WROTE MUCH OF HIS BODY OF WORK, INCLUDING THE DIVINE COMEDY.

THE ALLEGORICAL POEM WAS WRITTEN IN ITALIAN, THE LANGUAGE OF THE PEOPLE, INSTEAD OF LATIN. IT HAS AS ITS PROTAGONIST THE POET HIMSELF, A LIVING BEING EXPLORING THE UNKNOWN WORLD WITH THE SOULS OF VIRGIL, THE CLASSICAL POET, AND BEATRICE AS HIS GUIDES. HE WAS TOLD THAT IN ORDER TO FIND GOD HE HAD TO PASS THROUGH THE INFERNO, PURGATORY, AND PARADISE (HEAVEN). HE FINDS GOD WHILE DESCRIBING THE AMAZING DETAILS OF HIS JOURNEY TO ALL OF US.

IT IS COMPOSED OF ONE HUNDRED CANTOS AND TOLD IN TRIPLETS TO REPRESENT THE TRINITY. DANTE USES THE DIVINE COMEDY TO RAISE AWARENESS OF THE NEED FOR A MORAL LIFE AND FOR US TO TRUST IN THE GOD OF THE SCRIPTURES.

INFERNO

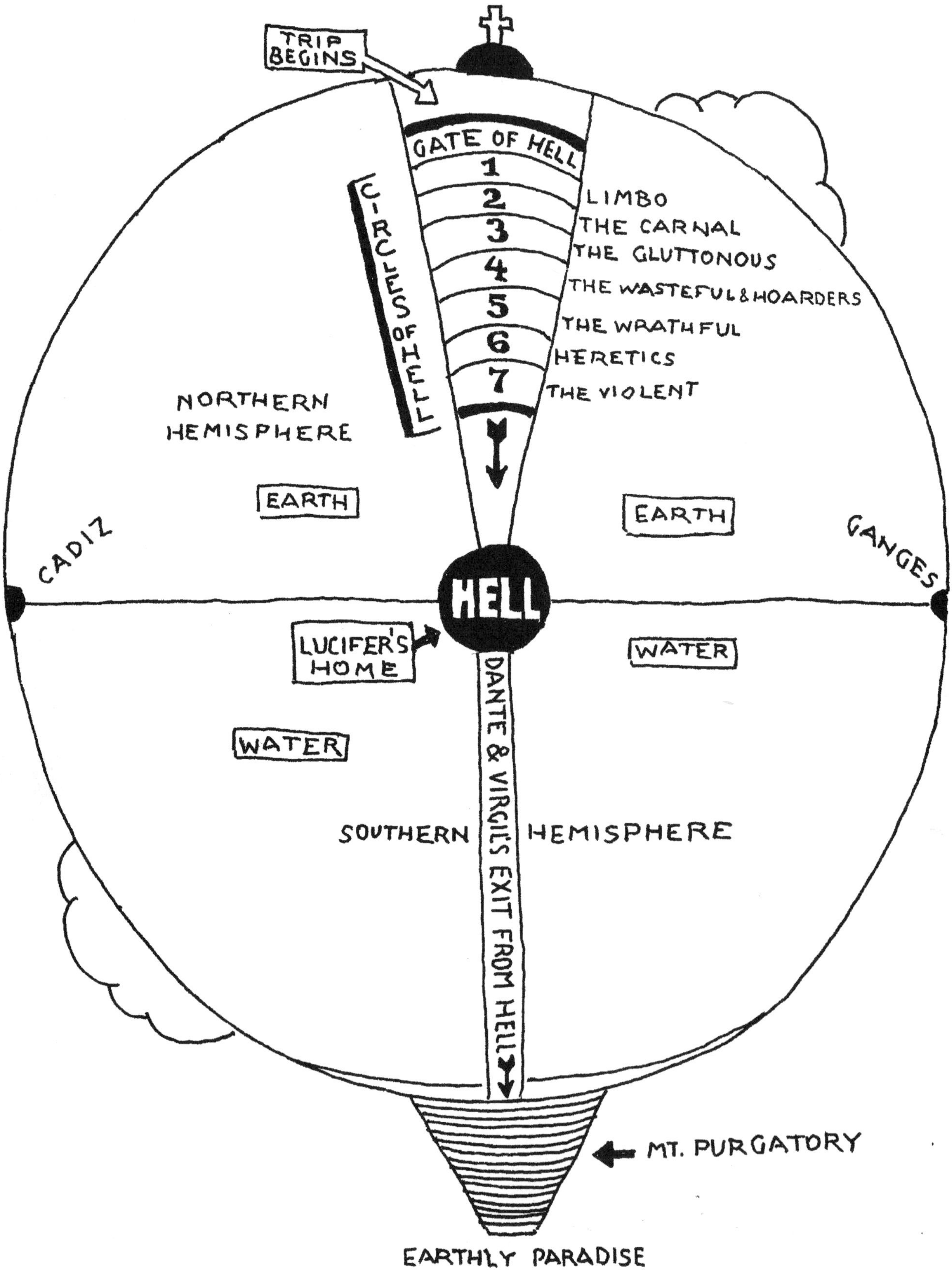

TRIP BEGINS
GATE OF HELL
CIRCLES OF HELL
1
2
3
4
5
6
7
LIMBO
THE CARNAL
THE GLUTTONOUS
THE WASTEFUL & HOARDERS
THE WRATHFUL
HERETICS
THE VIOLENT
NORTHERN HEMISPHERE
EARTH
EARTH
CADIZ
GANGES
HELL
LUCIFER'S HOME
WATER
WATER
DANTE & VIRGIL'S EXIT FROM HELL
SOUTHERN HEMISPHERE
MT. PURGATORY
EARTHLY PARADISE

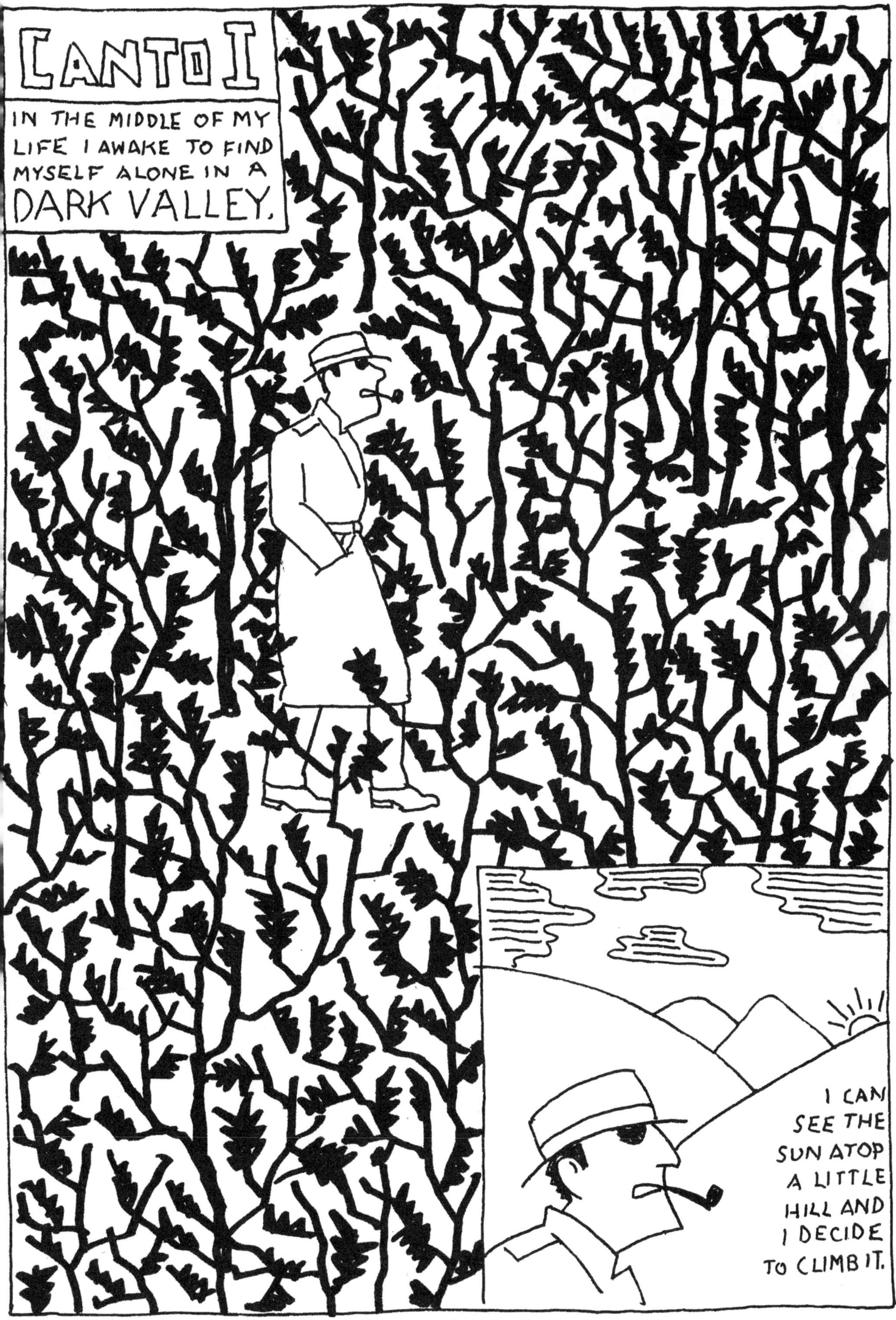
CANTO I
IN THE MIDDLE OF MY LIFE I AWAKE TO FIND MYSELF ALONE IN A DARK VALLEY.
I CAN SEE THE SUN ATOP A LITTLE HILL AND I DECIDE TO CLIMB IT.

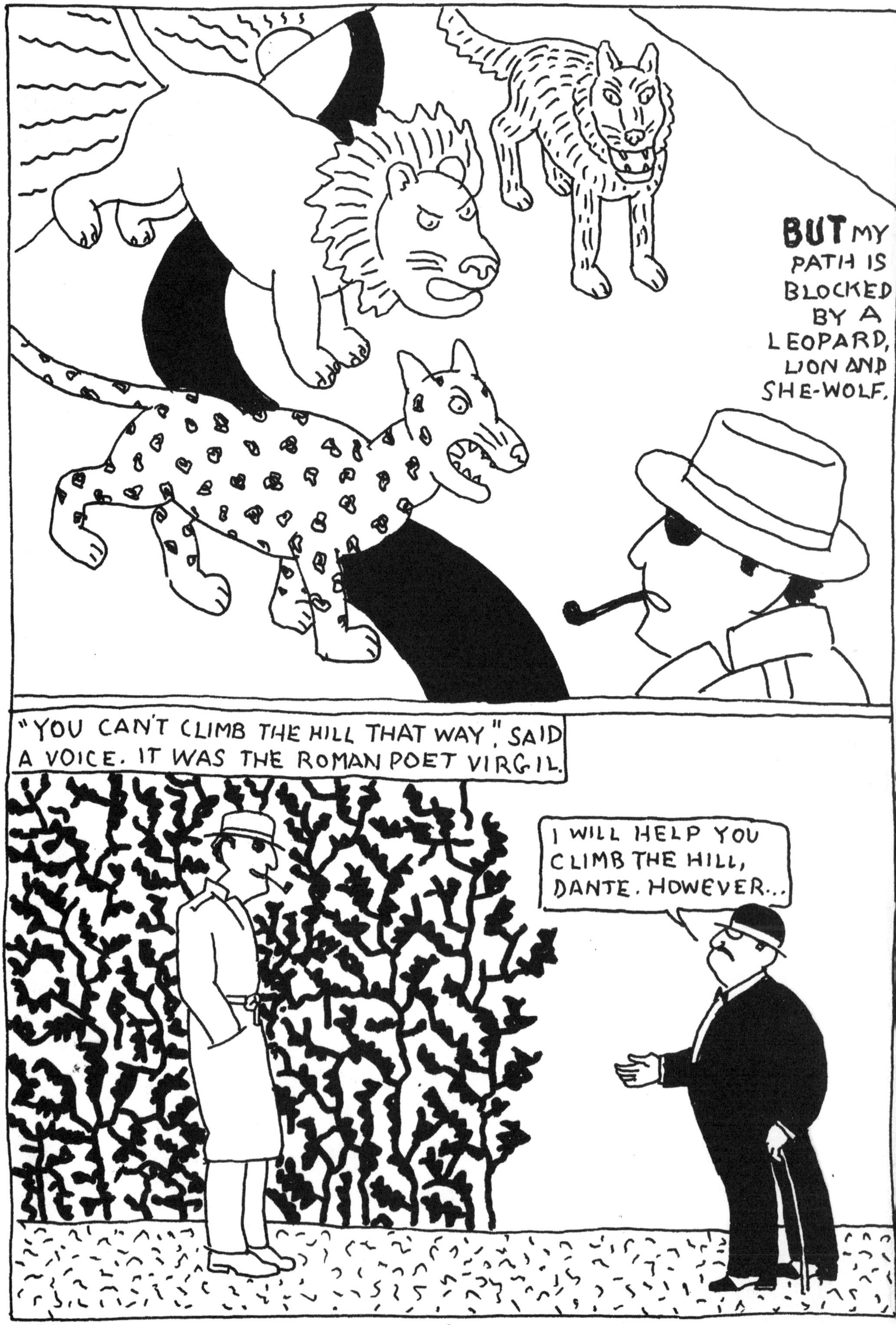
BUT MY PATH IS BLOCKED BY A LEOPARD, LION AND SHE-WOLF.
"YOU CAN'T CLIMB THE HILL THAT WAY", SAID A VOICE. IT WAS THE ROMAN POET VIRGIL.
I WILL HELP YOU CLIMB THE HILL, DANTE. HOWEVER...

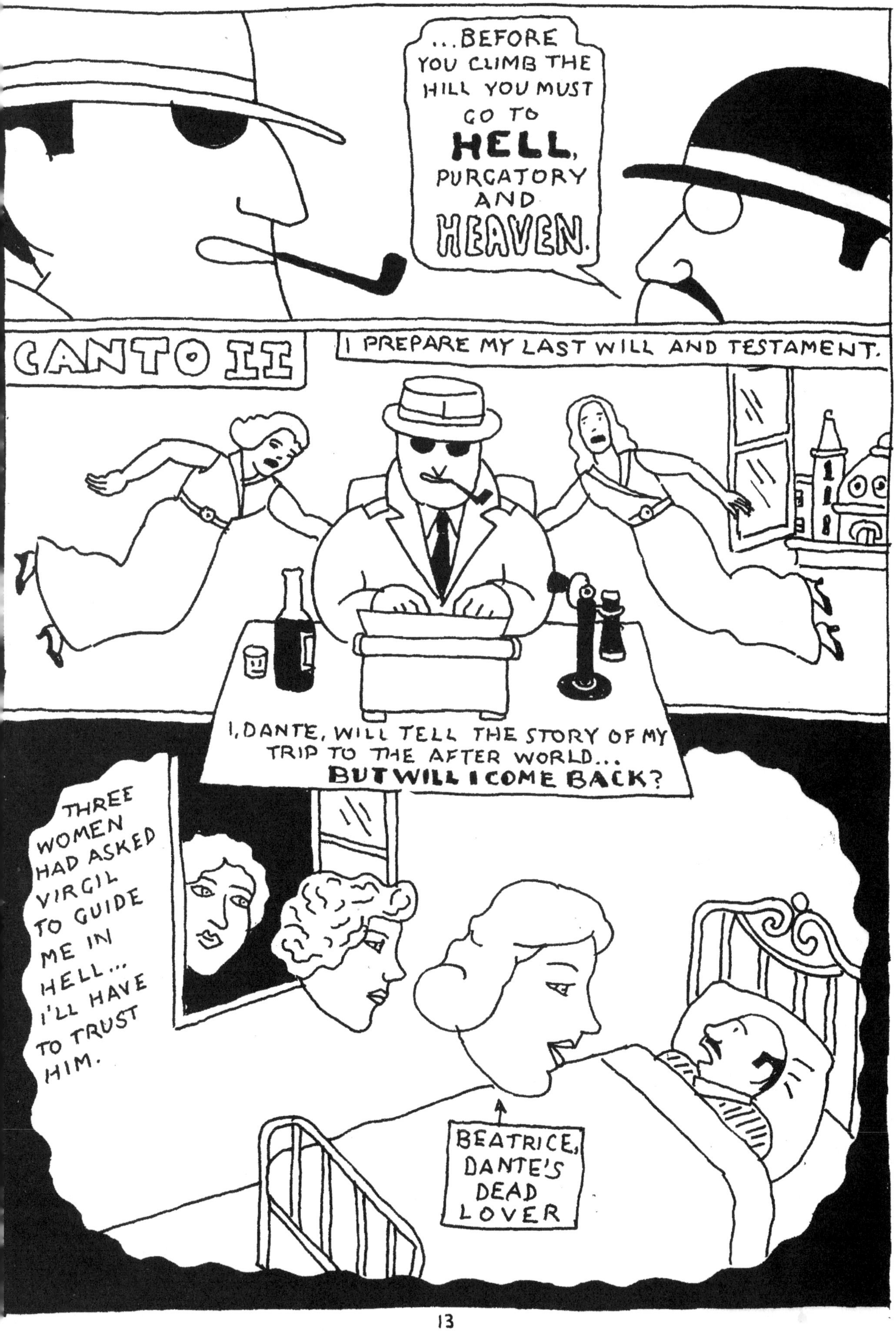

...BEFORE YOU CLIMB THE HILL YOU MUST GO TO HELL, PURGATORY AND HEAVEN.
CANTO II
I PREPARE MY LAST WILL AND TESTAMENT.
I, DANTE, WILL TELL THE STORY OF MY TRIP TO THE AFTER WORLD... BUT WILL I COME BACK?
THREE WOMEN HAD ASKED VIRGIL TO GUIDE ME IN HELL... I'LL HAVE TO TRUST HIM.
BEATRICE, DANTE'S DEAD LOVER

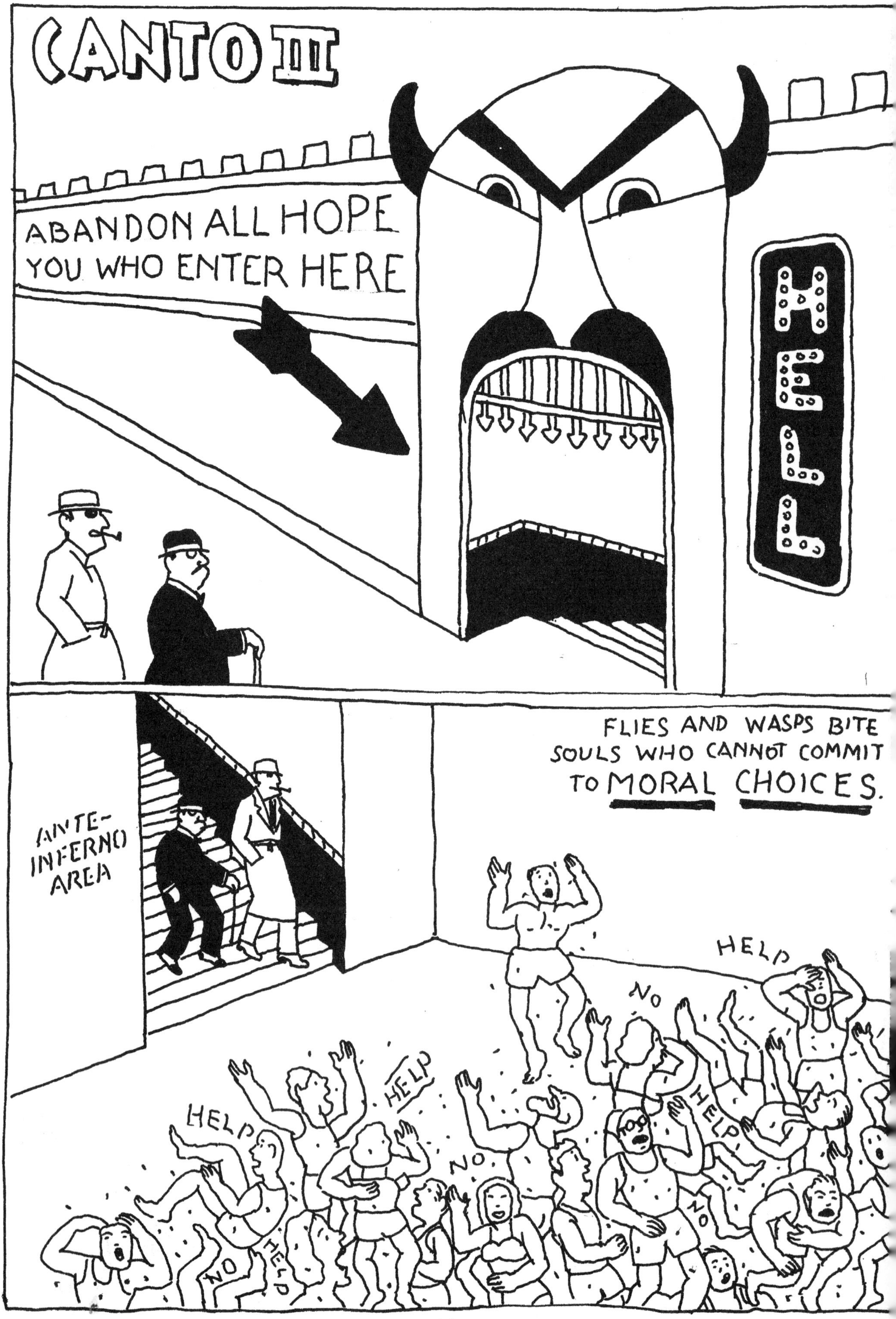
CANTO III
ABANDON ALL HOPE YOU WHO ENTER HERE
HELL
FLIES AND WASPS BITE SOULS WHO CANNOT COMMIT TO MORAL CHOICES.
ANTE-INFERNO AREA
HELP
NO
HELP
HELP
NO
HELP
NO
NO
HELP

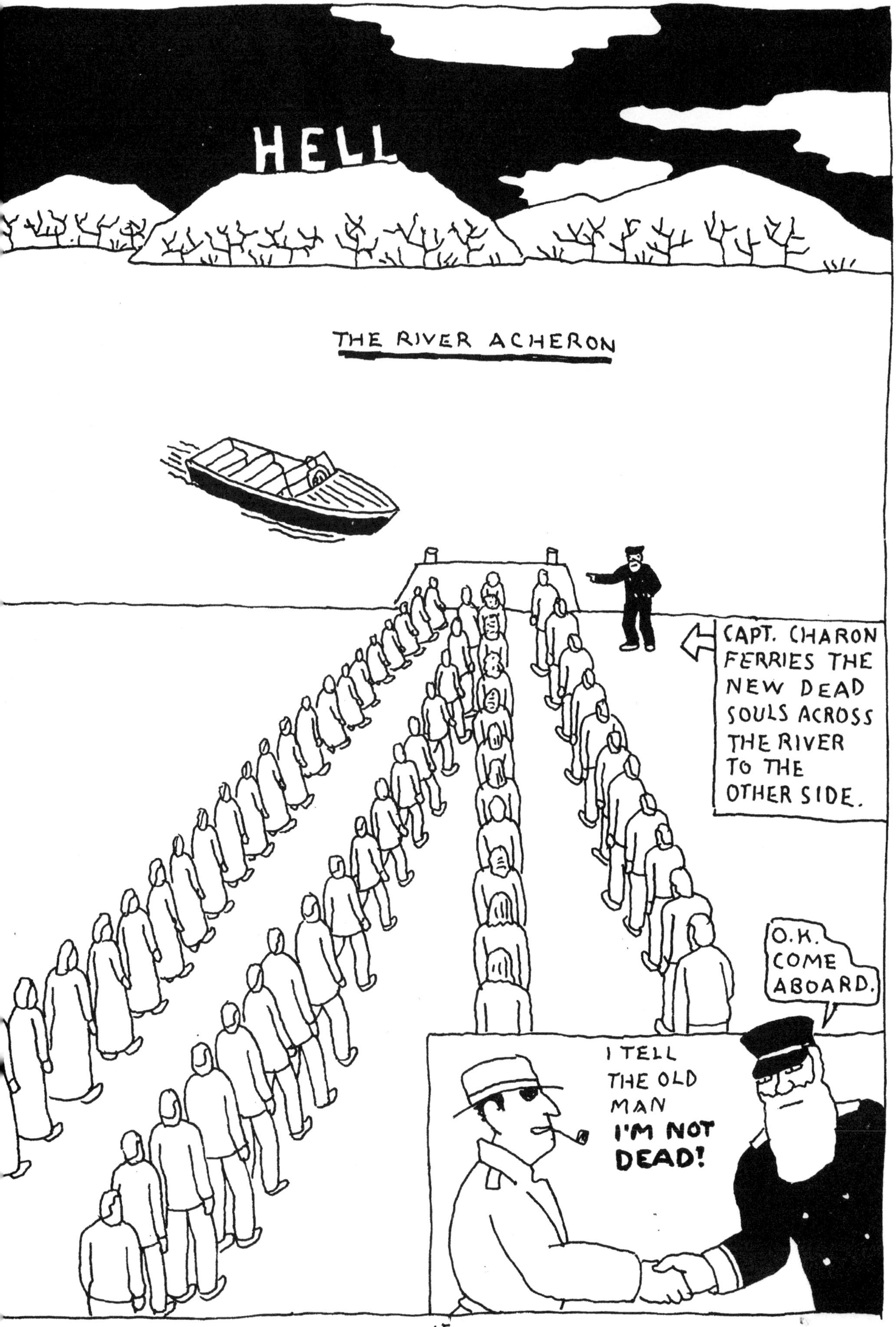
HELL
THE RIVER ACHERON
CAPT. CHARON FERRIES THE NEW DEAD SOULS ACROSS THE RIVER TO THE OTHER SIDE.
O.K. COME ABOARD.
I TELL THE OLD MAN **I'M NOT DEAD!**

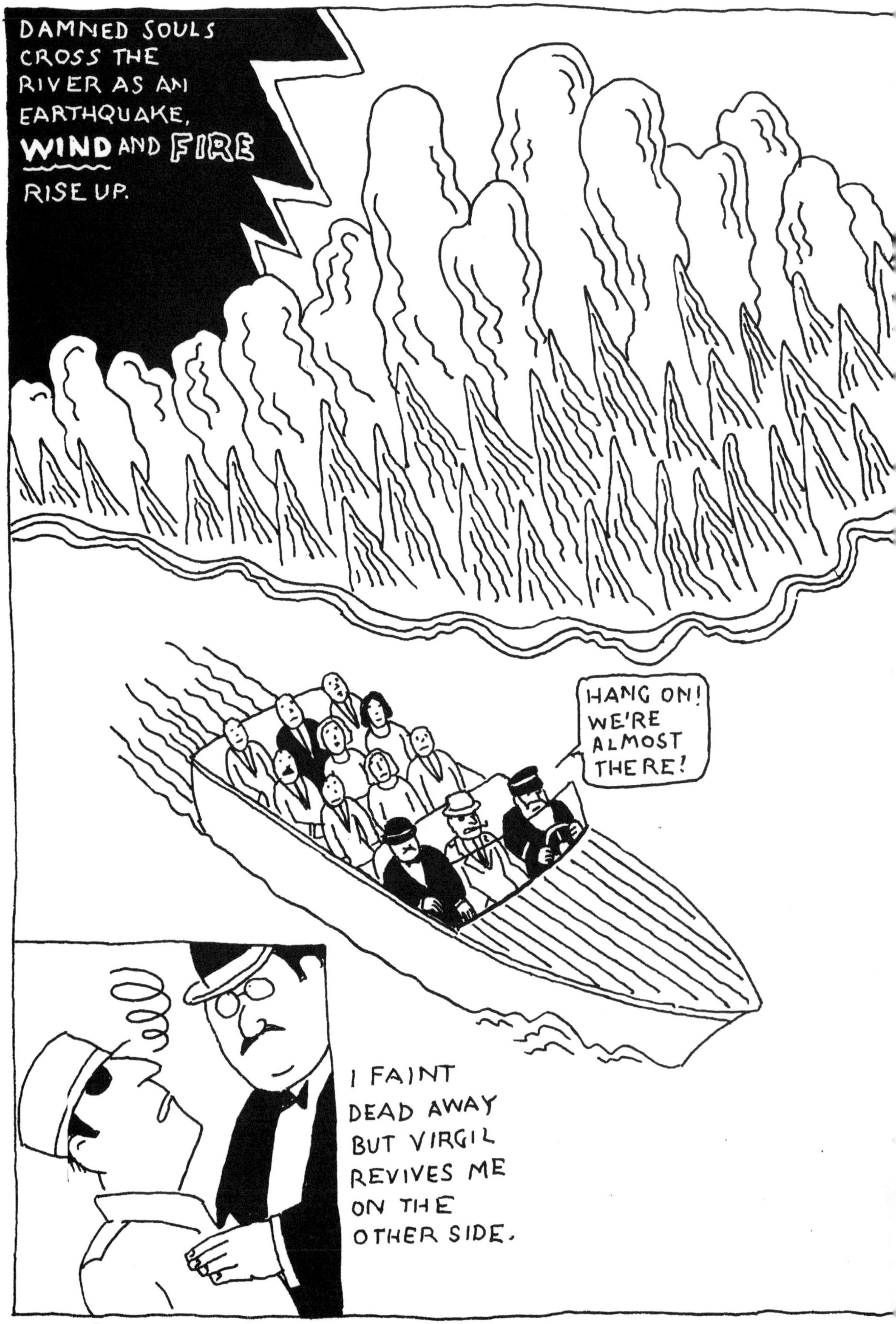
DAMNED SOULS CROSS THE RIVER AS AN EARTHQUAKE, WIND AND FIRE RISE UP.
HANG ON! WE'RE ALMOST THERE!
I FAINT DEAD AWAY BUT VIRGIL REVIVES ME ON THE OTHER SIDE.

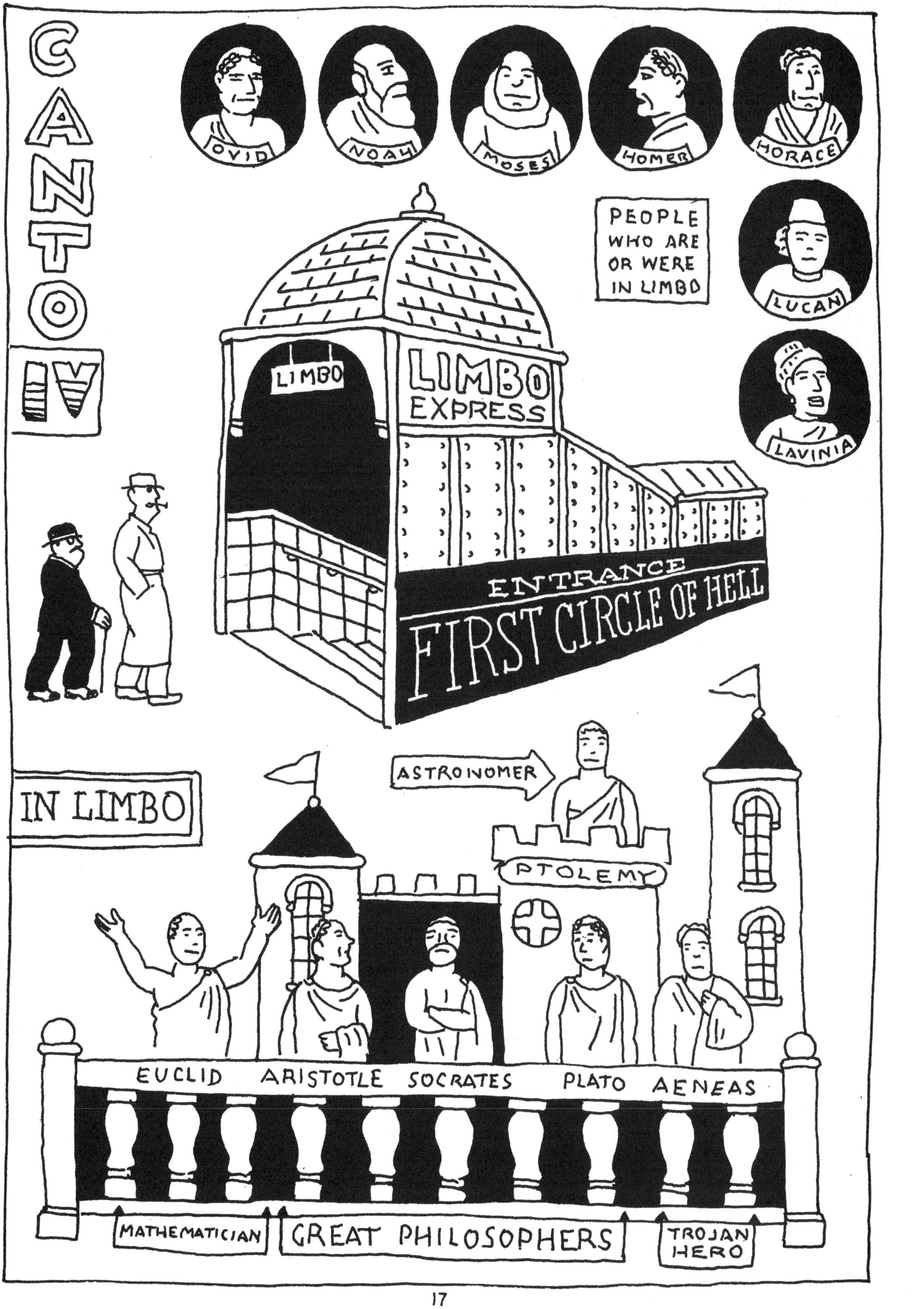
CANTO IV
OVID
NOAH
MOSES
HOMER
HORACE
PEOPLE WHO ARE OR WERE IN LIMBO
LUCAN
LAVINIA
LIMBO
LIMBO EXPRESS
ENTRANCE
FIRST CIRCLE OF HELL
IN LIMBO
ASTRONOMER
PTOLEMY
EUCLID
ARISTOTLE
SOCRATES
PLATO
AENEAS
MATHEMATICIAN
GREAT PHILOSOPHERS
TROJAN HERO

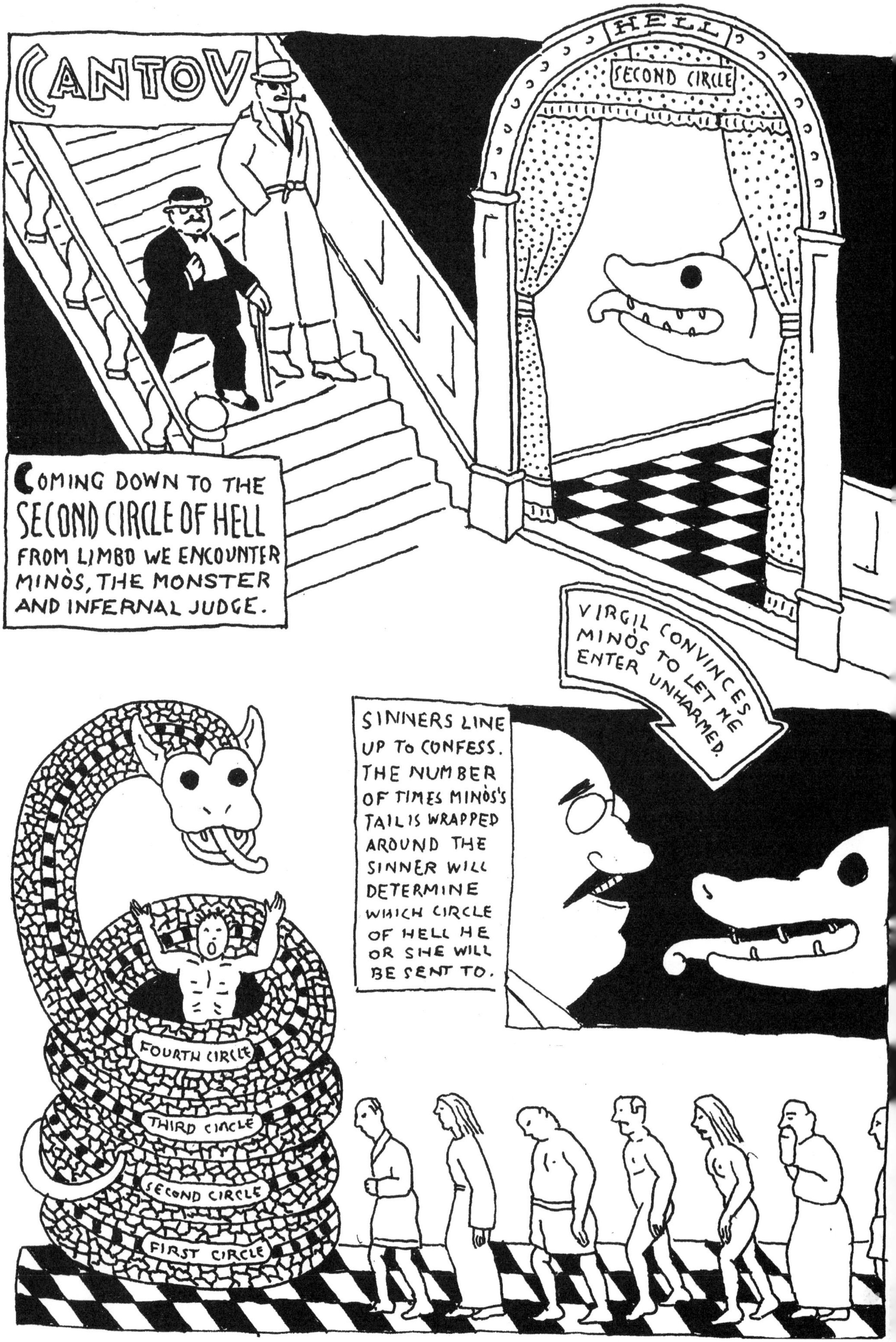
CANTO V
COMING DOWN TO THE SECOND CIRCLE OF HELL FROM LIMBO WE ENCOUNTER MINÒS, THE MONSTER AND INFERNAL JUDGE.
HELL
SECOND CIRCLE
VIRGIL CONVINCES MINÒS TO LET ME ENTER UNHARMED.
SINNERS LINE UP TO CONFESS. THE NUMBER OF TIMES MINÒS'S TAIL IS WRAPPED AROUND THE SINNER WILL DETERMINE WHICH CIRCLE OF HELL HE OR SHE WILL BE SENT TO.
FOURTH CIRCLE
THIRD CIRCLE
SECOND CIRCLE
FIRST CIRCLE

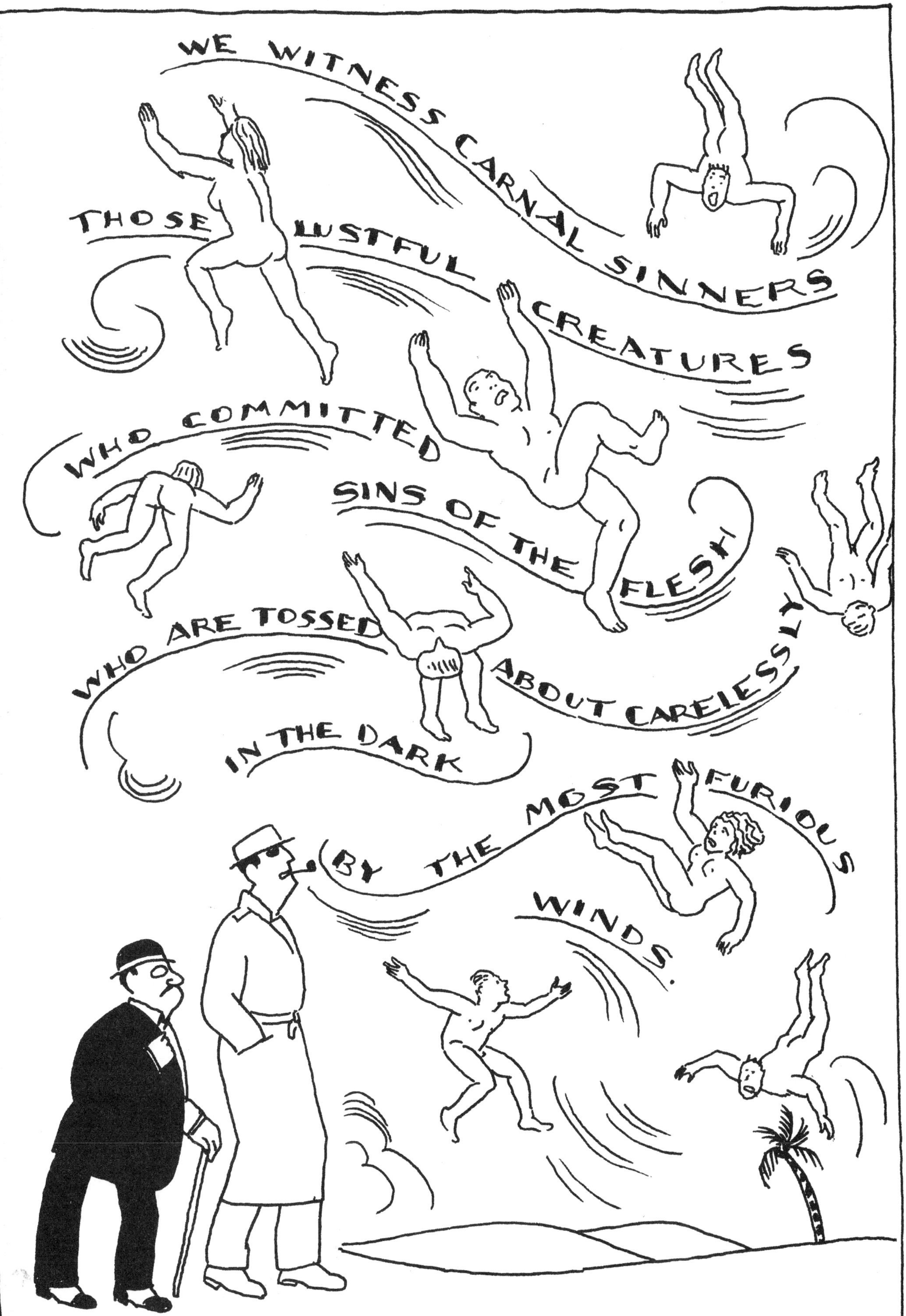
WE WITNESS CARNAL SINNERS
THOSE LUSTFUL CREATURES
WHO COMMITTED SINS OF THE FLESH
WHO ARE TOSSED ABOUT CARELESSLY
IN THE DARK
BY THE MOST FURIOUS WINDS.

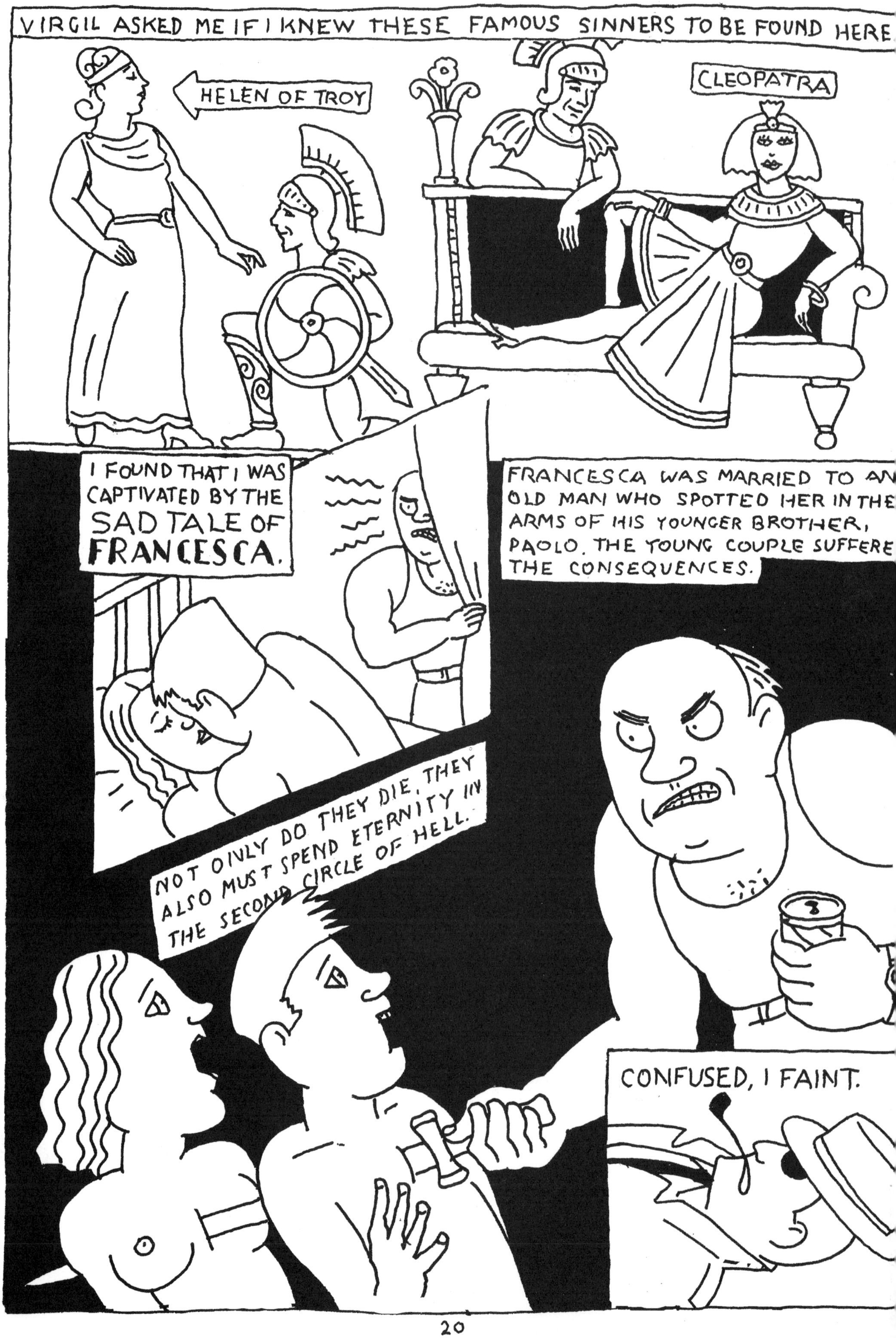
VIRGIL ASKED ME IF I KNEW THESE FAMOUS SINNERS TO BE FOUND HERE
HELEN OF TROY
CLEOPATRA
I FOUND THAT I WAS CAPTIVATED BY THE SAD TALE OF FRANCESCA.
FRANCESCA WAS MARRIED TO AN OLD MAN WHO SPOTTED HER IN THE ARMS OF HIS YOUNGER BROTHER, PAOLO. THE YOUNG COUPLE SUFFERE THE CONSEQUENCES.
NOT ONLY DO THEY DIE, THEY ALSO MUST SPEND ETERNITY IN THE SECOND CIRCLE OF HELL.
CONFUSED, I FAINT.

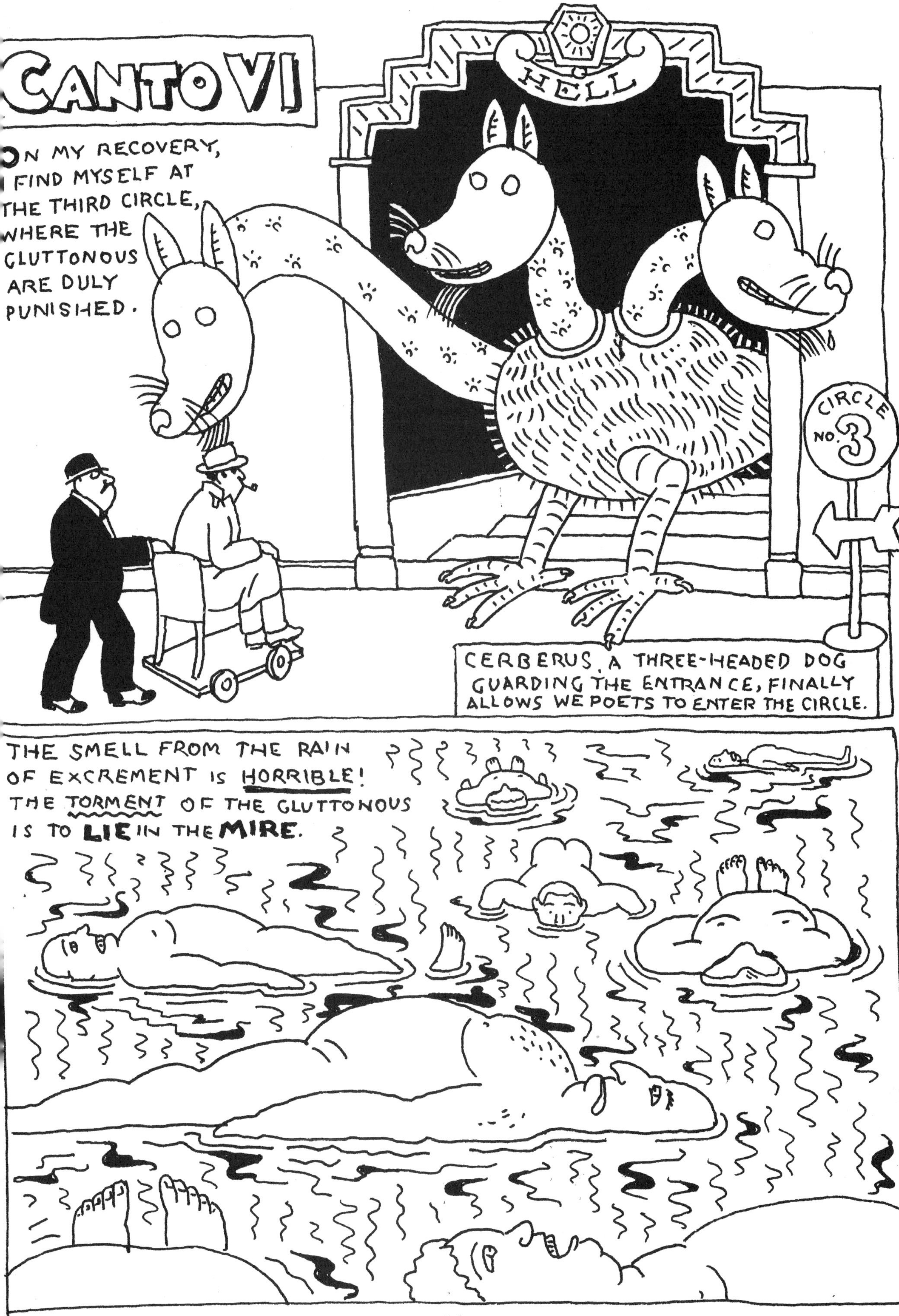
CANTO VI
ON MY RECOVERY, I FIND MYSELF AT THE THIRD CIRCLE, WHERE THE GLUTTONOUS ARE DULY PUNISHED.
HELL
CIRCLE NO. 3
CERBERUS, A THREE-HEADED DOG GUARDING THE ENTRANCE, FINALLY ALLOWS WE POETS TO ENTER THE CIRCLE.
THE SMELL FROM THE RAIN OF EXCREMENT IS HORRIBLE! THE TORMENT OF THE GLUTTONOUS IS TO LIE IN THE MIRE.

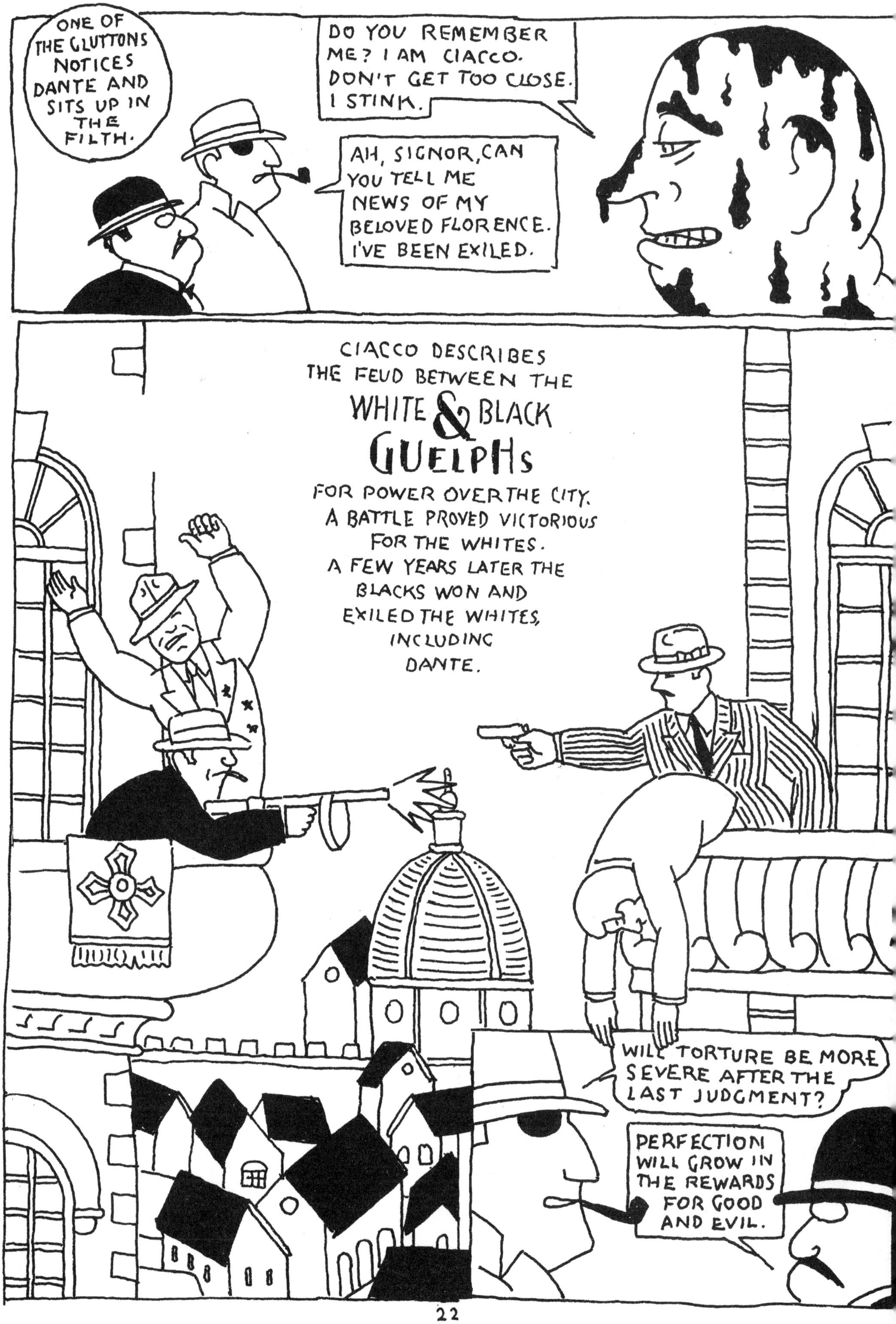
ONE OF THE GLUTTONS NOTICES DANTE AND SITS UP IN THE FILTH.
DO YOU REMEMBER ME? I AM CIACCO. DON'T GET TOO CLOSE. I STINK.
AH, SIGNOR, CAN YOU TELL ME NEWS OF MY BELOVED FLORENCE. I'VE BEEN EXILED.
CIACCO DESCRIBES THE FEUD BETWEEN THE WHITE & BLACK GUELPHS FOR POWER OVER THE CITY. A BATTLE PROVED VICTORIOUS FOR THE WHITES. A FEW YEARS LATER THE BLACKS WON AND EXILED THE WHITES, INCLUDING DANTE.
WILL TORTURE BE MORE SEVERE AFTER THE LAST JUDGMENT?
PERFECTION WILL GROW IN THE REWARDS FOR GOOD AND EVIL.

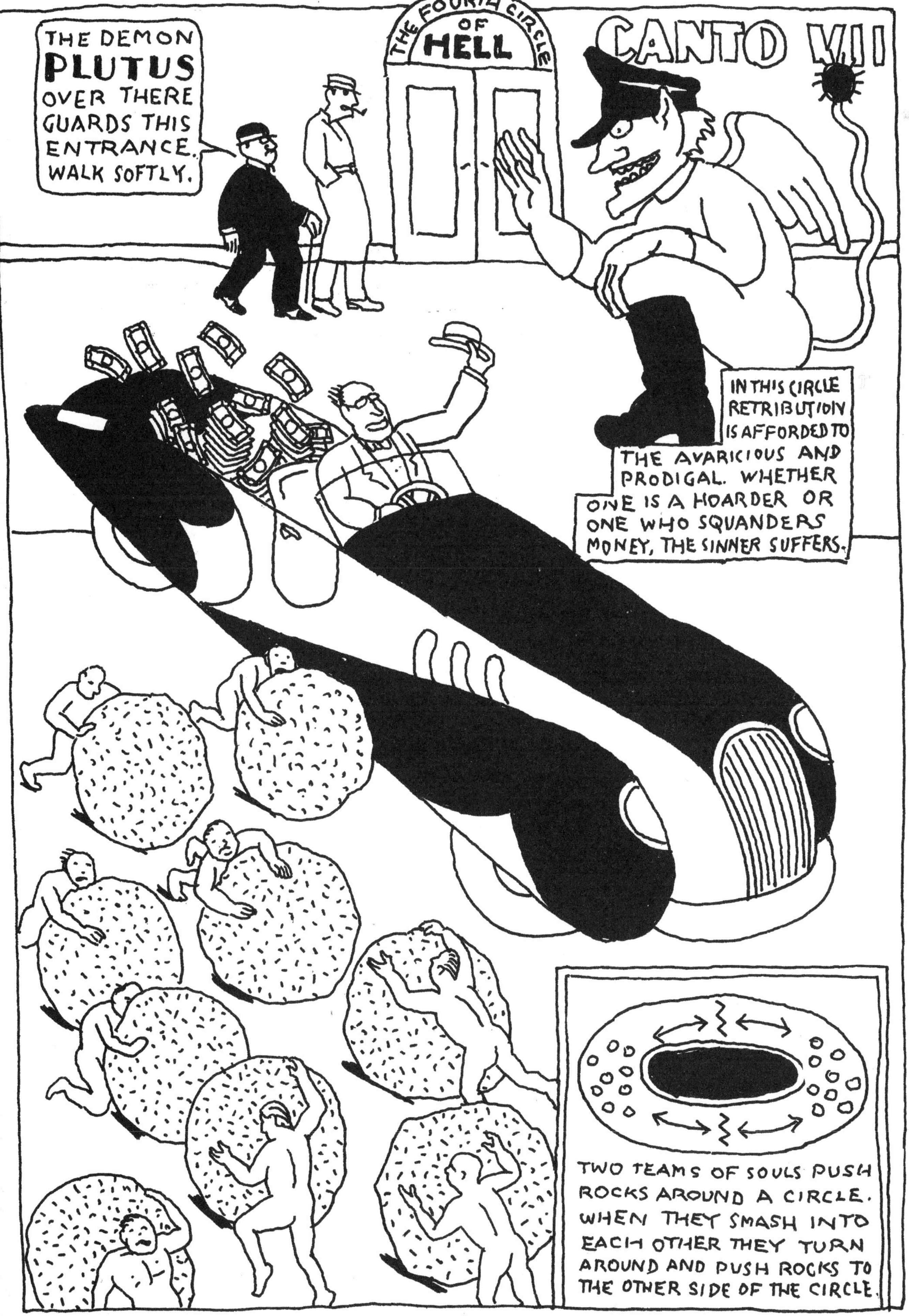

THE DEMON PLUTUS OVER THERE GUARDS THIS ENTRANCE. WALK SOFTLY.
THE FOURTH CIRCLE OF HELL
CANTO VII
IN THIS CIRCLE RETRIBUTION IS AFFORDED TO THE AVARICIOUS AND PRODIGAL. WHETHER ONE IS A HOARDER OR ONE WHO SQUANDERS MONEY, THE SINNER SUFFERS.
TWO TEAMS OF SOULS PUSH ROCKS AROUND A CIRCLE. WHEN THEY SMASH INTO EACH OTHER THEY TURN AROUND AND PUSH ROCKS TO THE OTHER SIDE OF THE CIRCLE.

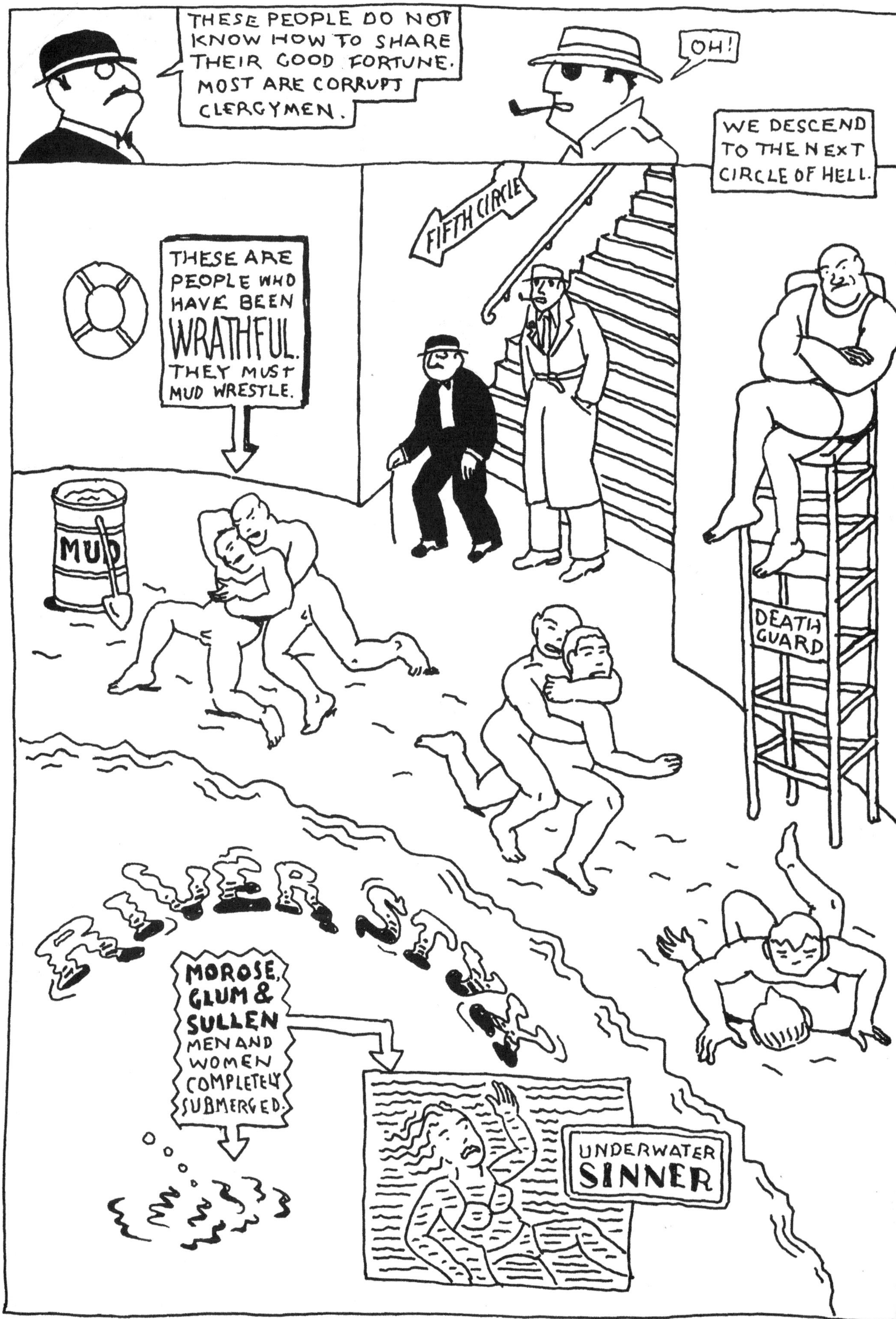

THESE PEOPLE DO NOT KNOW HOW TO SHARE THEIR GOOD FORTUNE. MOST ARE CORRUPT CLERGYMEN.
OH!
WE DESCEND TO THE NEXT CIRCLE OF HELL.
FIFTH CIRCLE
THESE ARE PEOPLE WHO HAVE BEEN WRATHFUL. THEY MUST MUD WRESTLE.
MUD
DEATH GUARD
RIVER STYX
MOROSE, GLUM & SULLEN MEN AND WOMEN COMPLETELY SUBMERGED.
UNDERWATER SINNER

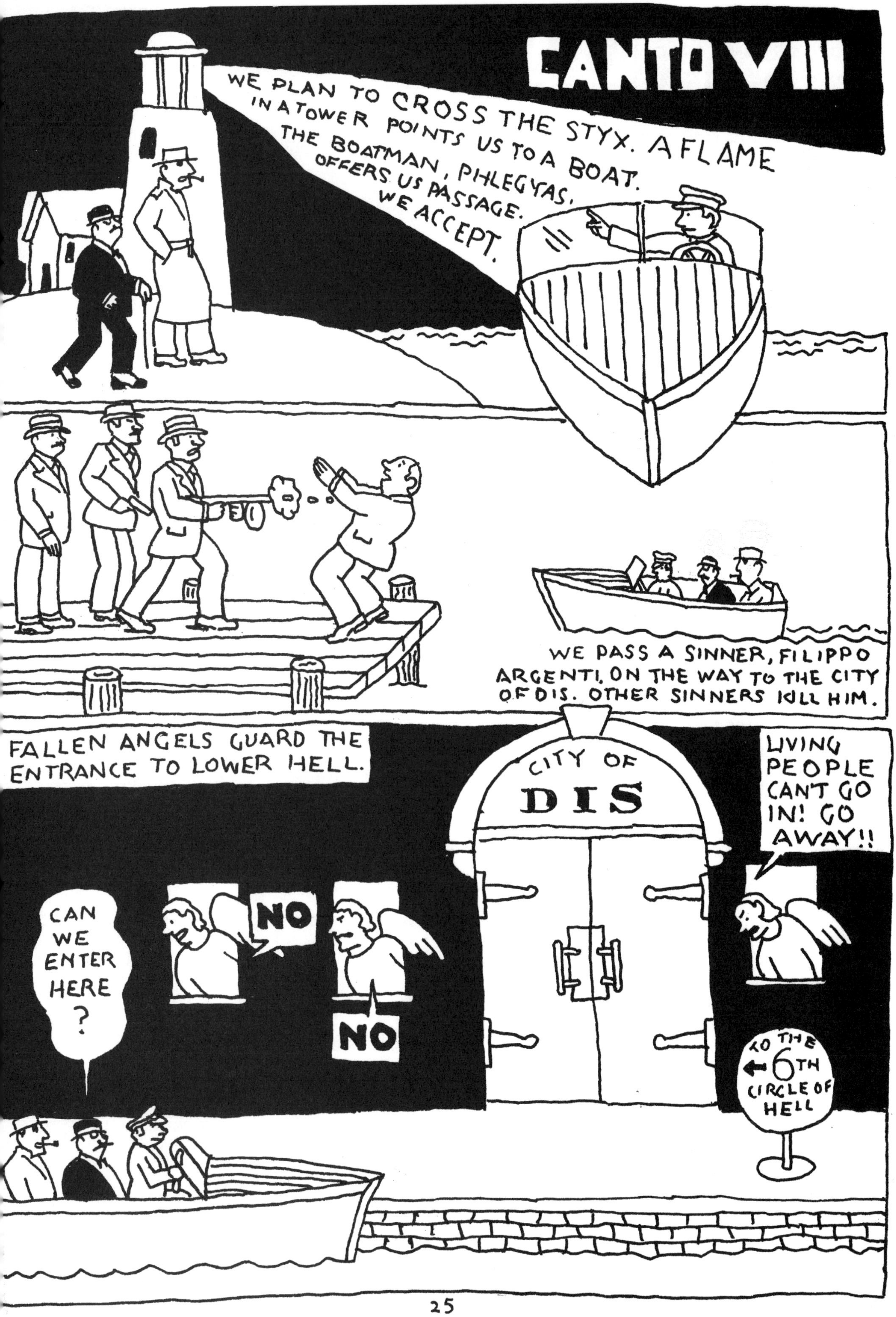
CANTO VIII
WE PLAN TO CROSS THE STYX. A FLAME IN A TOWER POINTS US TO A BOAT. THE BOATMAN, PHLEGYAS, OFFERS US PASSAGE. WE ACCEPT.
WE PASS A SINNER, FILIPPO ARGENTI, ON THE WAY TO THE CITY OF DIS. OTHER SINNERS KILL HIM.
FALLEN ANGELS GUARD THE ENTRANCE TO LOWER HELL.
CITY OF DIS
LIVING PEOPLE CAN'T GO IN! GO AWAY!!
CAN WE ENTER HERE?
NO
NO
TO THE 6TH CIRCLE OF HELL

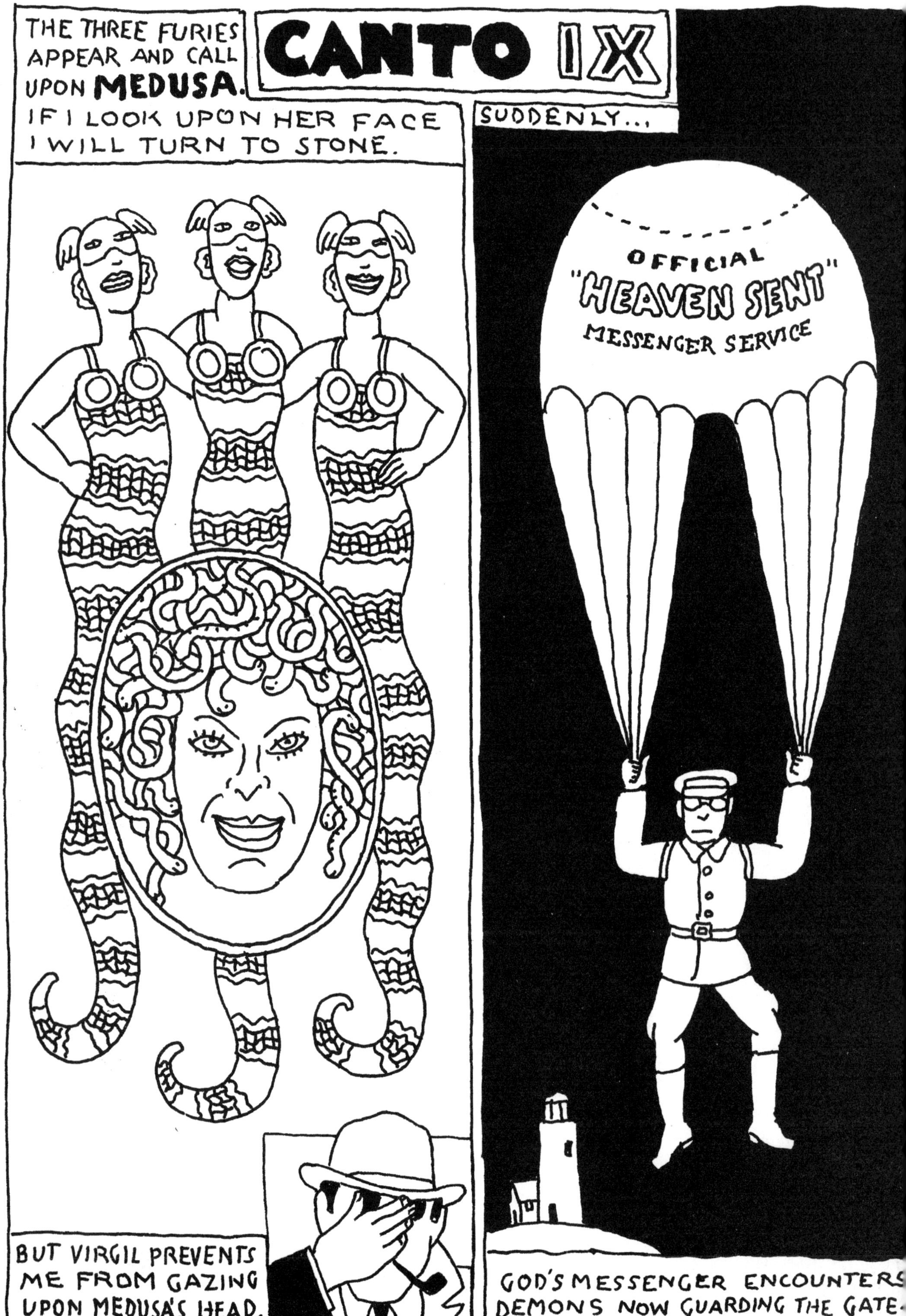
THE THREE FURIES APPEAR AND CALL UPON MEDUSA.
CANTO IX
IF I LOOK UPON HER FACE I WILL TURN TO STONE.
SUDDENLY...
OFFICIAL "HEAVEN SENT" MESSENGER SERVICE
BUT VIRGIL PREVENTS ME FROM GAZING UPON MEDUSA'S HEAD.
GOD'S MESSENGER ENCOUNTERS DEMONS NOW GUARDING THE GATE.

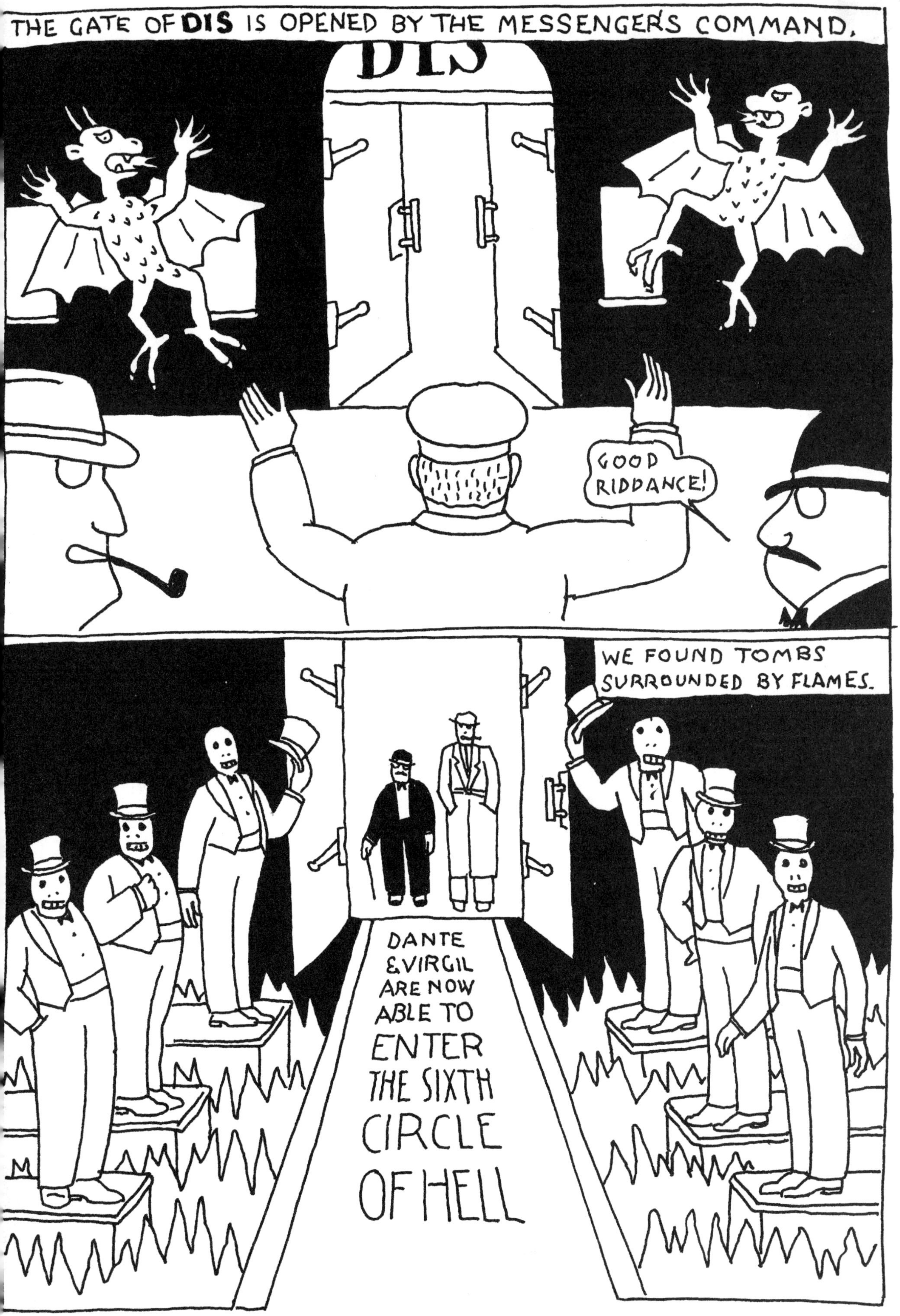
THE GATE OF DIS IS OPENED BY THE MESSENGER'S COMMAND.
DIS
GOOD RIDDANCE!
WE FOUND TOMBS SURROUNDED BY FLAMES.
DANTE & VIRGIL ARE NOW ABLE TO ENTER THE SIXTH CIRCLE OF HELL

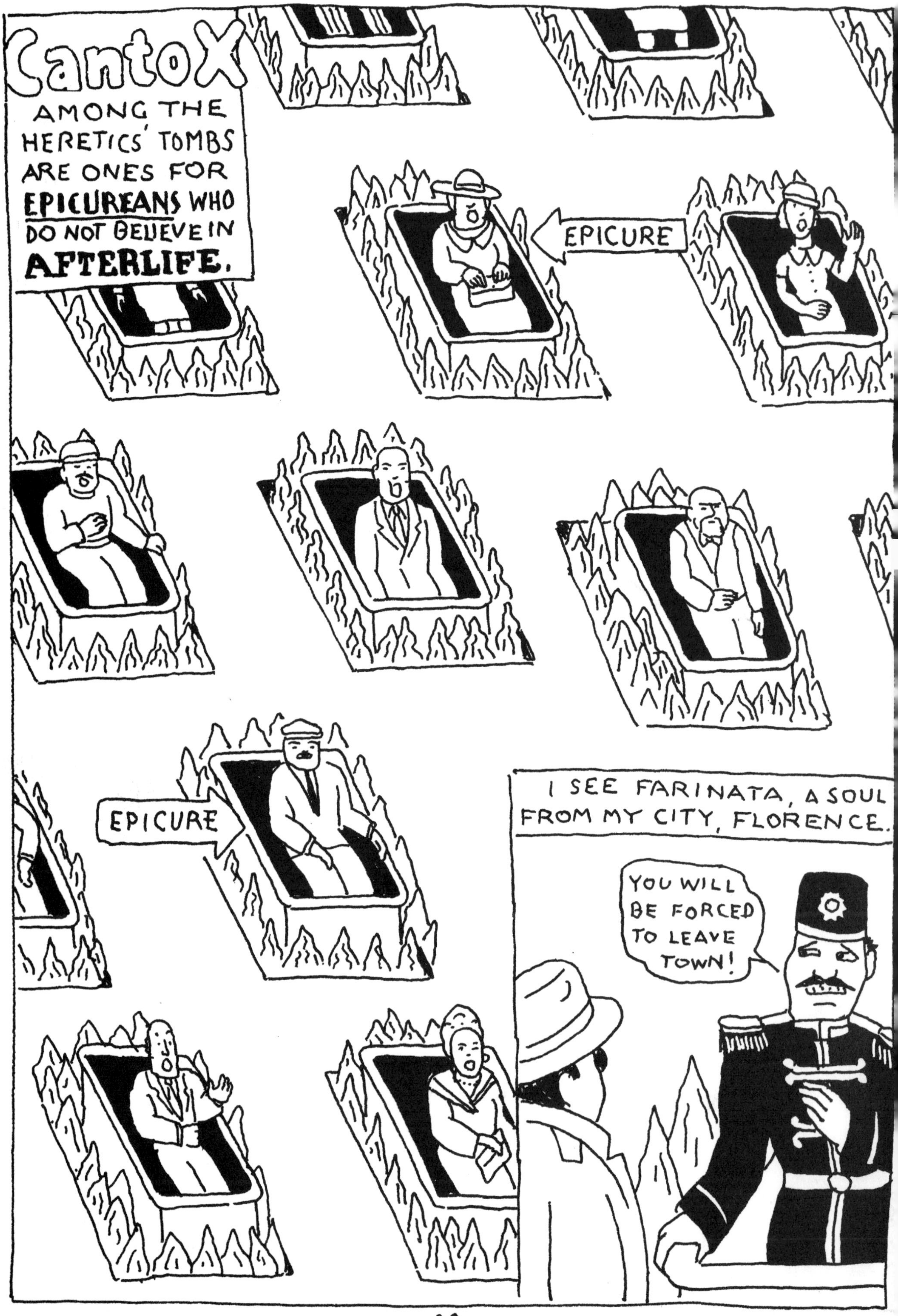
Canto X
AMONG THE HERETICS' TOMBS ARE ONES FOR EPICUREANS WHO DO NOT BELIEVE IN AFTERLIFE.
EPICURE
EPICURE
I SEE FARINATA, A SOUL FROM MY CITY, FLORENCE.
YOU WILL BE FORCED TO LEAVE TOWN!

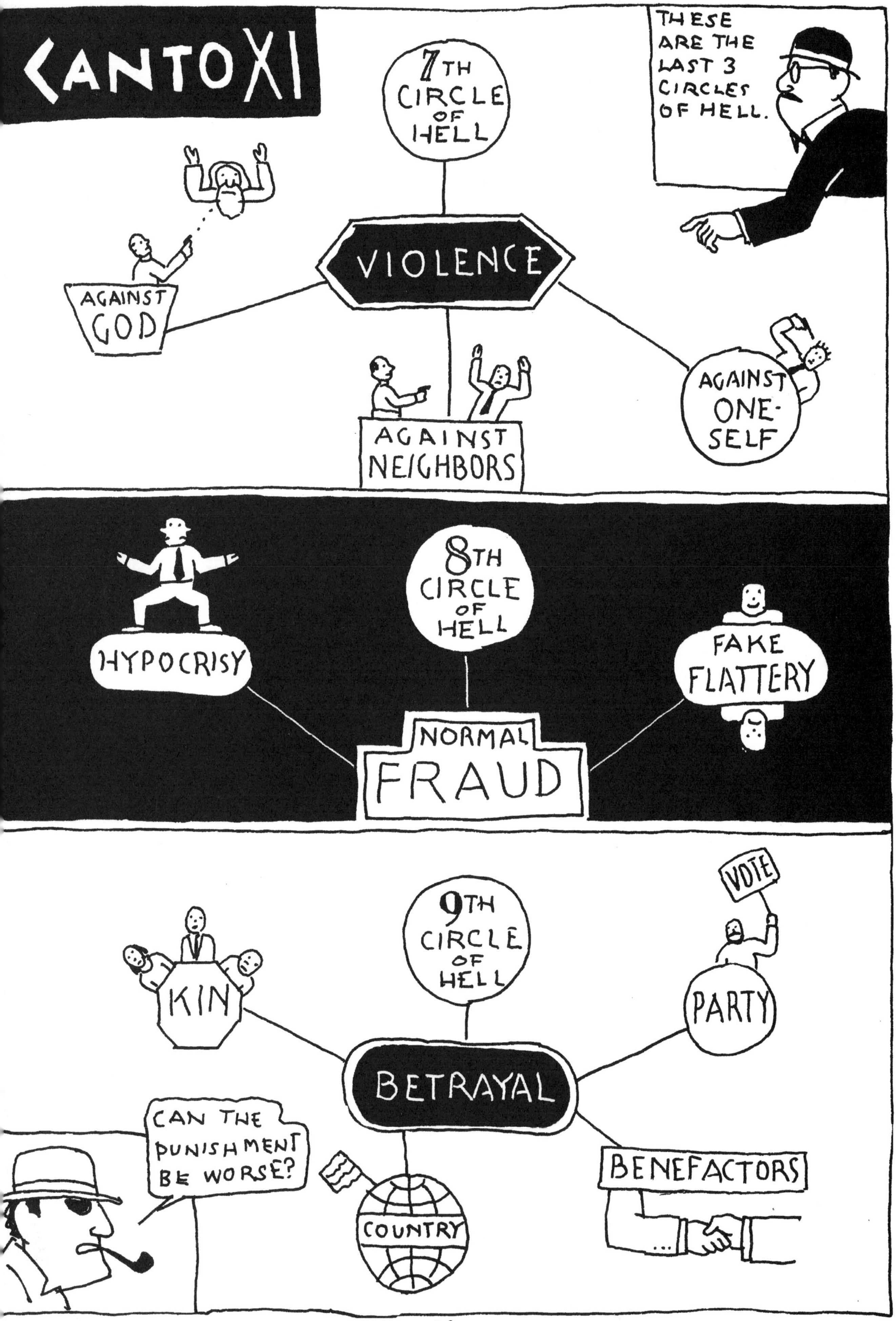
CANTO XI
7TH CIRCLE OF HELL
THESE ARE THE LAST 3 CIRCLES OF HELL.
VIOLENCE
AGAINST GOD
AGAINST NEIGHBORS
AGAINST ONE-SELF
8TH CIRCLE OF HELL
HYPOCRISY
FAKE FLATTERY
NORMAL FRAUD
9TH CIRCLE OF HELL
VOTE
KIN
PARTY
BETRAYAL
CAN THE PUNISHMENT BE WORSE?
COUNTRY
BENEFACTORS

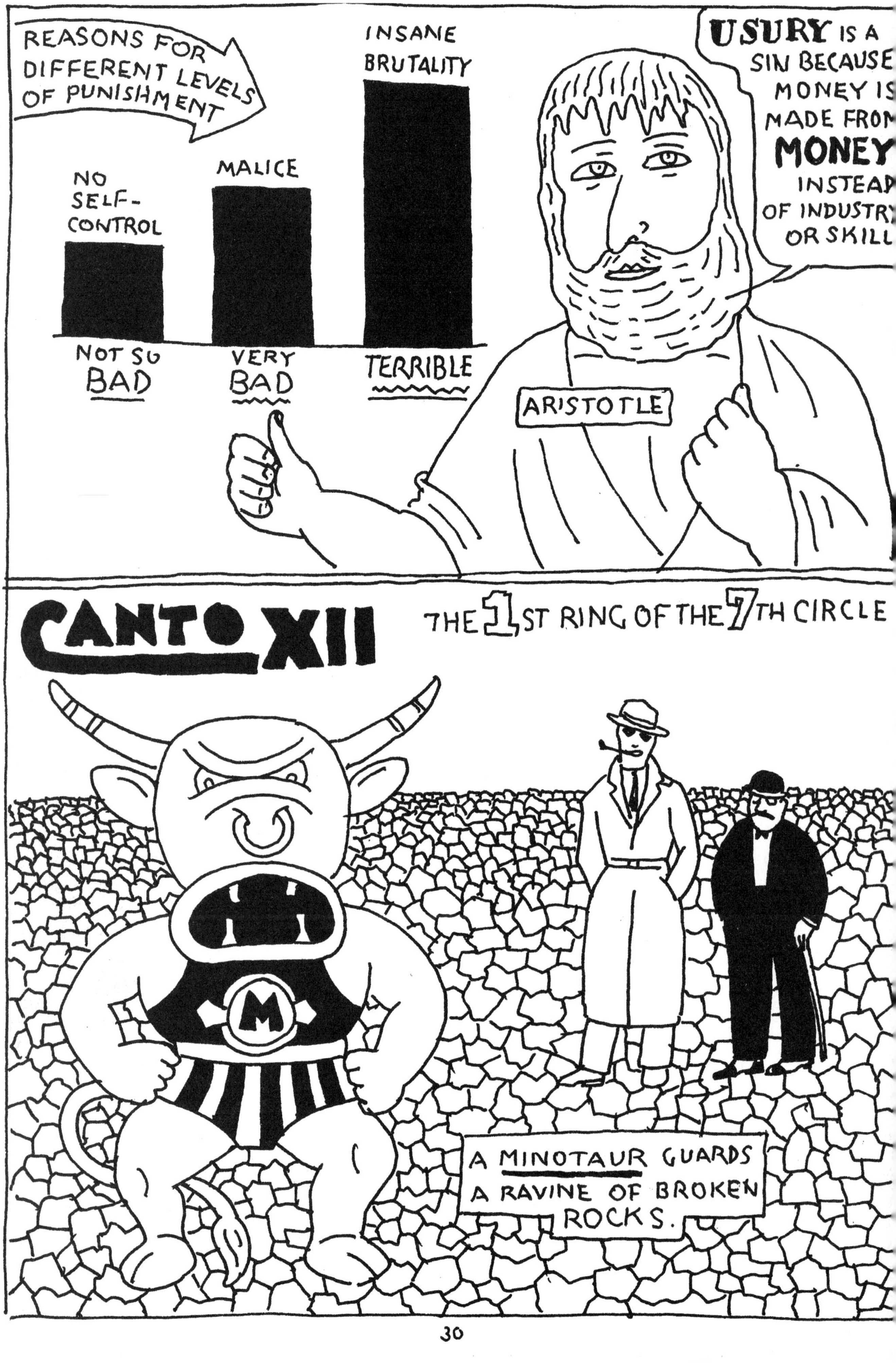
REASONS FOR DIFFERENT LEVELS OF PUNISHMENT
NO SELF-CONTROL
MALICE
INSANE BRUTALITY
NOT SO BAD
VERY BAD
TERRIBLE
USURY IS A SIN BECAUSE MONEY IS MADE FROM MONEY INSTEAD OF INDUSTRY OR SKILL
ARISTOTLE
CANTO XII
THE 1ST RING OF THE 7TH CIRCLE
M
A MINOTAUR GUARDS A RAVINE OF BROKEN ROCKS.

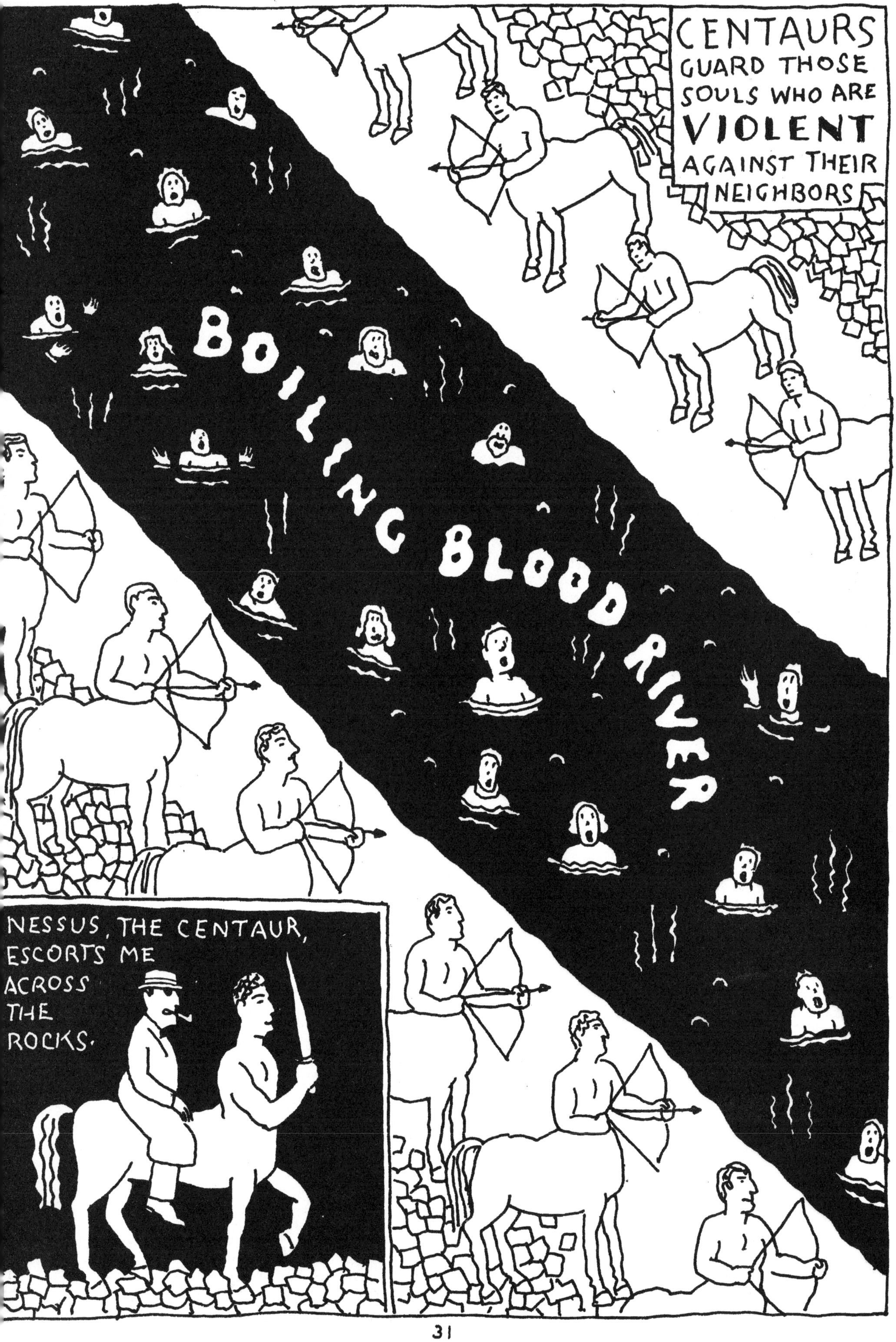

CENTAURS GUARD THOSE SOULS WHO ARE VIOLENT AGAINST THEIR NEIGHBORS
BOILING BLOOD RIVER
NESSUS, THE CENTAUR, ESCORTS ME ACROSS THE ROCKS.

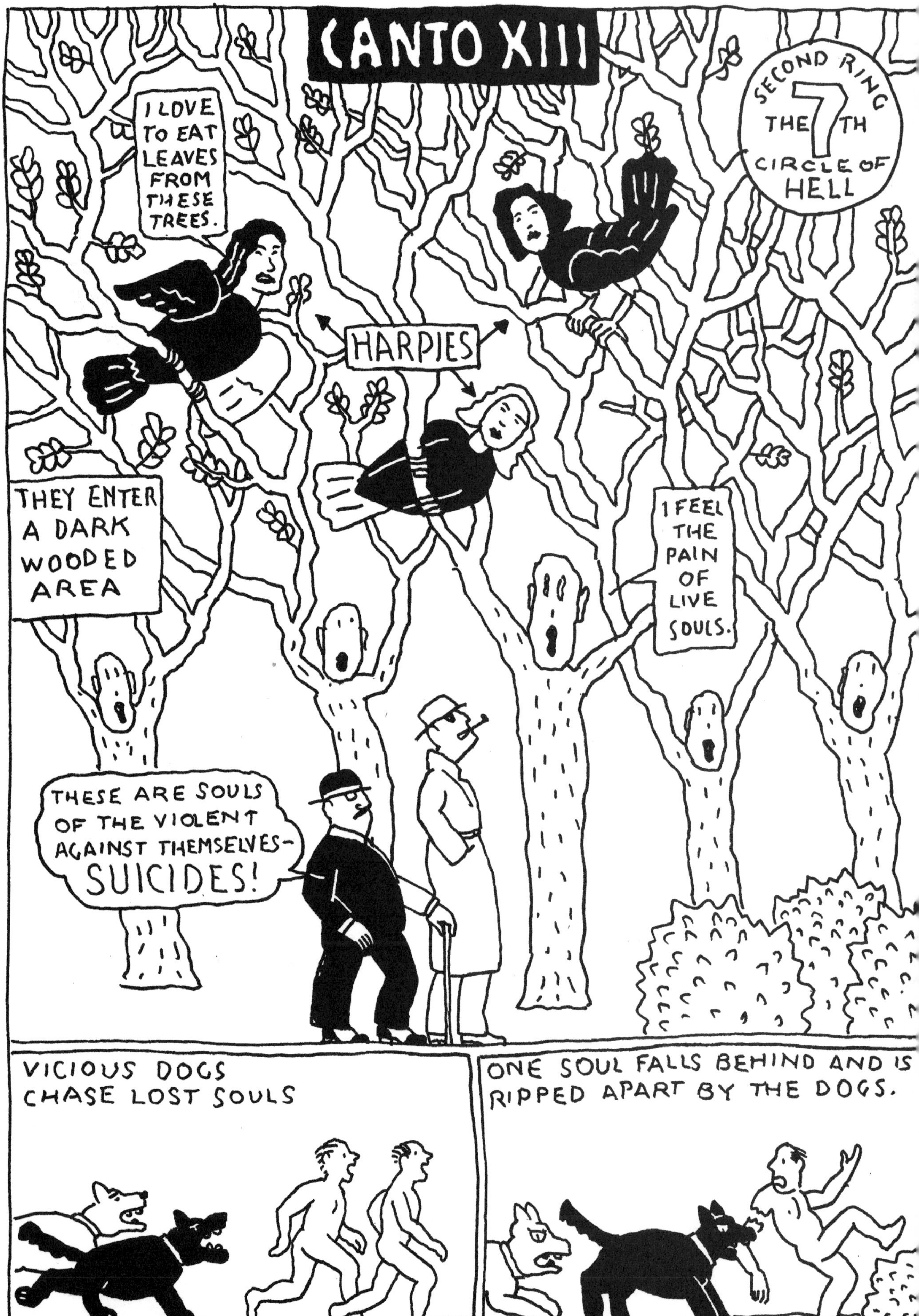
CANTO XIII
SECOND RING THE 7TH CIRCLE OF HELL
THEY ENTER A DARK WOODED AREA
I LOVE TO EAT LEAVES FROM THESE TREES.
HARPIES
I FEEL THE PAIN OF LIVE SOULS.
THESE ARE SOULS OF THE VIOLENT AGAINST THEMSELVES- SUICIDES!
VICIOUS DOGS CHASE LOST SOULS
ONE SOUL FALLS BEHIND AND IS RIPPED APART BY THE DOGS.

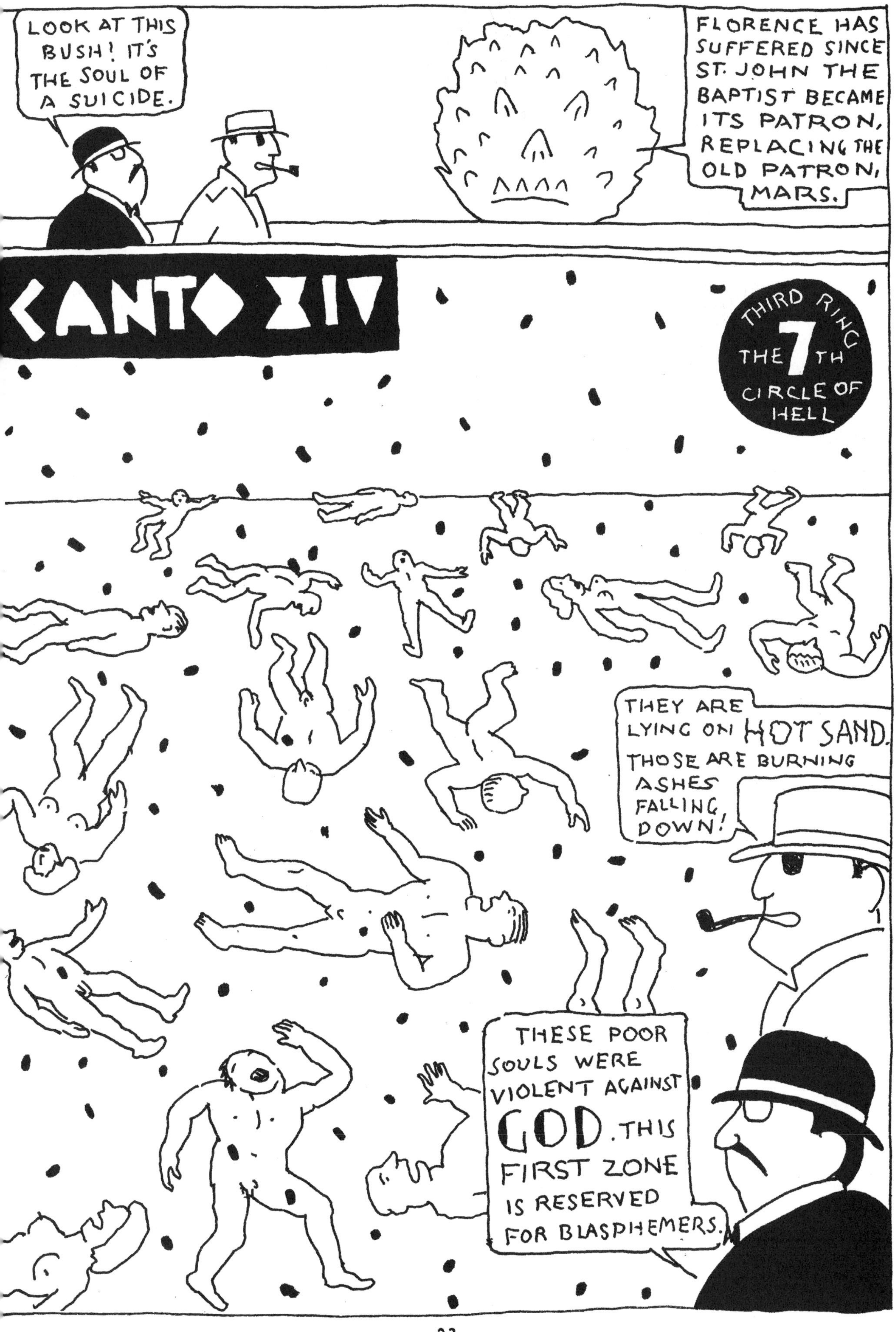
LOOK AT THIS BUSH! IT'S THE SOUL OF A SUICIDE.
FLORENCE HAS SUFFERED SINCE ST. JOHN THE BAPTIST BECAME ITS PATRON, REPLACING THE OLD PATRON, MARS.
CANTO XIV
THIRD RING
THE 7TH CIRCLE OF HELL
THEY ARE LYING ON HOT SAND. THOSE ARE BURNING ASHES FALLING DOWN!
THESE POOR SOULS WERE VIOLENT AGAINST GOD. THIS FIRST ZONE IS RESERVED FOR BLASPHEMERS.

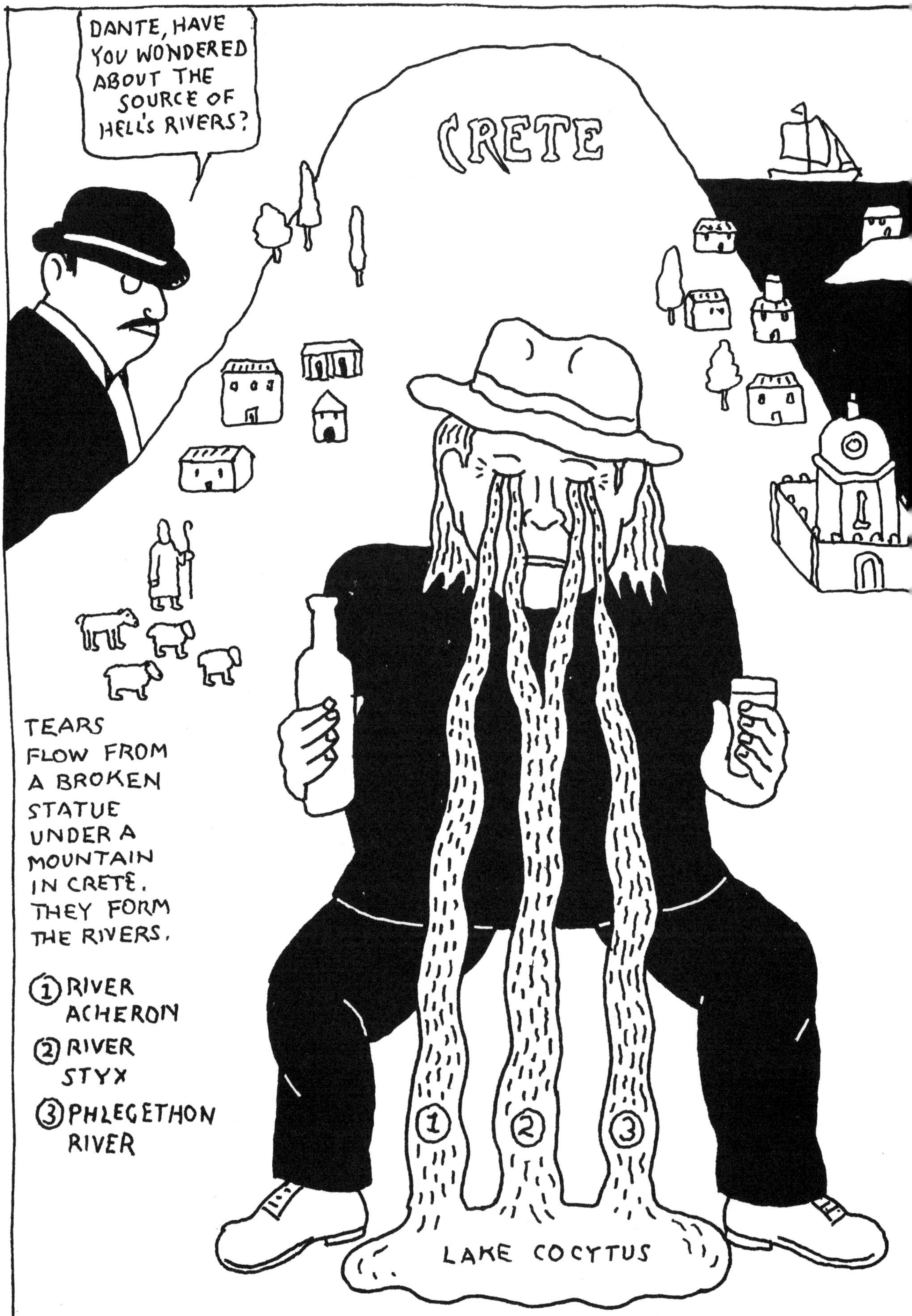
DANTE, HAVE YOU WONDERED ABOUT THE SOURCE OF HELL'S RIVERS?
CRETE
TEARS FLOW FROM A BROKEN STATUE UNDER A MOUNTAIN IN CRETE. THEY FORM THE RIVERS.
1 RIVER ACHERON
2 RIVER STYX
3 PHLEGETHON RIVER
1
2
3
LAKE COCYTUS

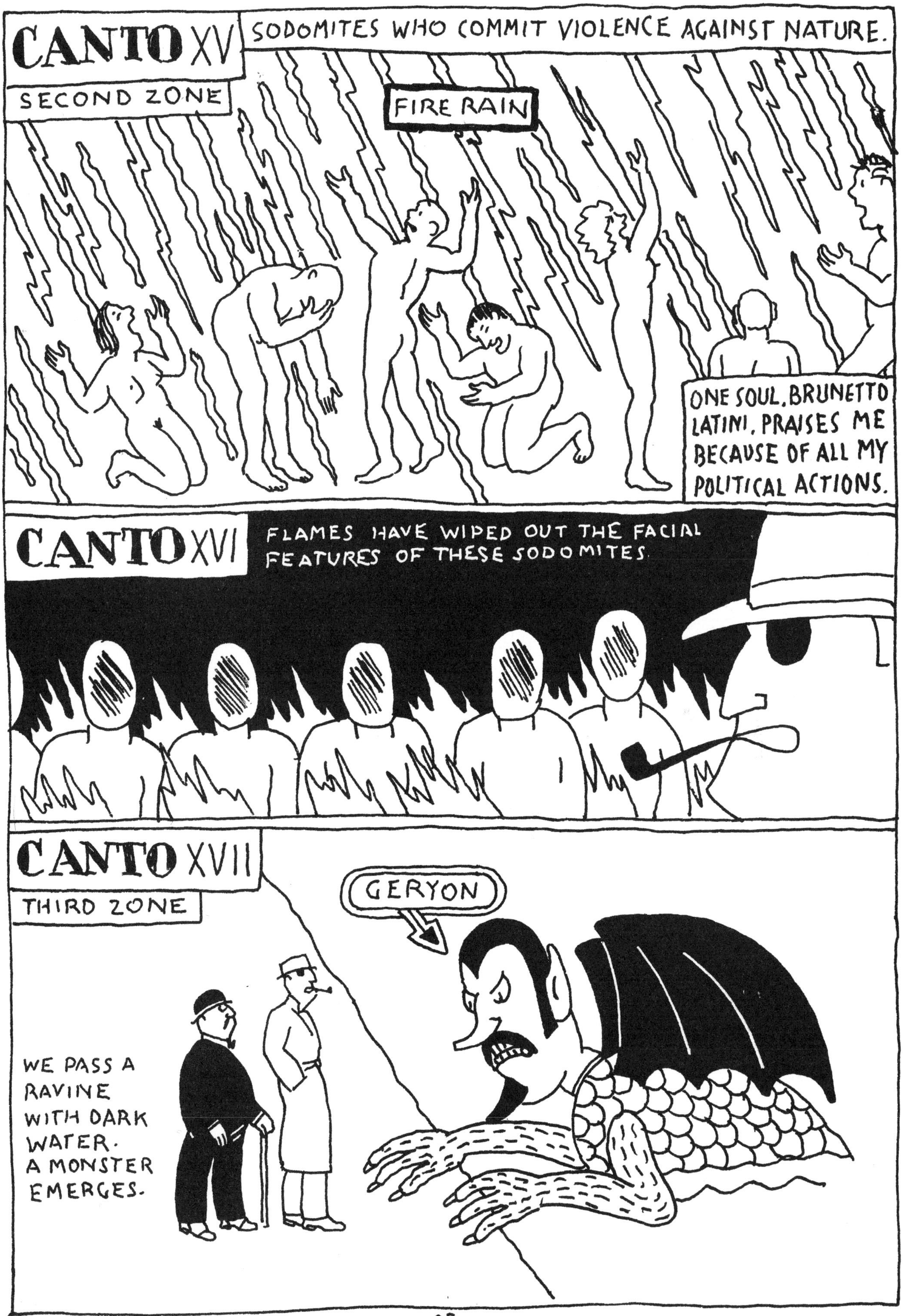
CANTO XV
SODOMITES WHO COMMIT VIOLENCE AGAINST NATURE.
SECOND ZONE
FIRE RAIN
ONE SOUL, BRUNETTO LATINI, PRAISES ME BECAUSE OF ALL MY POLITICAL ACTIONS.
CANTO XVI
FLAMES HAVE WIPED OUT THE FACIAL FEATURES OF THESE SODOMITES.
CANTO XVII
THIRD ZONE
GERYON
WE PASS A RAVINE WITH DARK WATER. A MONSTER EMERGES.

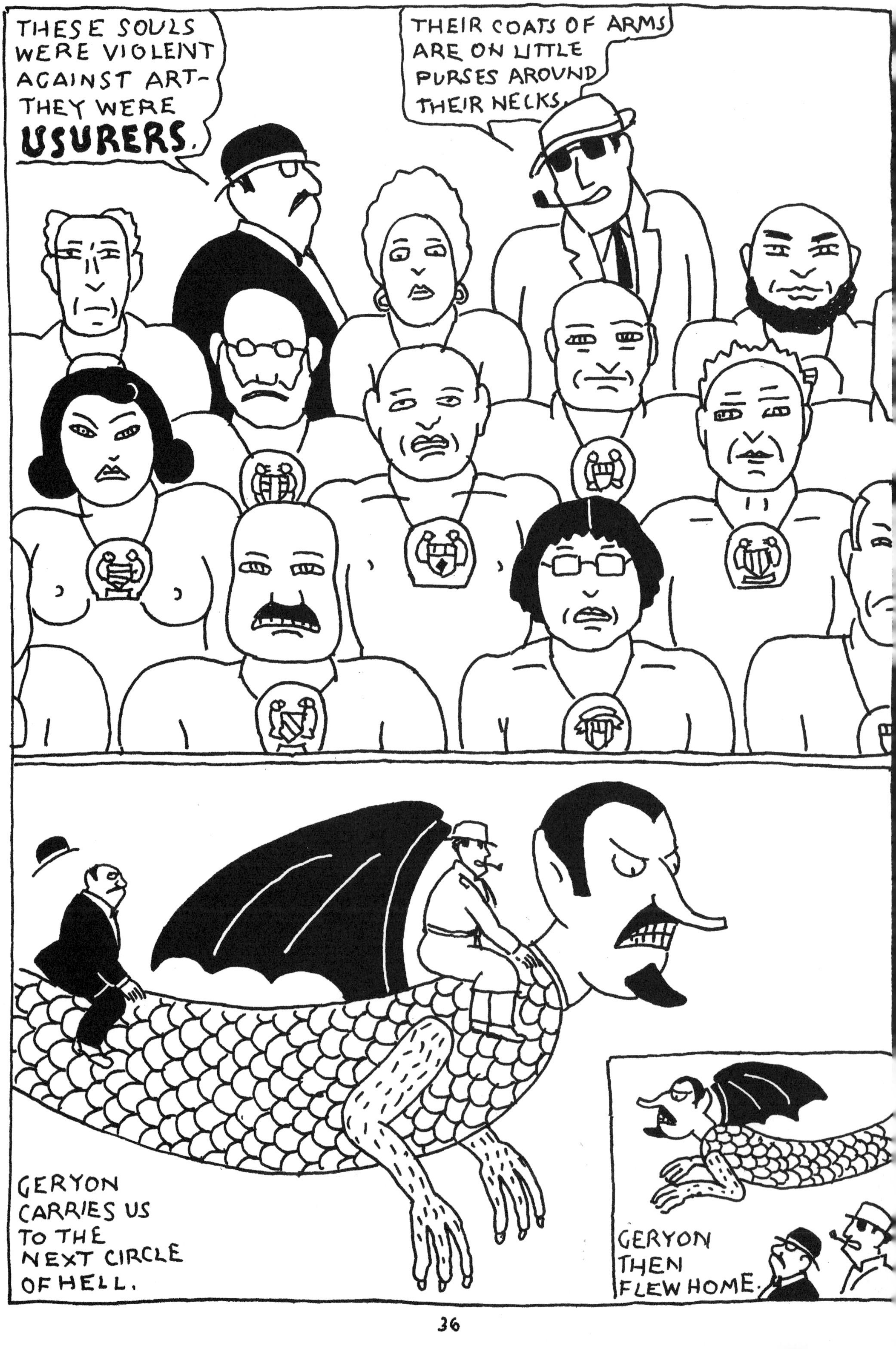
THESE SOULS WERE VIOLENT AGAINST ART- THEY WERE **USURERS**.
THEIR COATS OF ARMS ARE ON LITTLE PURSES AROUND THEIR NECKS.
GERYON CARRIES US TO THE NEXT CIRCLE OF HELL.
GERYON THEN FLEW HOME.

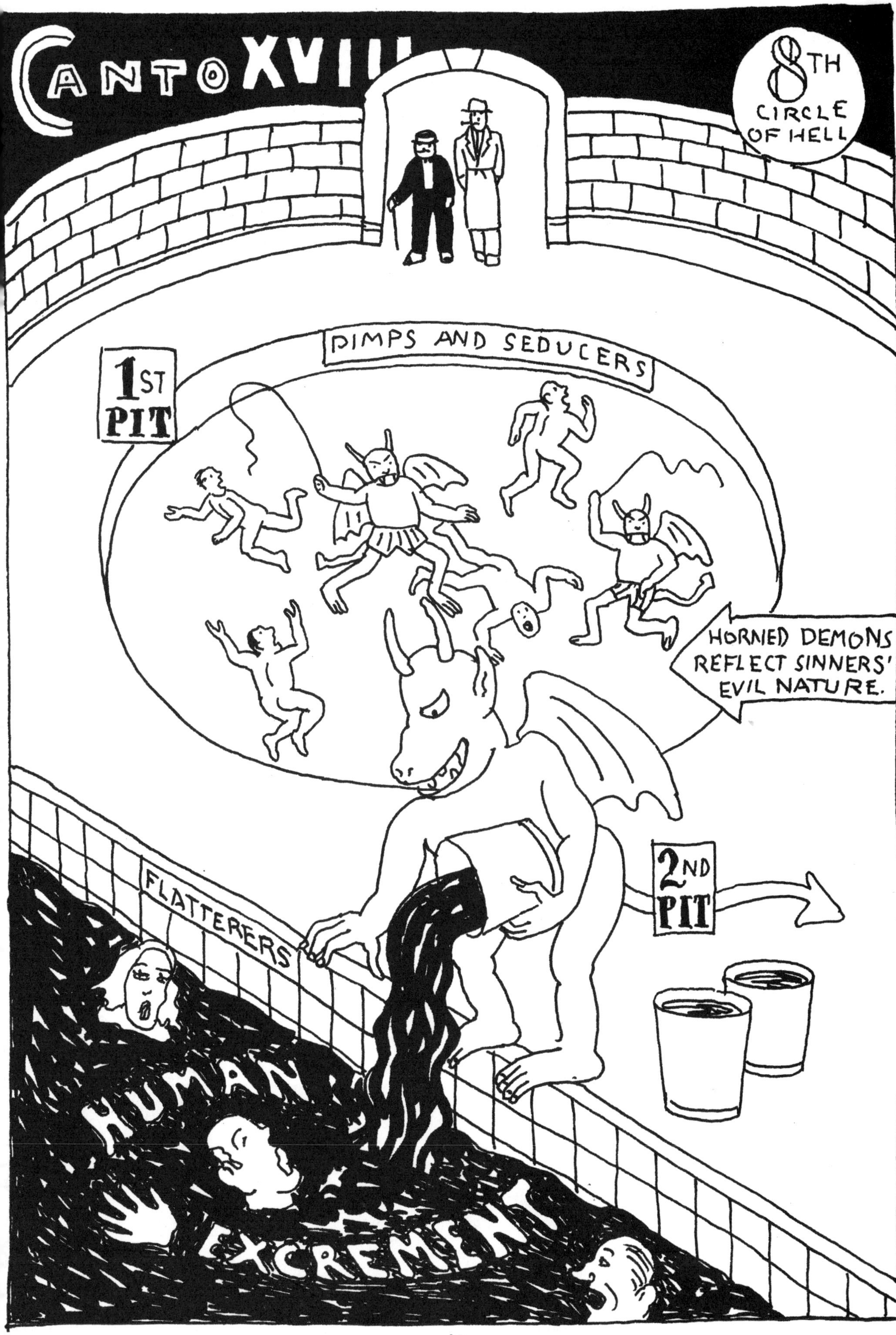
CANTO XVIII
8TH CIRCLE OF HELL
PIMPS AND SEDUCERS
1ST PIT
HORNED DEMONS REFLECT SINNERS' EVIL NATURE.
FLATTERERS
2ND PIT
HUMAN EXCREMENT

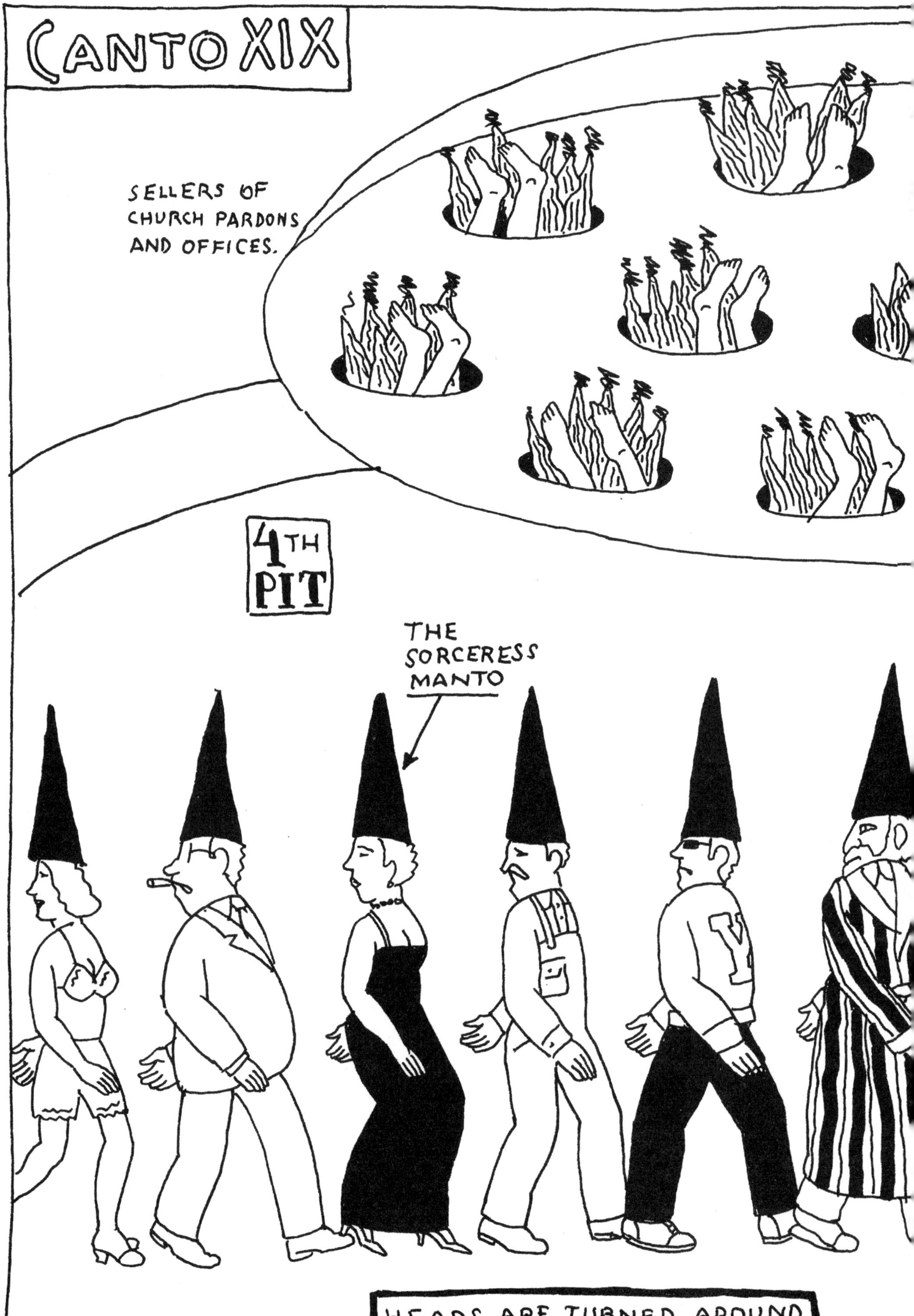
CANTO XIX
SELLERS OF CHURCH PARDONS AND OFFICES.
4TH PIT
THE SORCERESS MANTO
HEADS ARE TURNED AROUND

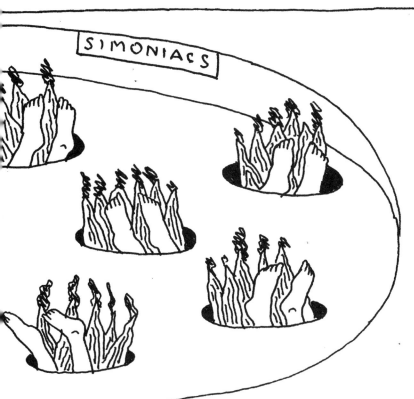

SIMONIACS

3RD PIT

SINNERS IN FIERY TUBES, THEIR FEET ABLAZE

CANTO XX — SOULS WHO ARE ASTROLOGERS, DIVINERS AND MAGICIANS

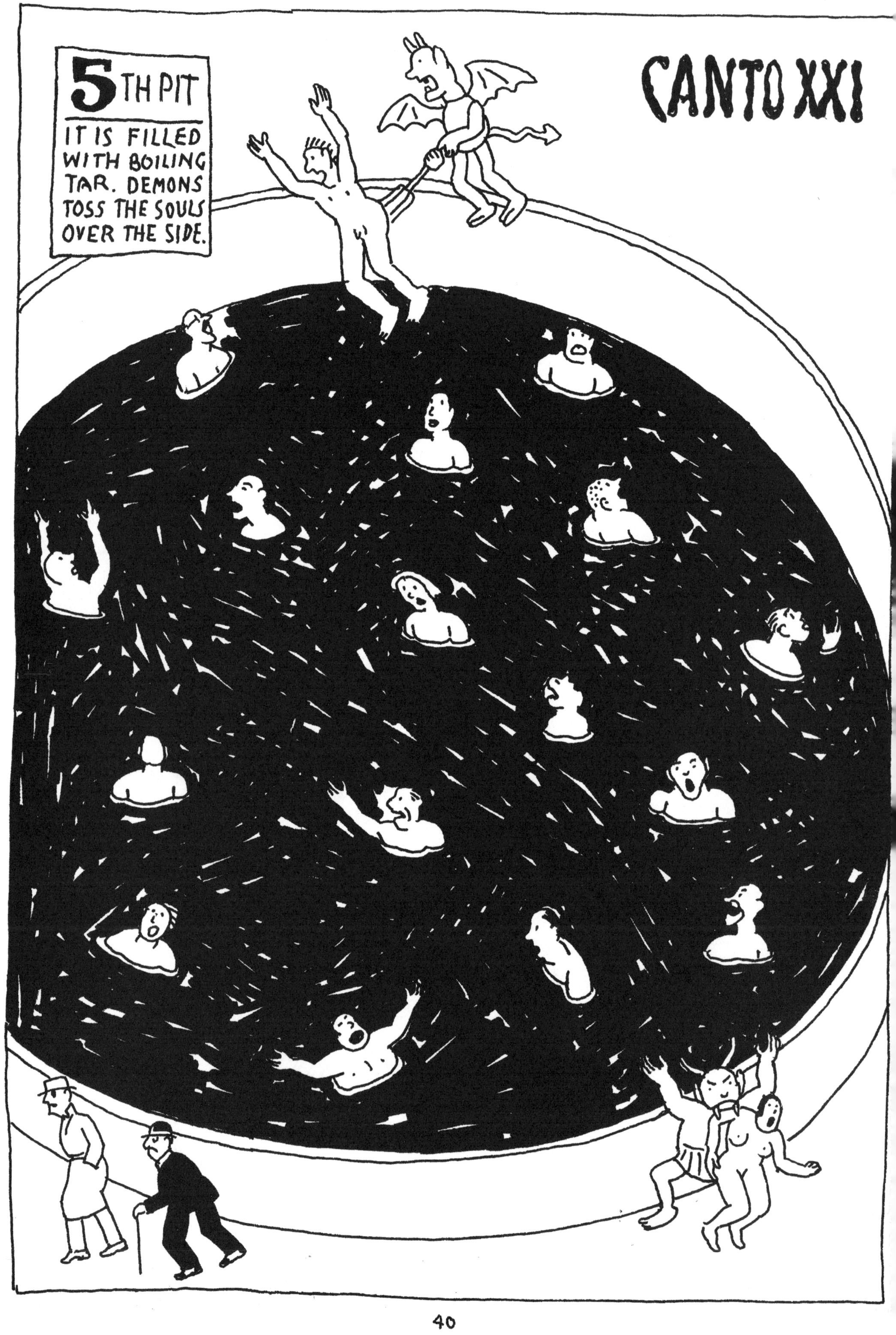
5TH PIT
IT IS FILLED WITH BOILING TAR. DEMONS TOSS THE SOULS OVER THE SIDE.
CANTO XXI

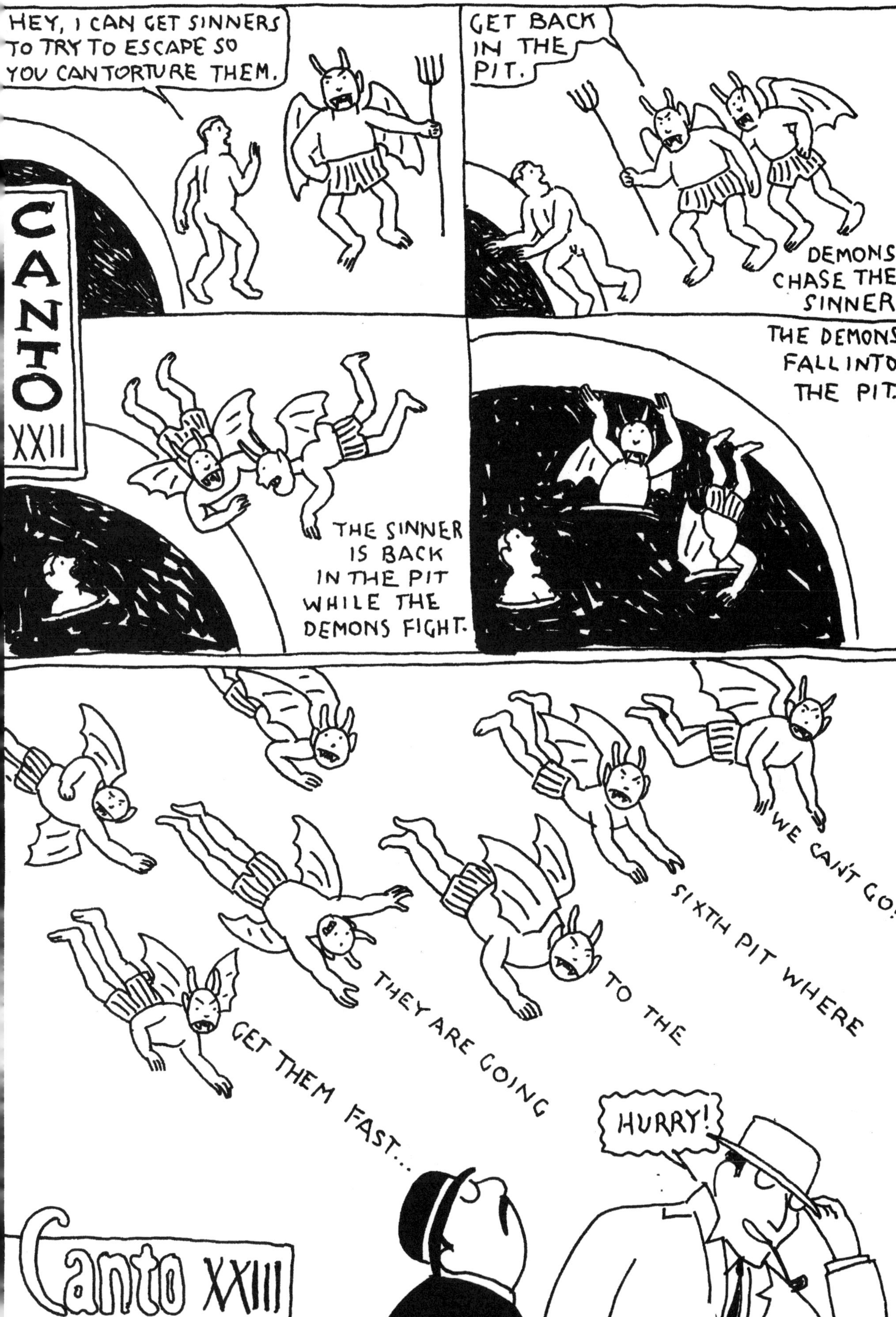
HEY, I CAN GET SINNERS TO TRY TO ESCAPE SO YOU CAN TORTURE THEM.
GET BACK IN THE PIT.
DEMONS CHASE THE SINNER.
CANTO XXII
THE SINNER IS BACK IN THE PIT WHILE THE DEMONS FIGHT.
THE DEMONS FALL INTO THE PIT.
GET THEM FAST...
THEY ARE GOING TO THE SIXTH PIT WHERE WE CAN'T GO!
HURRY!
Canto XXIII

6TH PIT
HYPOCRITES
CAIAPHAS HIGH PRIEST TO PONTIUS PILATE
THESE CLOTHES ARE VERY HEAVY... THEY ARE LINED IN LEAD.

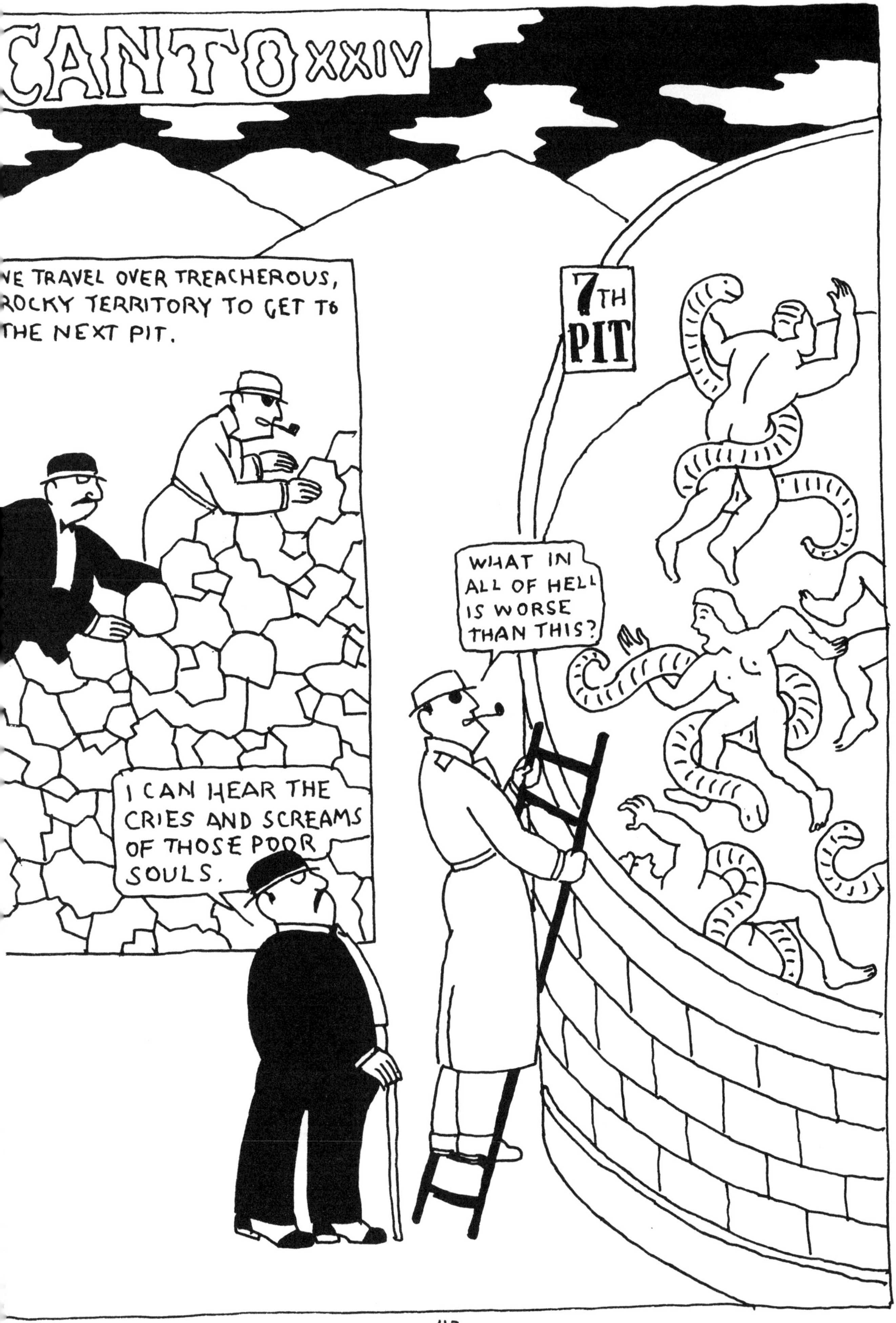

CANTO XXIV
WE TRAVEL OVER TREACHEROUS, ROCKY TERRITORY TO GET TO THE NEXT PIT.
I CAN HEAR THE CRIES AND SCREAMS OF THOSE POOR SOULS.
7TH PIT
WHAT IN ALL OF HELL IS WORSE THAN THIS?

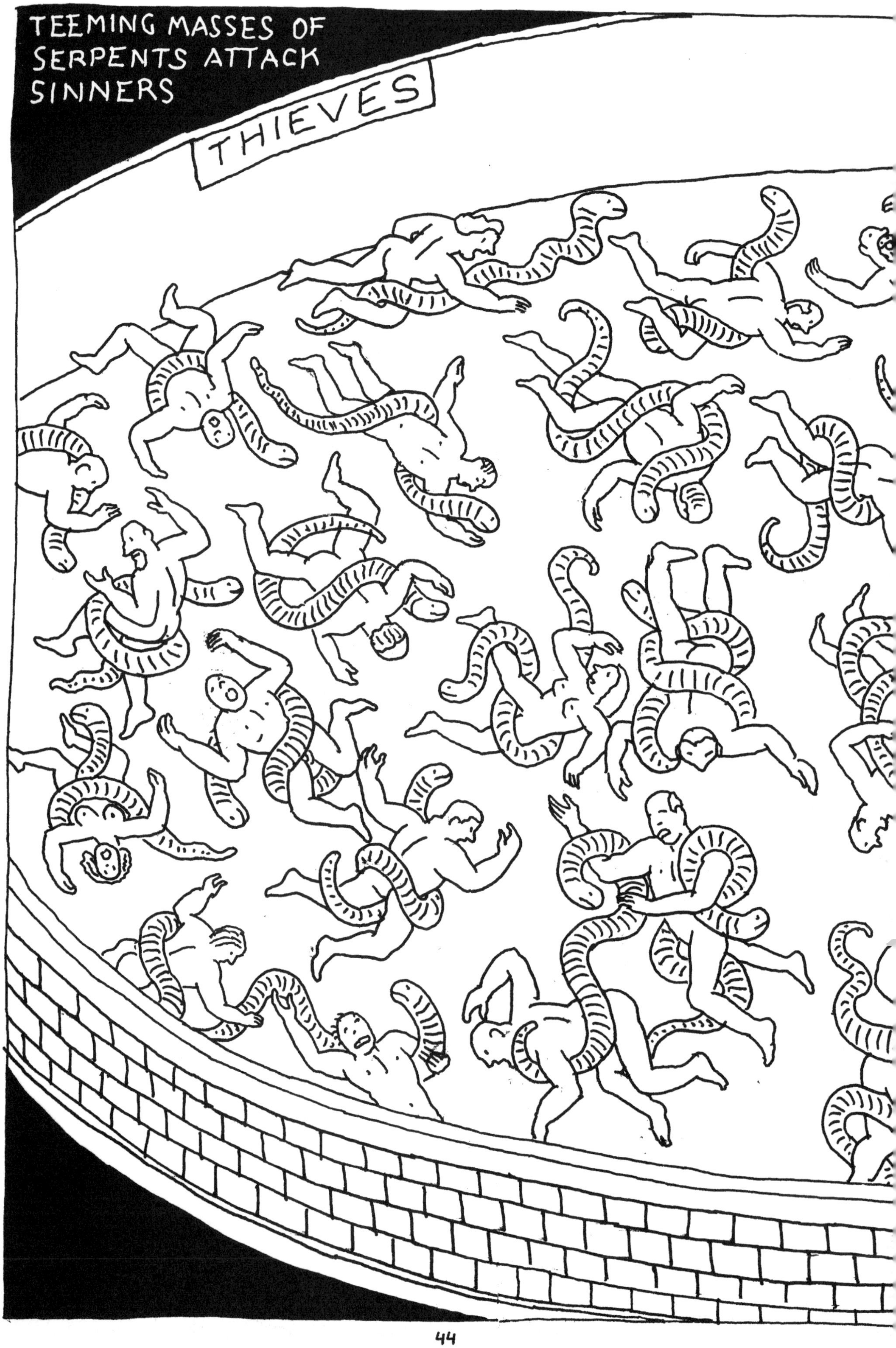
TEEMING MASSES OF SERPENTS ATTACK SINNERS
THIEVES

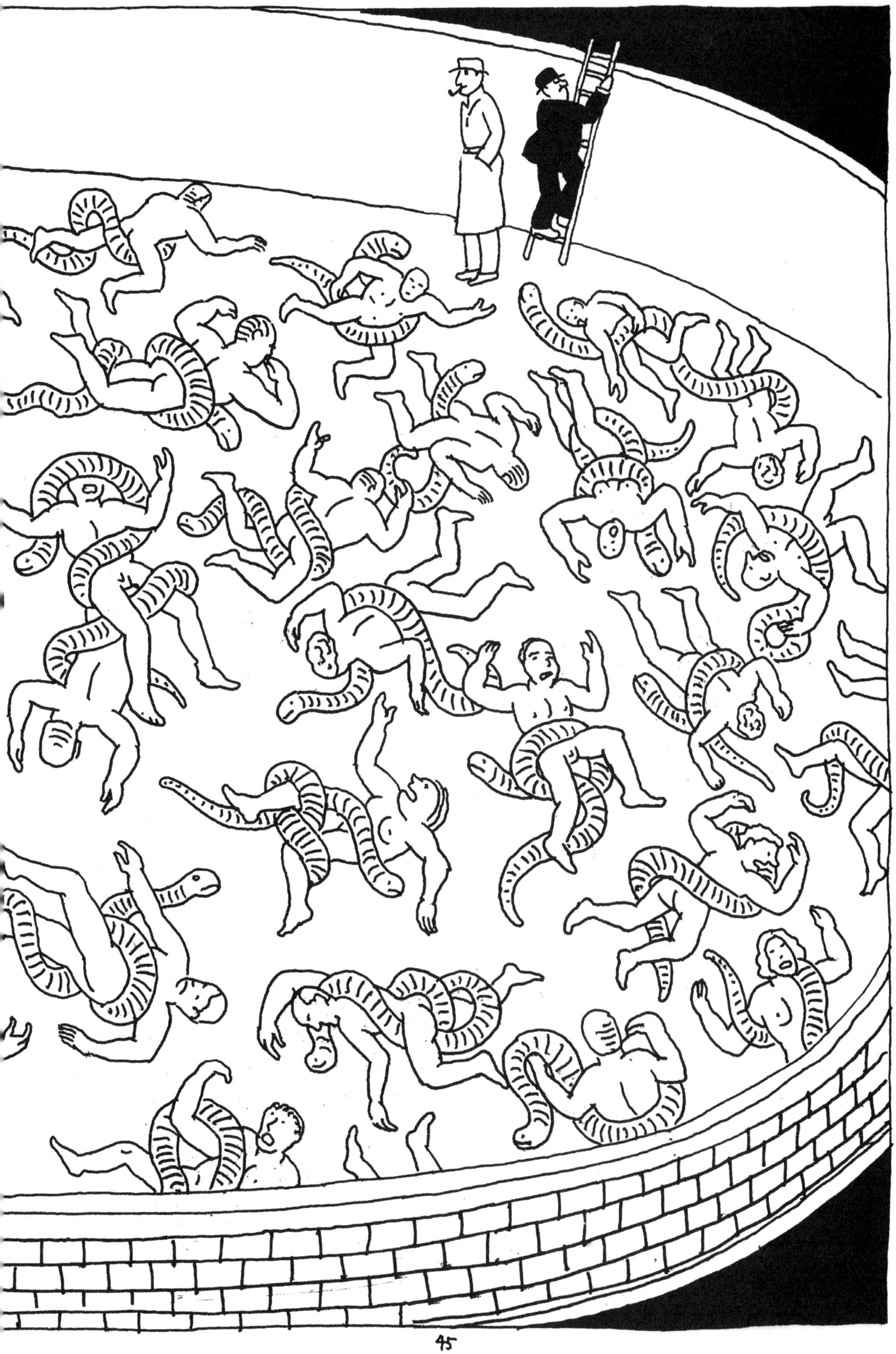

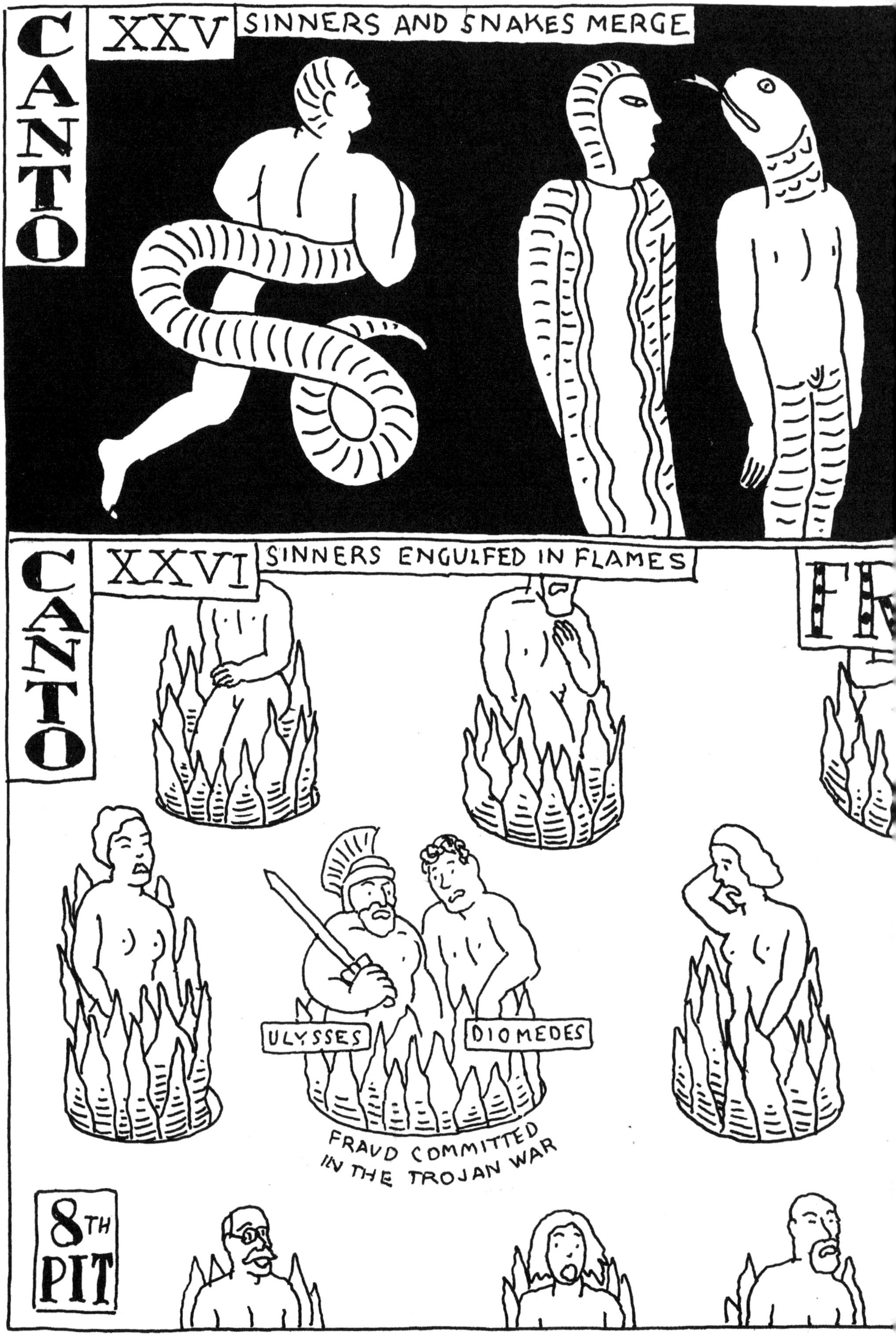
CANTO XXV
SINNERS AND SNAKES MERGE
CANTO XXVI
SINNERS ENGULFED IN FLAMES
ULYSSES
DIOMEDES
FRAUD COMMITTED IN THE TROJAN WAR
8TH PIT

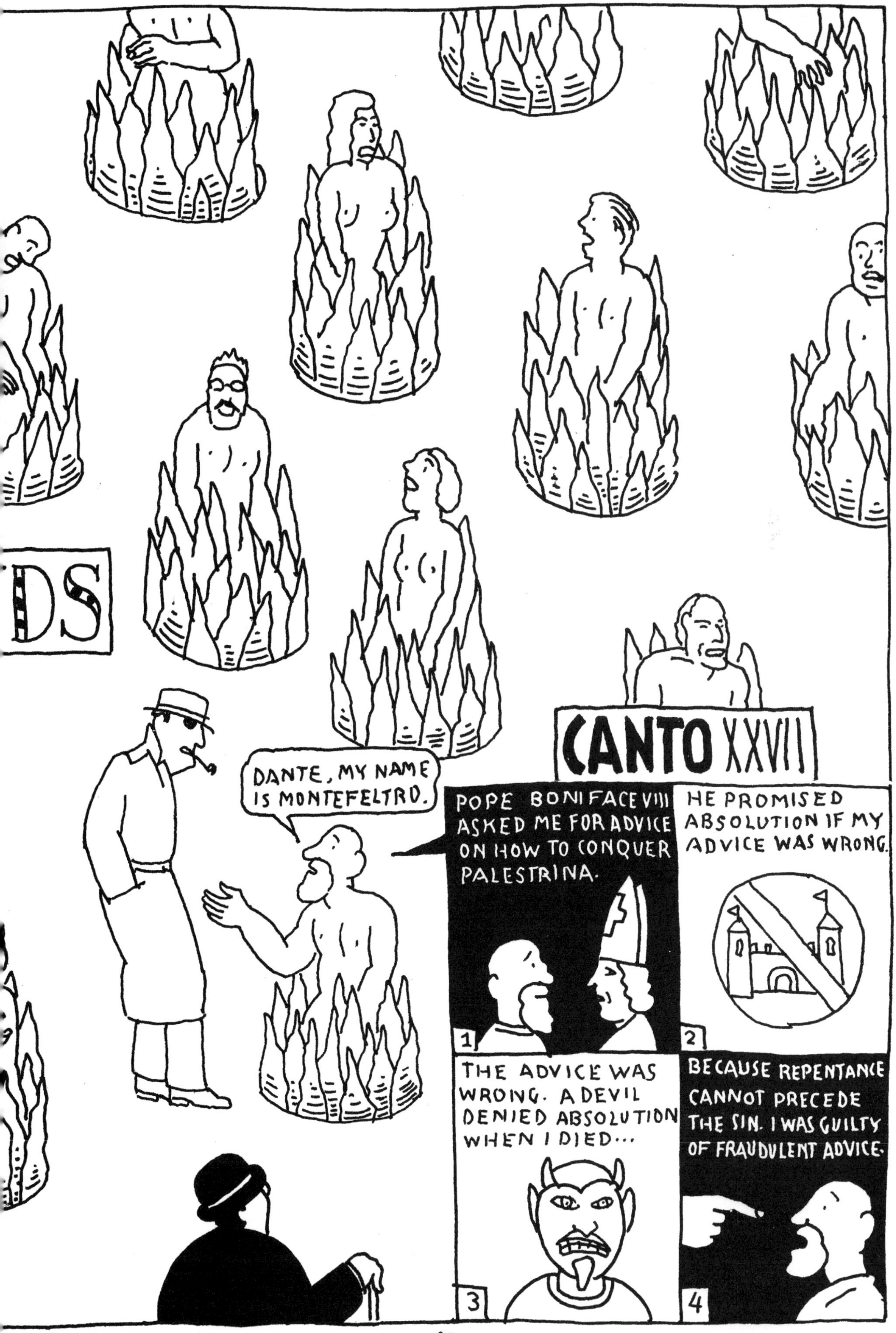
DS
CANTO XXVII
DANTE, MY NAME IS MONTEFELTRO.
POPE BONIFACE VIII ASKED ME FOR ADVICE ON HOW TO CONQUER PALESTRINA.
1
HE PROMISED ABSOLUTION IF MY ADVICE WAS WRONG.
2
THE ADVICE WAS WRONG. A DEVIL DENIED ABSOLUTION WHEN I DIED...
3
BECAUSE REPENTANCE CANNOT PRECEDE THE SIN. I WAS GUILTY OF FRAUDULENT ADVICE.
4

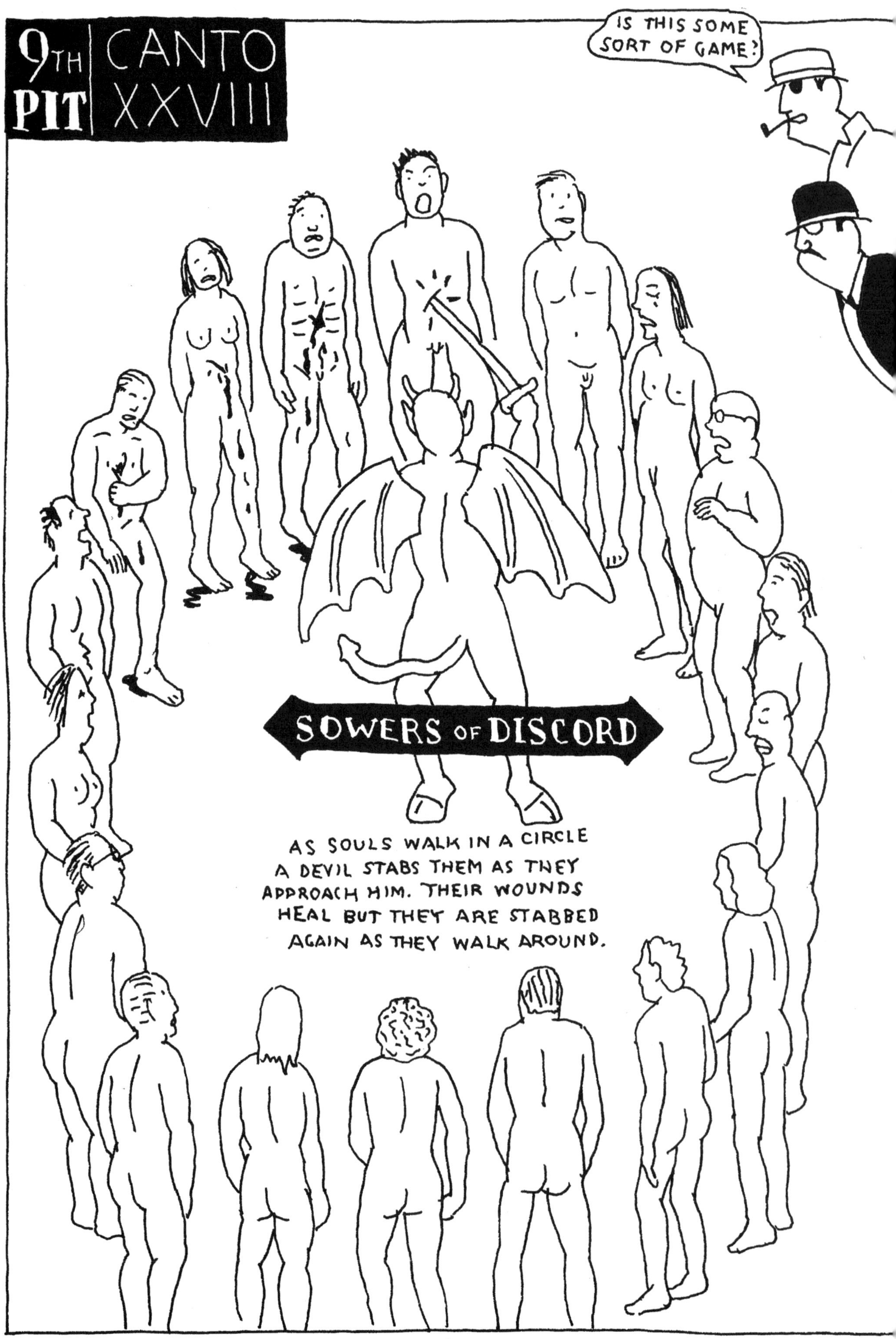
9TH PIT
CANTO XXVIII
IS THIS SOME SORT OF GAME?
SOWERS OF DISCORD
AS SOULS WALK IN A CIRCLE A DEVIL STABS THEM AS THEY APPROACH HIM. THEIR WOUNDS HEAL BUT THEY ARE STABBED AGAIN AS THEY WALK AROUND.

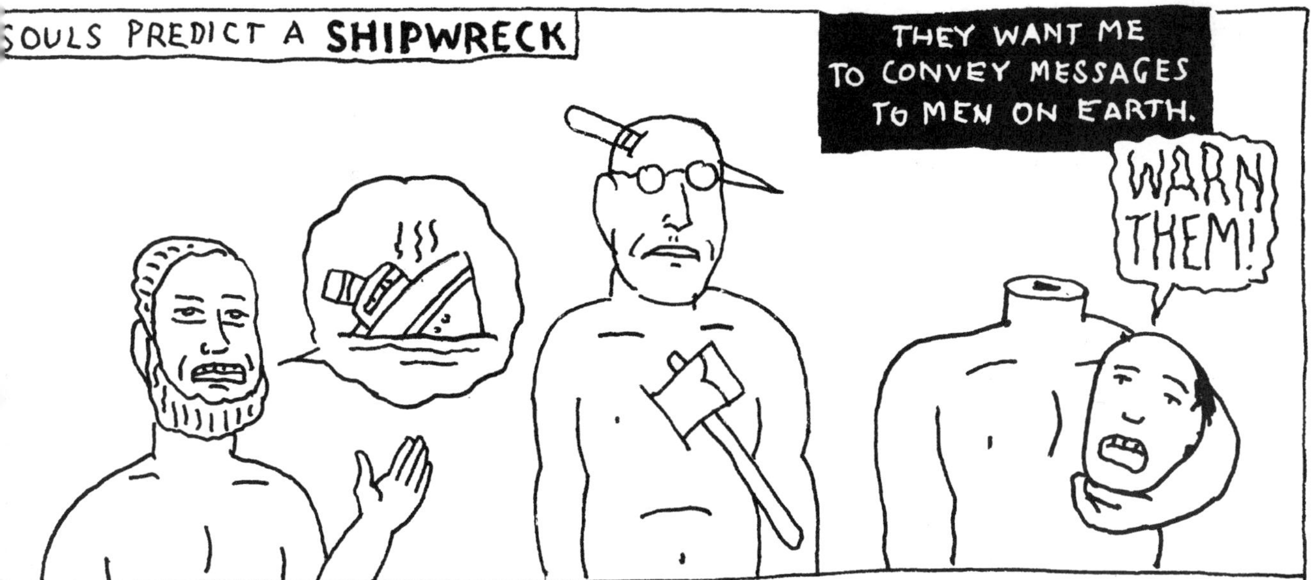
SOULS PREDICT A SHIPWRECK
THEY WANT ME TO CONVEY MESSAGES TO MEN ON EARTH.
WARN THEM!

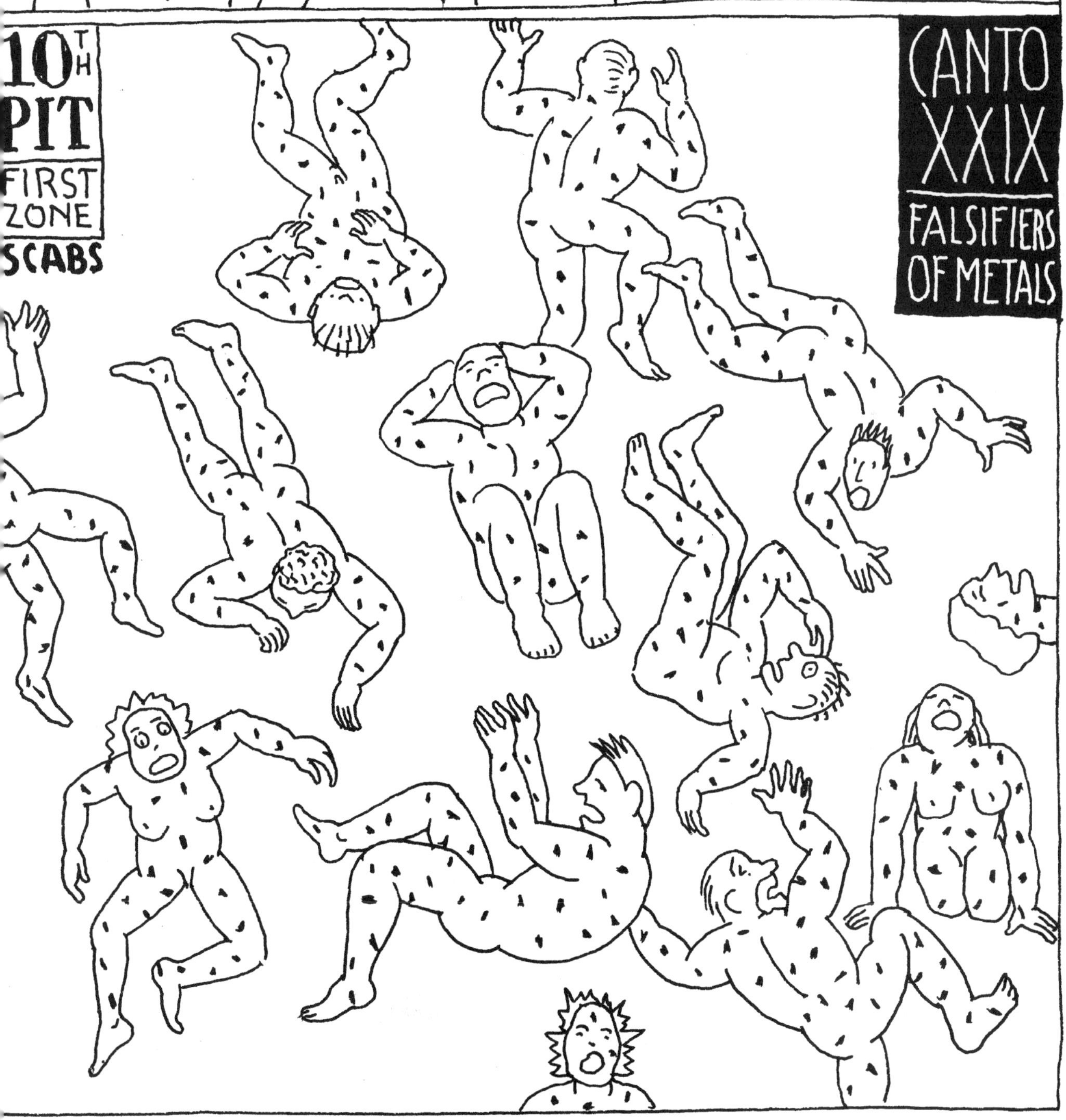
10TH PIT
FIRST ZONE
SCABS
CANTO XXIX
FALSIFIERS OF METALS

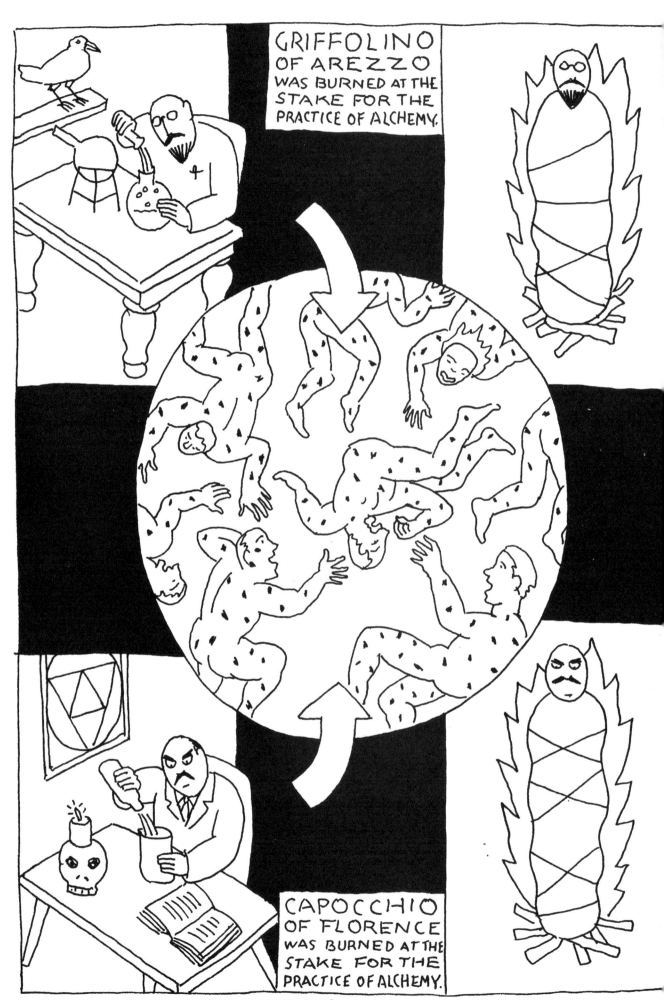

GRIFFOLINO OF AREZZO WAS BURNED AT THE STAKE FOR THE PRACTICE OF ALCHEMY.

CAPOCCHIO OF FLORENCE WAS BURNED AT THE STAKE FOR THE PRACTICE OF ALCHEMY.

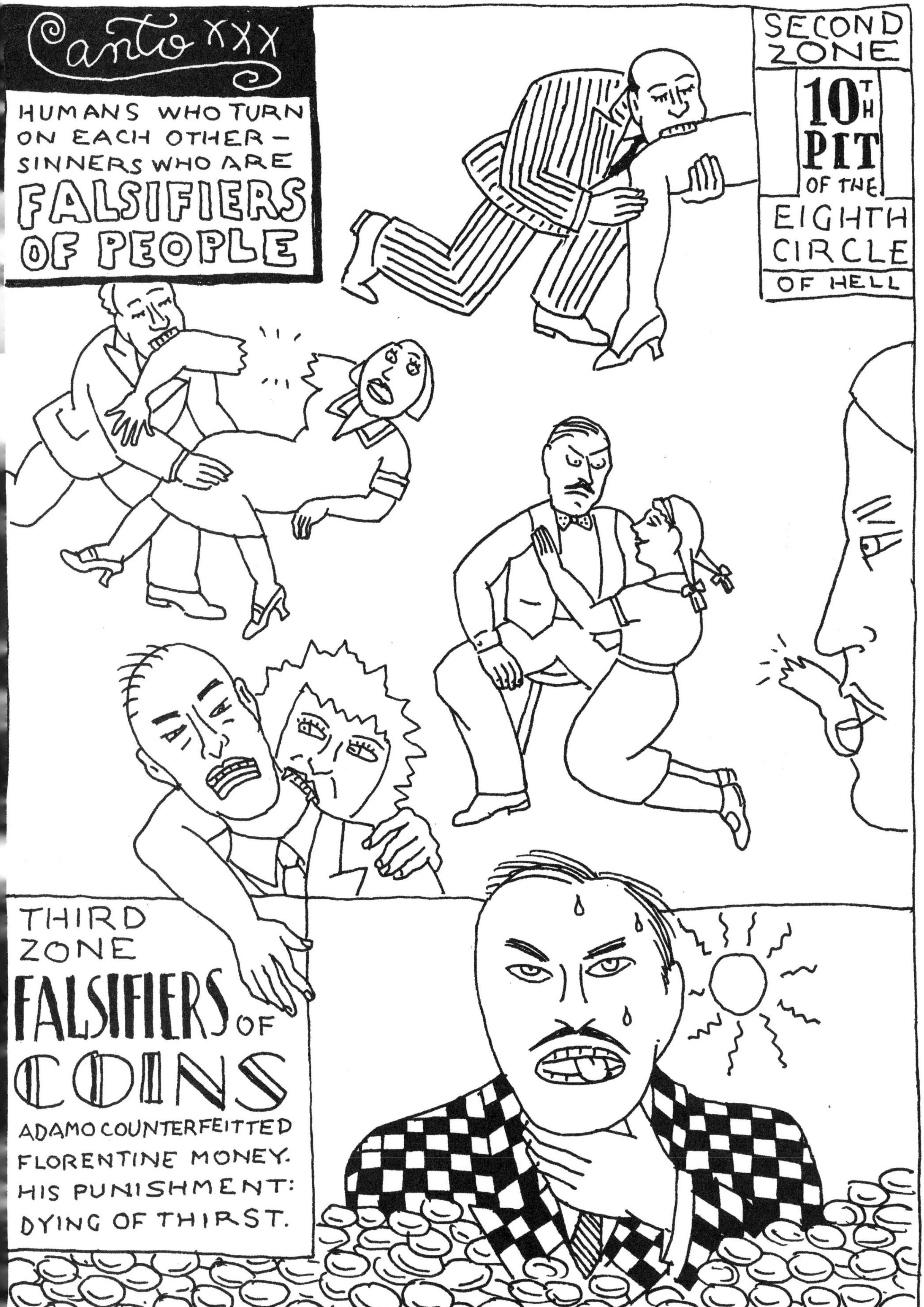
Canto XXX
HUMANS WHO TURN ON EACH OTHER – SINNERS WHO ARE FALSIFIERS OF PEOPLE
SECOND ZONE
10TH PIT OF THE EIGHTH CIRCLE OF HELL
THIRD ZONE
FALSIFIERS OF COINS
ADAMO COUNTERFEITTED FLORENTINE MONEY. HIS PUNISHMENT: DYING OF THIRST.

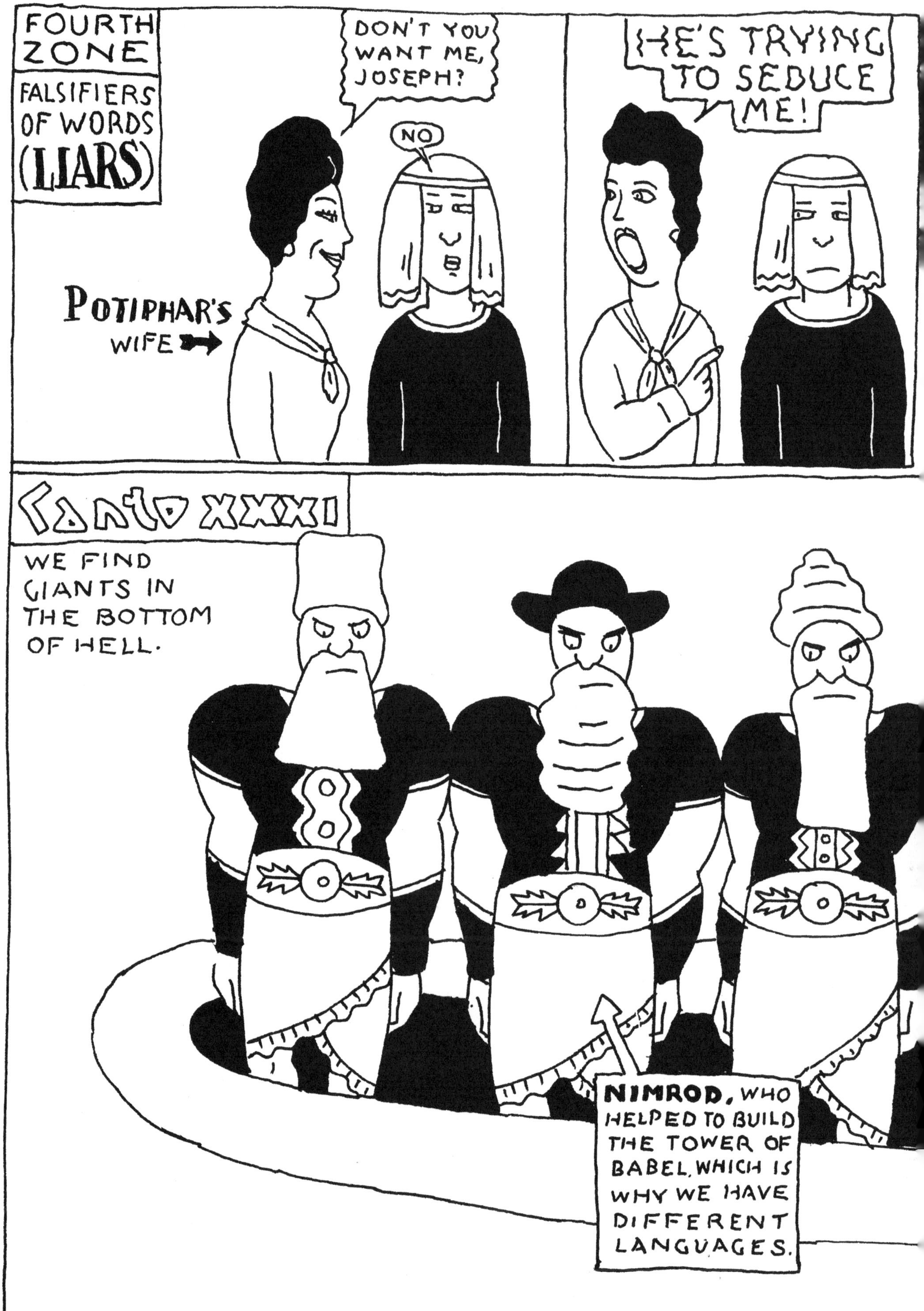
FOURTH ZONE
FALSIFIERS OF WORDS (LIARS)
DON'T YOU WANT ME, JOSEPH?
NO
POTIPHAR'S WIFE
HE'S TRYING TO SEDUCE ME!
CANTO XXXI
WE FIND GIANTS IN THE BOTTOM OF HELL.
NIMROD, WHO HELPED TO BUILD THE TOWER OF BABEL, WHICH IS WHY WE HAVE DIFFERENT LANGUAGES.

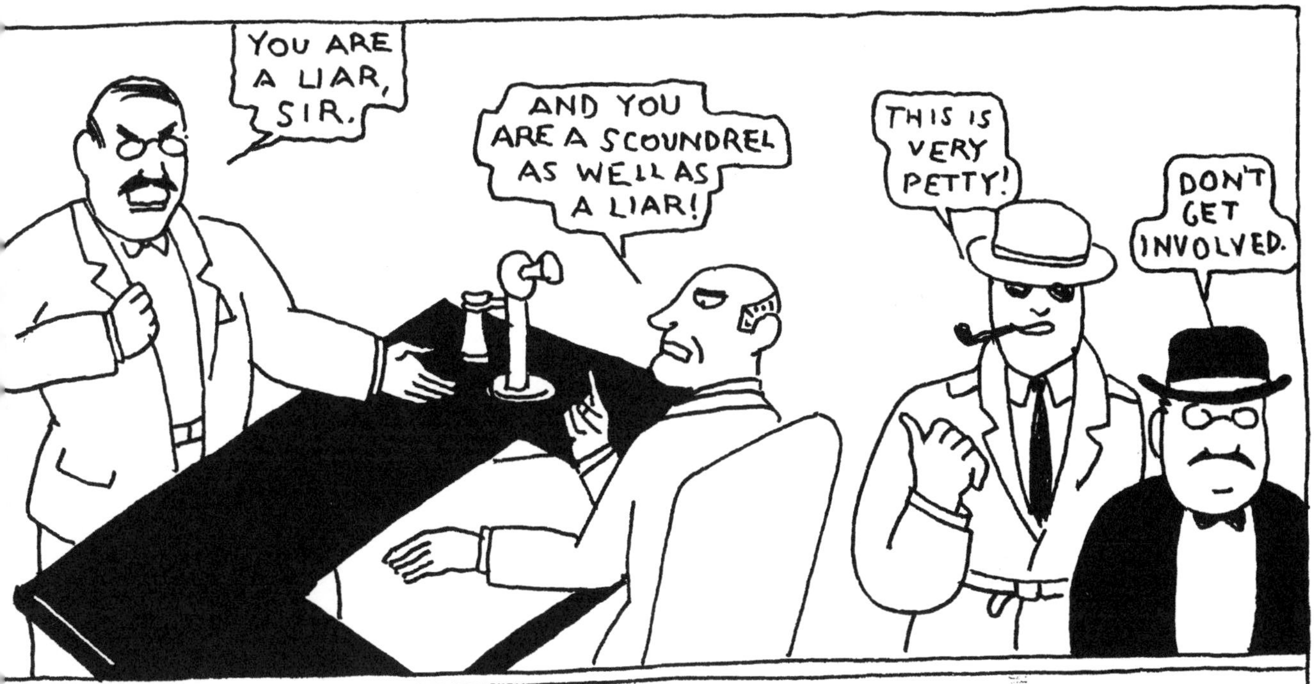
YOU ARE A LIAR, SIR.
AND YOU ARE A SCOUNDREL AS WELL AS A LIAR!
THIS IS VERY PETTY!
DON'T GET INVOLVED.

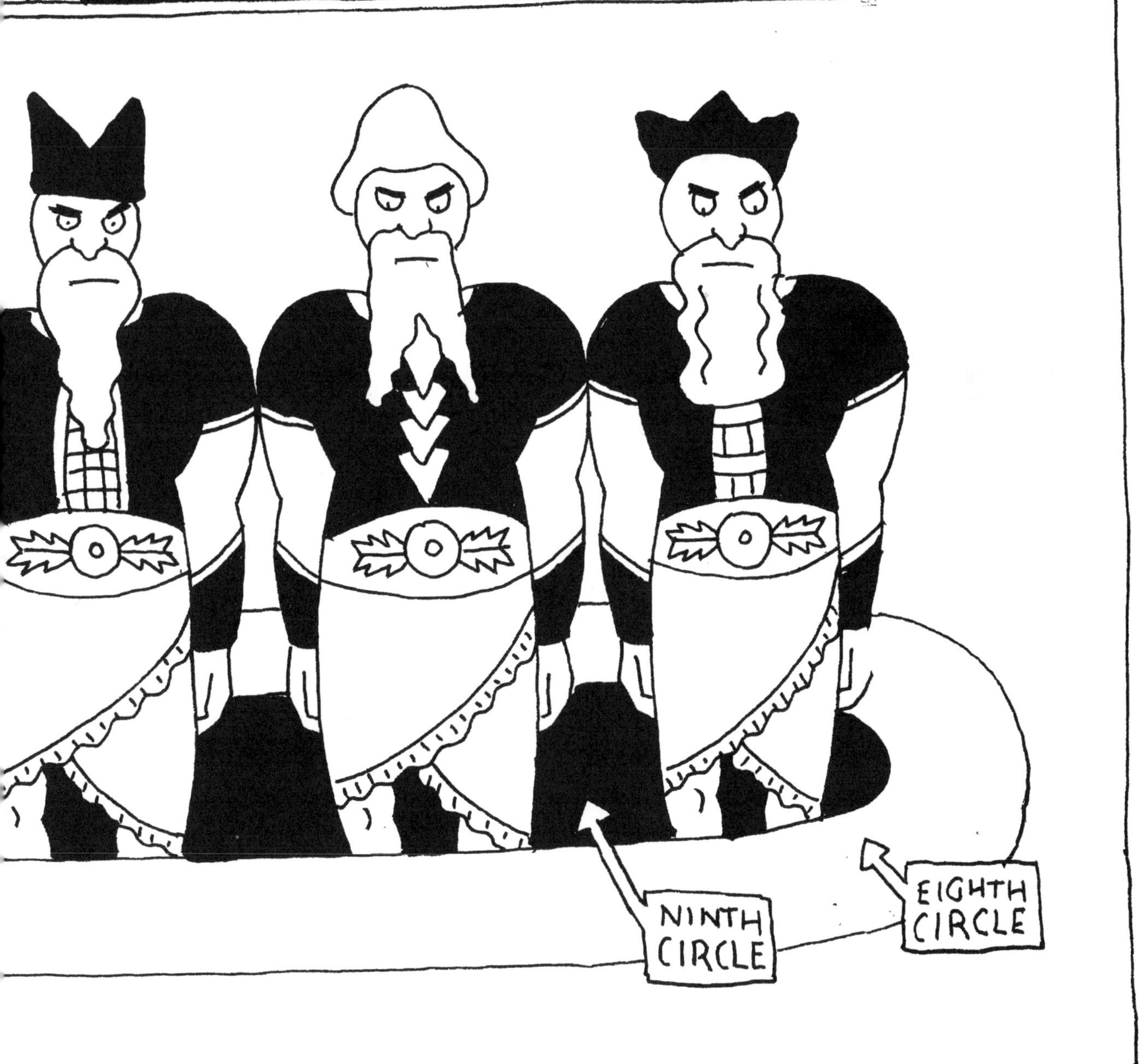
NINTH CIRCLE
EIGHTH CIRCLE

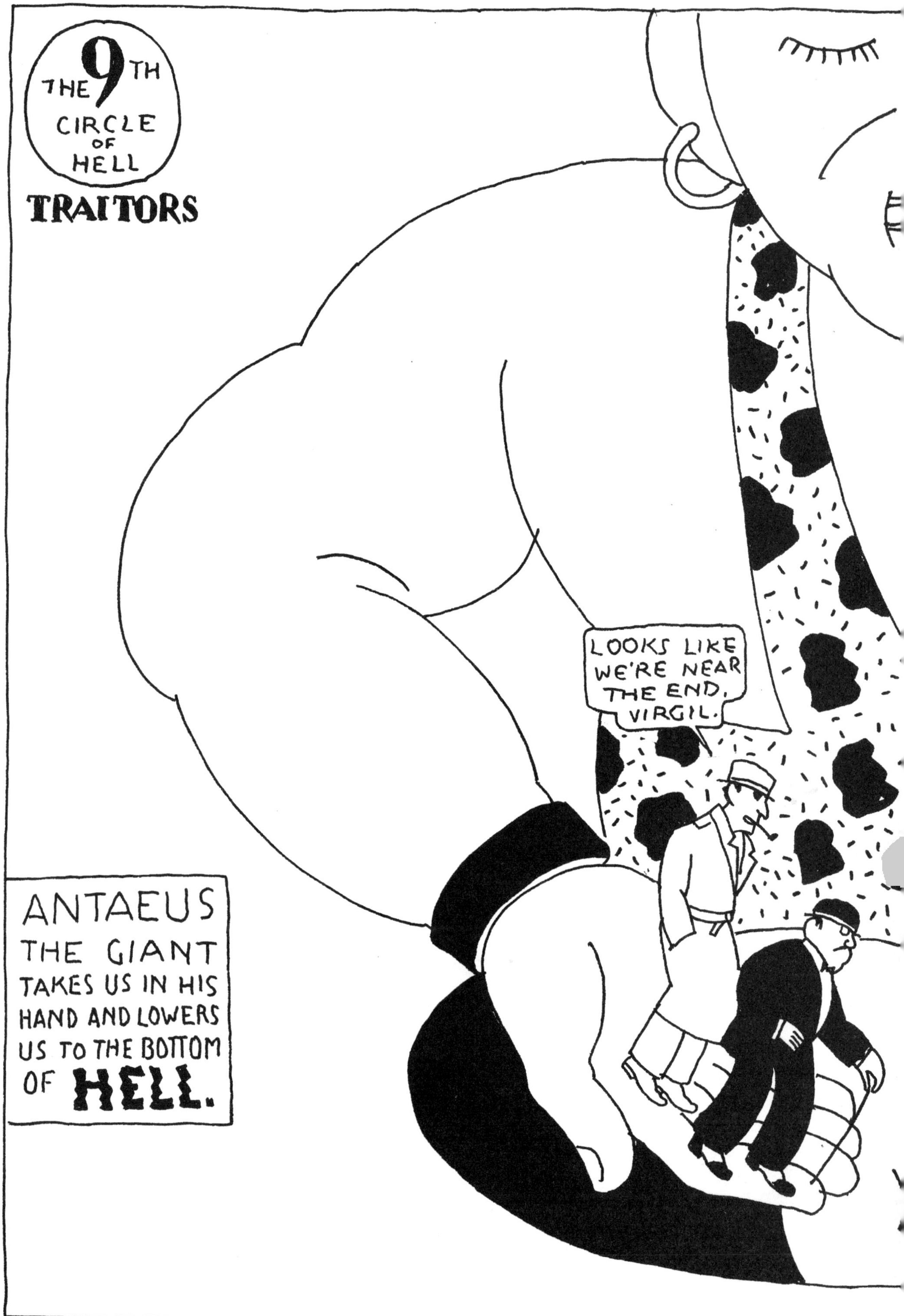
THE 9TH CIRCLE OF HELL
TRAITORS
LOOKS LIKE WE'RE NEAR THE END, VIRGIL.
ANTAEUS THE GIANT TAKES US IN HIS HAND AND LOWERS US TO THE BOTTOM OF HELL.

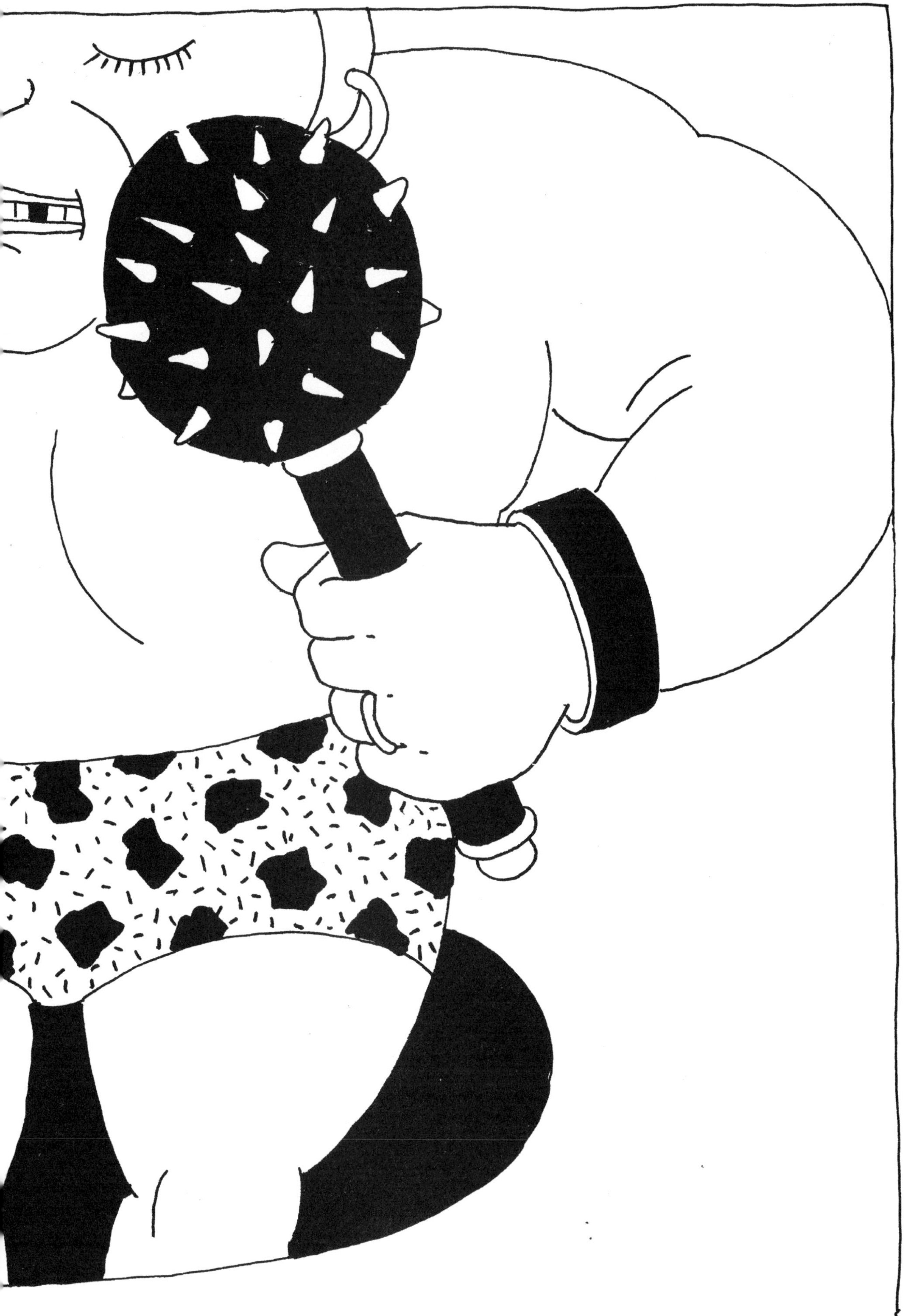

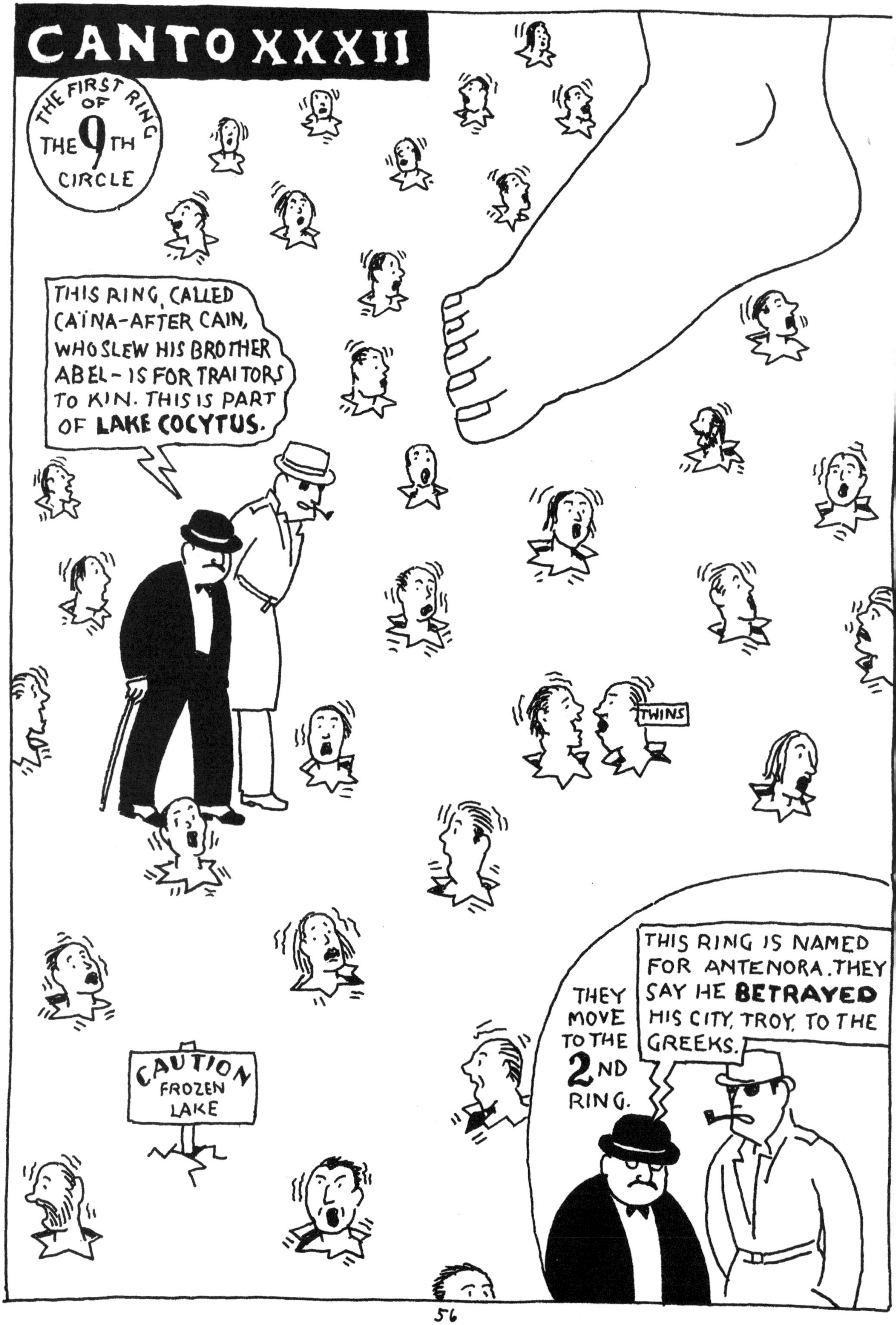
CANTO XXXII
THE FIRST RING OF THE 9TH CIRCLE
THIS RING, CALLED CAÏNA-AFTER CAIN, WHO SLEW HIS BROTHER ABEL - IS FOR TRAITORS TO KIN. THIS IS PART OF LAKE COCYTUS.
TWINS
CAUTION FROZEN LAKE
THEY MOVE TO THE 2ND RING.
THIS RING IS NAMED FOR ANTENORA. THEY SAY HE BETRAYED HIS CITY, TROY, TO THE GREEKS.

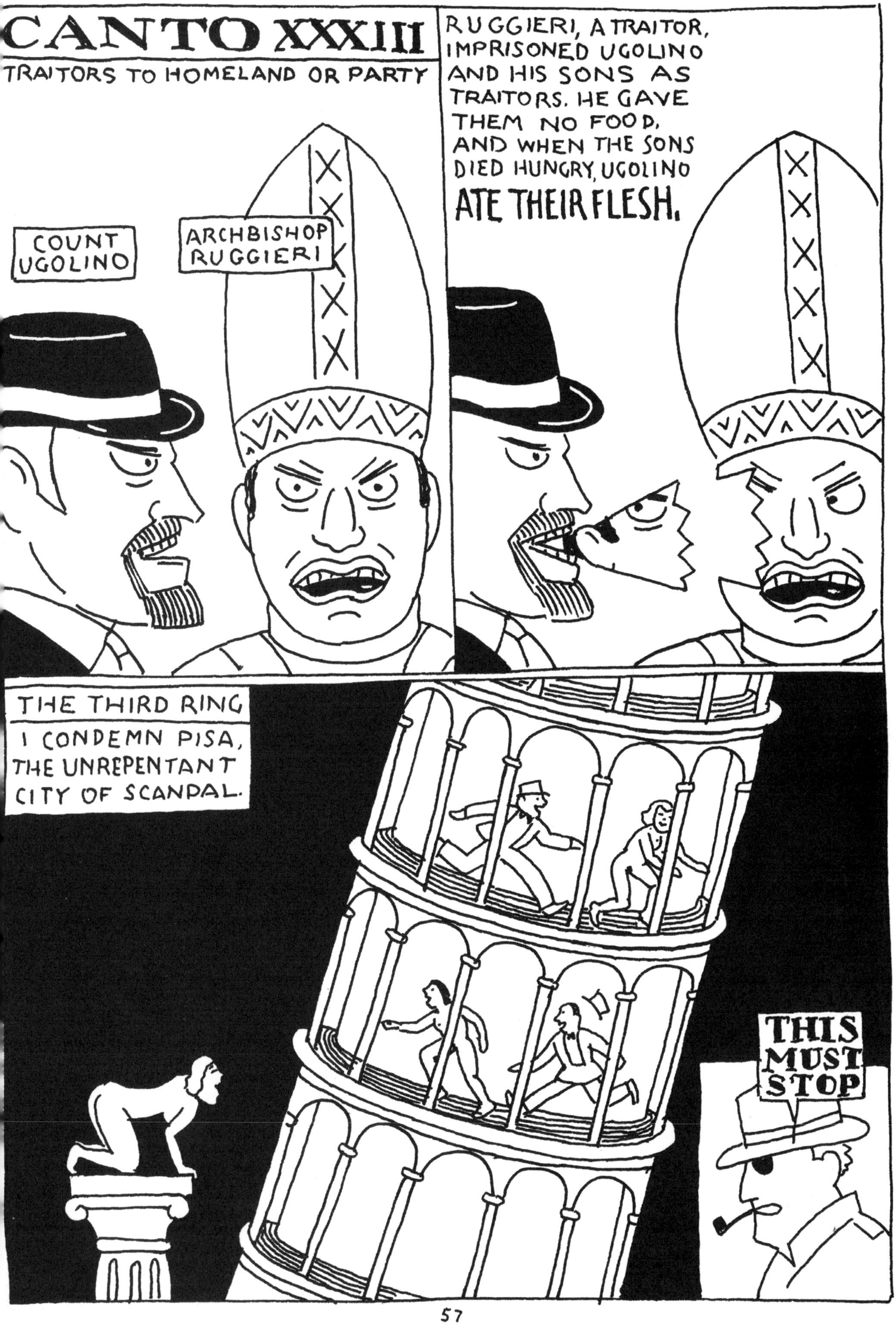
CANTO XXXIII
TRAITORS TO HOMELAND OR PARTY
COUNT UGOLINO
ARCHBISHOP RUGGIERI
RUGGIERI, A TRAITOR, IMPRISONED UGOLINO AND HIS SONS AS TRAITORS. HE GAVE THEM NO FOOD, AND WHEN THE SONS DIED HUNGRY, UGOLINO ATE THEIR FLESH.
THE THIRD RING
I CONDEMN PISA, THE UNREPENTANT CITY OF SCANDAL.
THIS MUST STOP

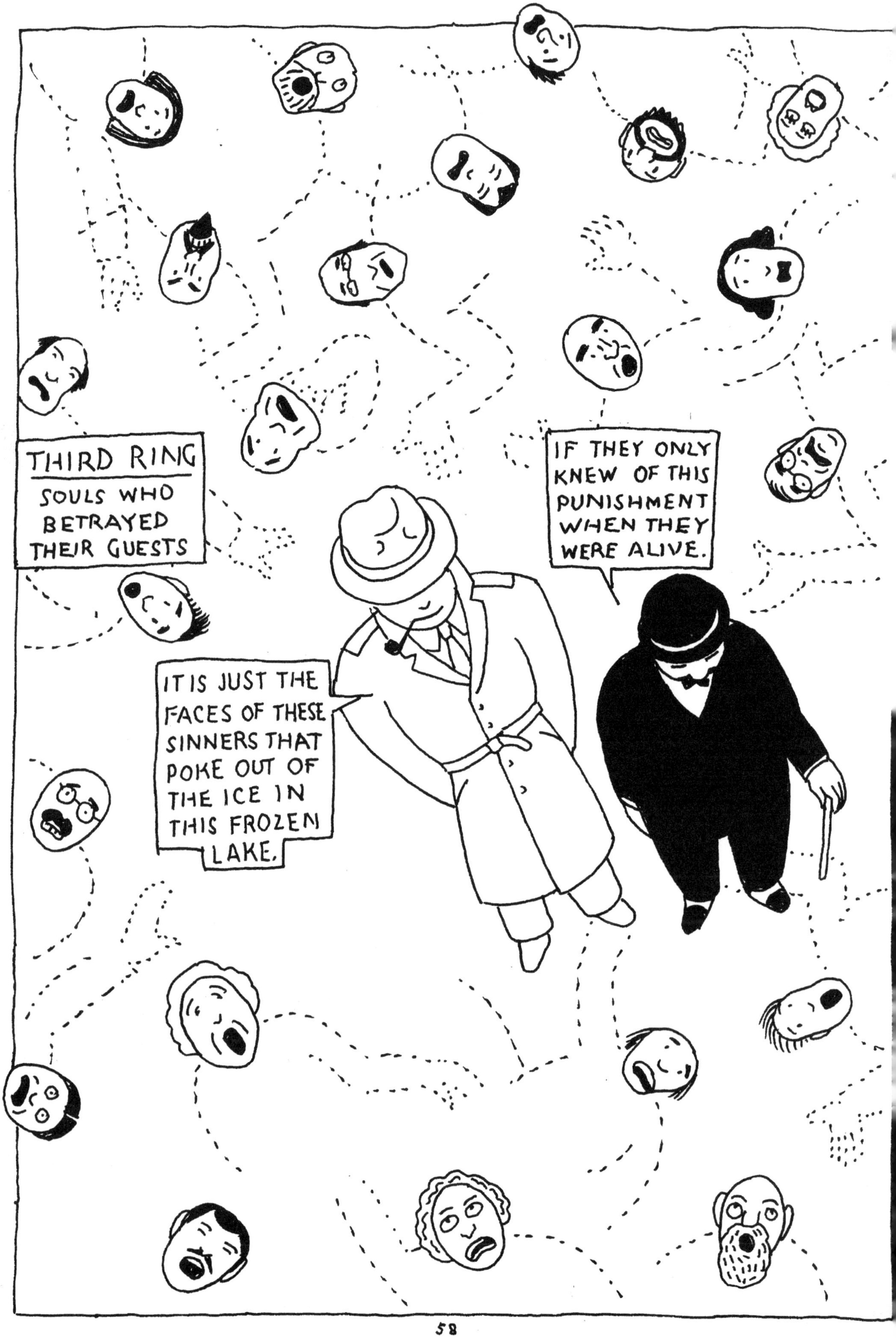
THIRD RING
SOULS WHO BETRAYED THEIR GUESTS
IF THEY ONLY KNEW OF THIS PUNISHMENT WHEN THEY WERE ALIVE.
IT IS JUST THE FACES OF THESE SINNERS THAT POKE OUT OF THE ICE IN THIS FROZEN LAKE.

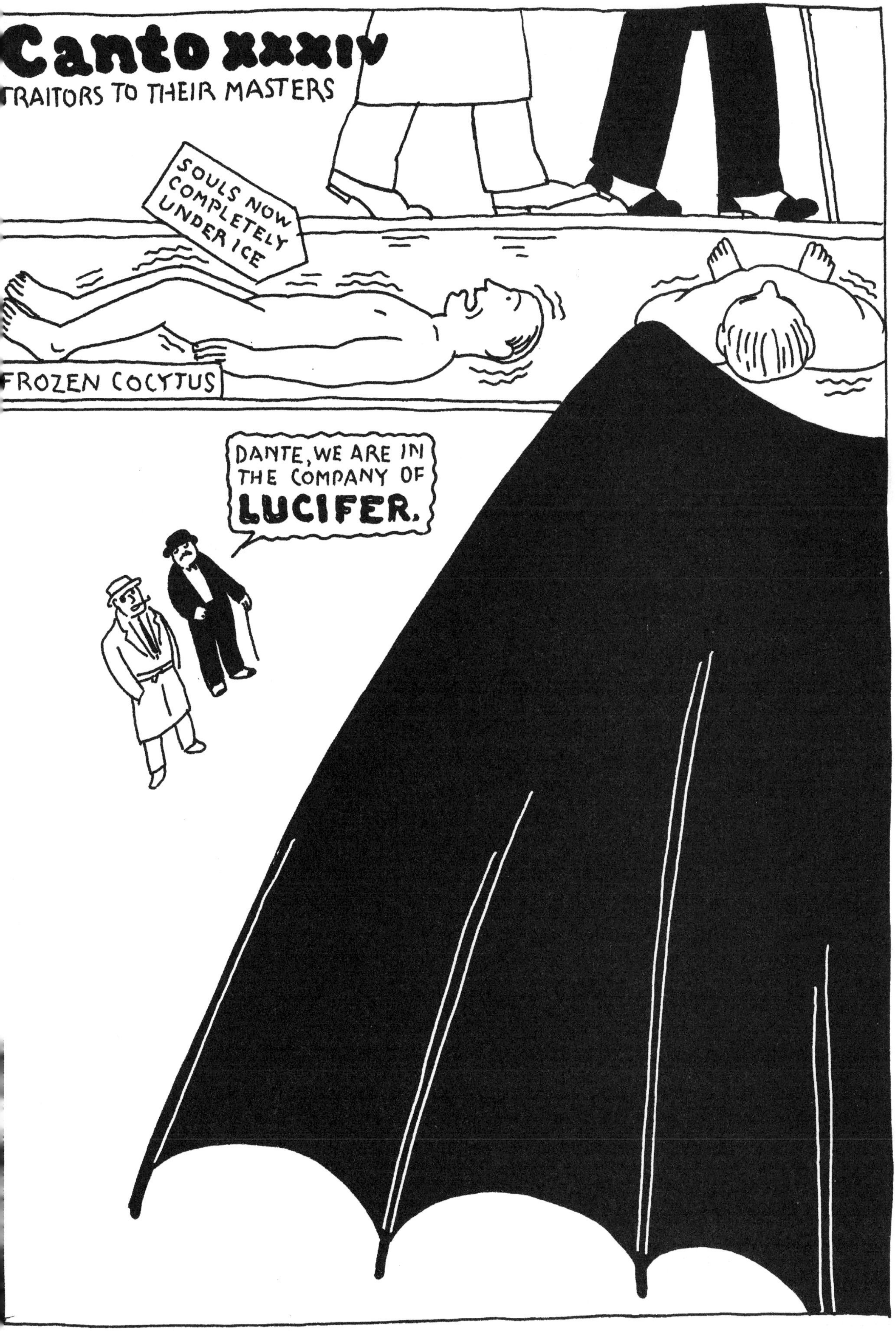
Canto XXXIV
TRAITORS TO THEIR MASTERS
SOULS NOW COMPLETELY UNDER ICE
FROZEN COCYTUS
DANTE, WE ARE IN THE COMPANY OF LUCIFER.

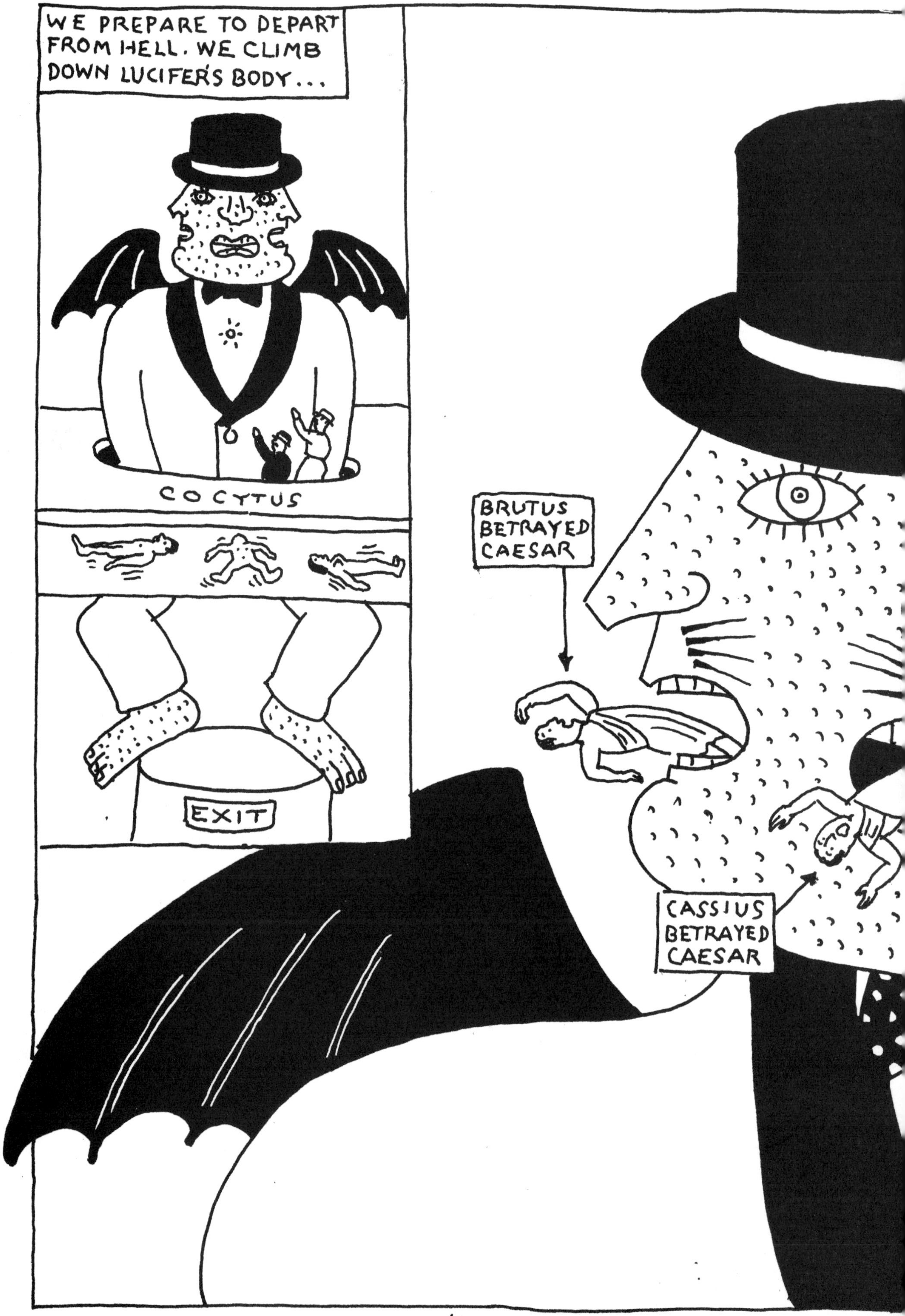
WE PREPARE TO DEPART FROM HELL. WE CLIMB DOWN LUCIFER'S BODY...
COCYTUS
EXIT
BRUTUS BETRAYED CAESAR
CASSIUS BETRAYED CAESAR

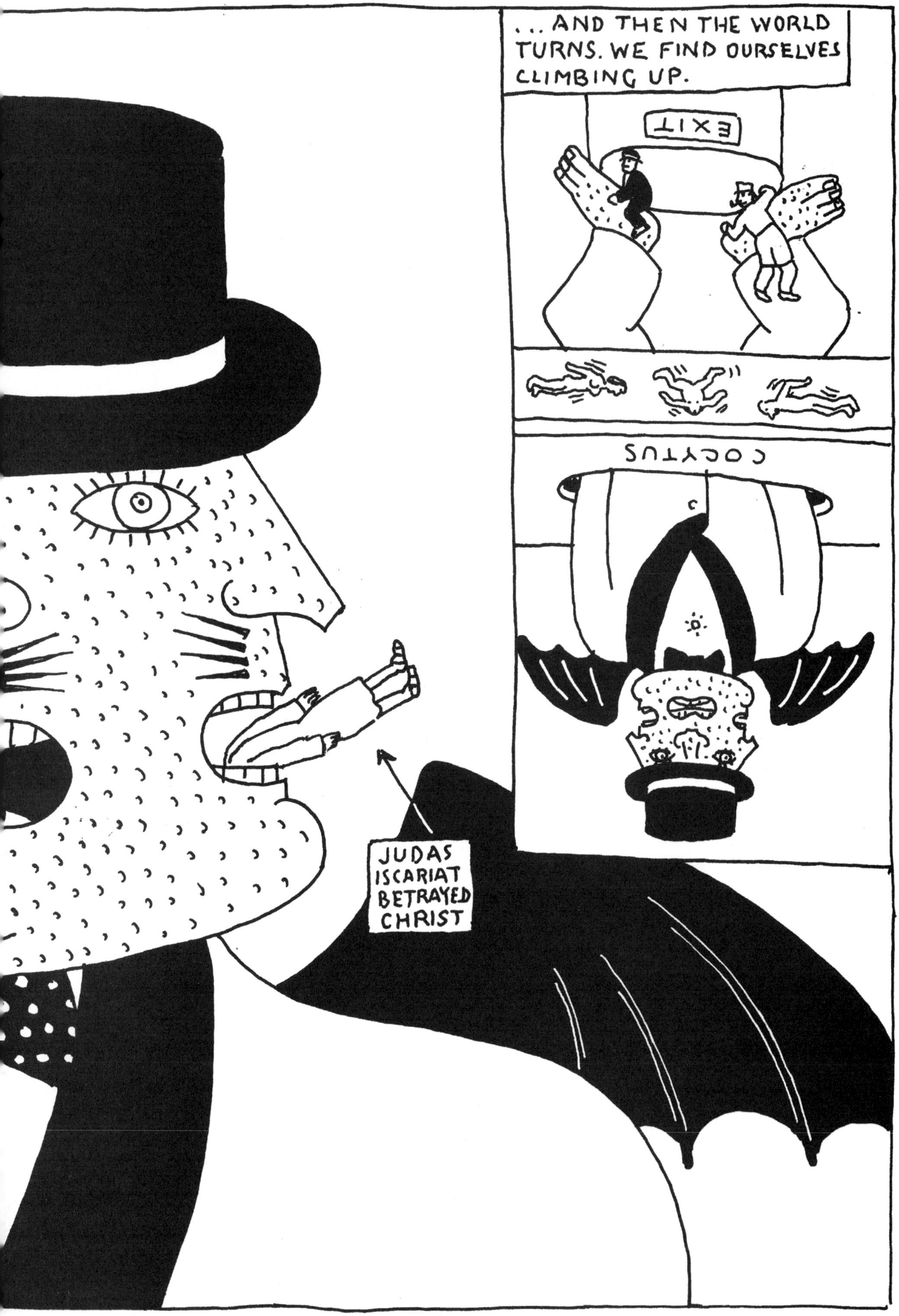
...AND THEN THE WORLD TURNS. WE FIND OURSELVES CLIMBING UP.
EXIT
COCYTUS
JUDAS ISCARIAT BETRAYED CHRIST

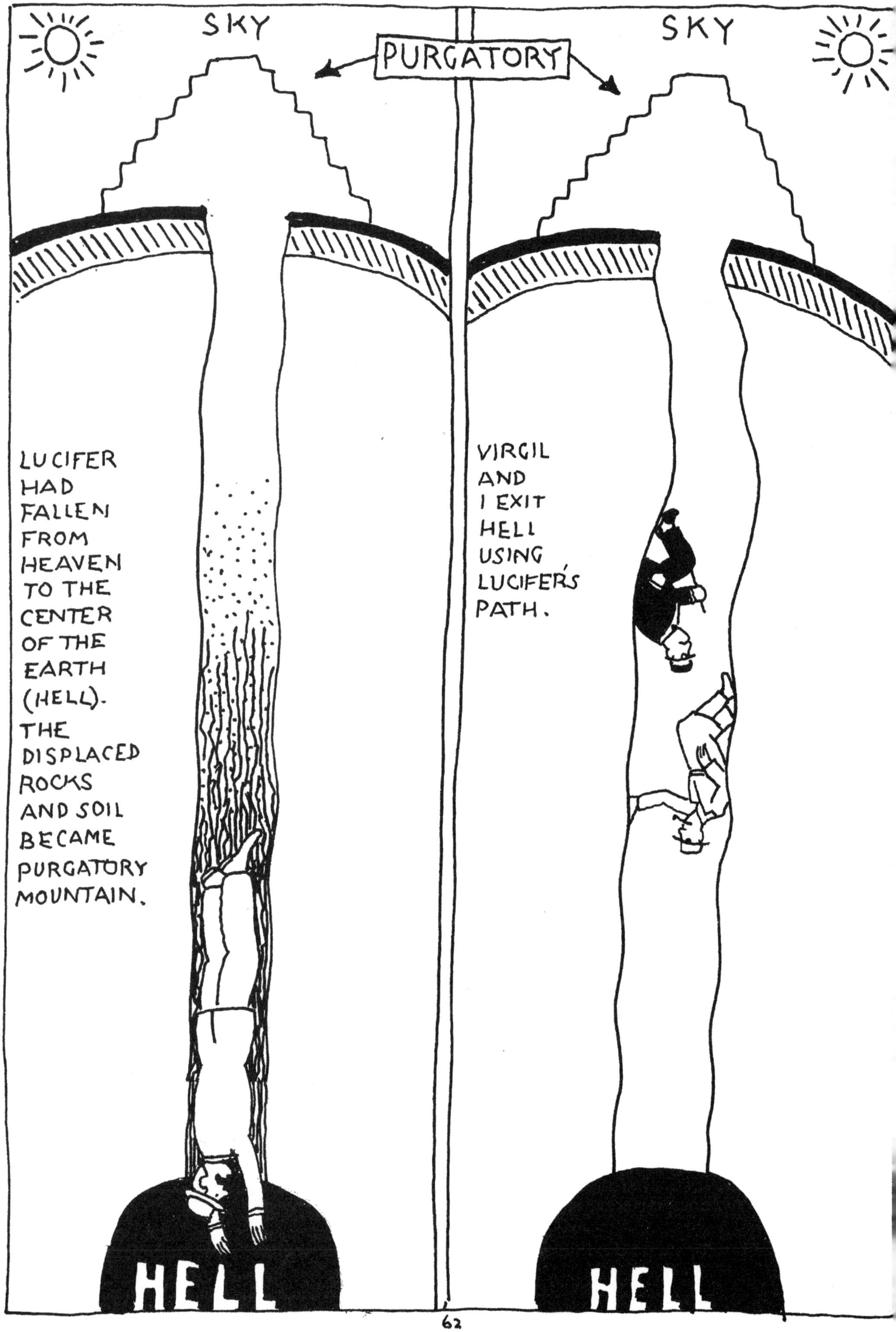
SKY
PURGATORY
SKY
LUCIFER HAD FALLEN FROM HEAVEN TO THE CENTER OF THE EARTH (HELL). THE DISPLACED ROCKS AND SOIL BECAME PURGATORY MOUNTAIN.
VIRGIL AND I EXIT HELL USING LUCIFER'S PATH.
HELL
HELL

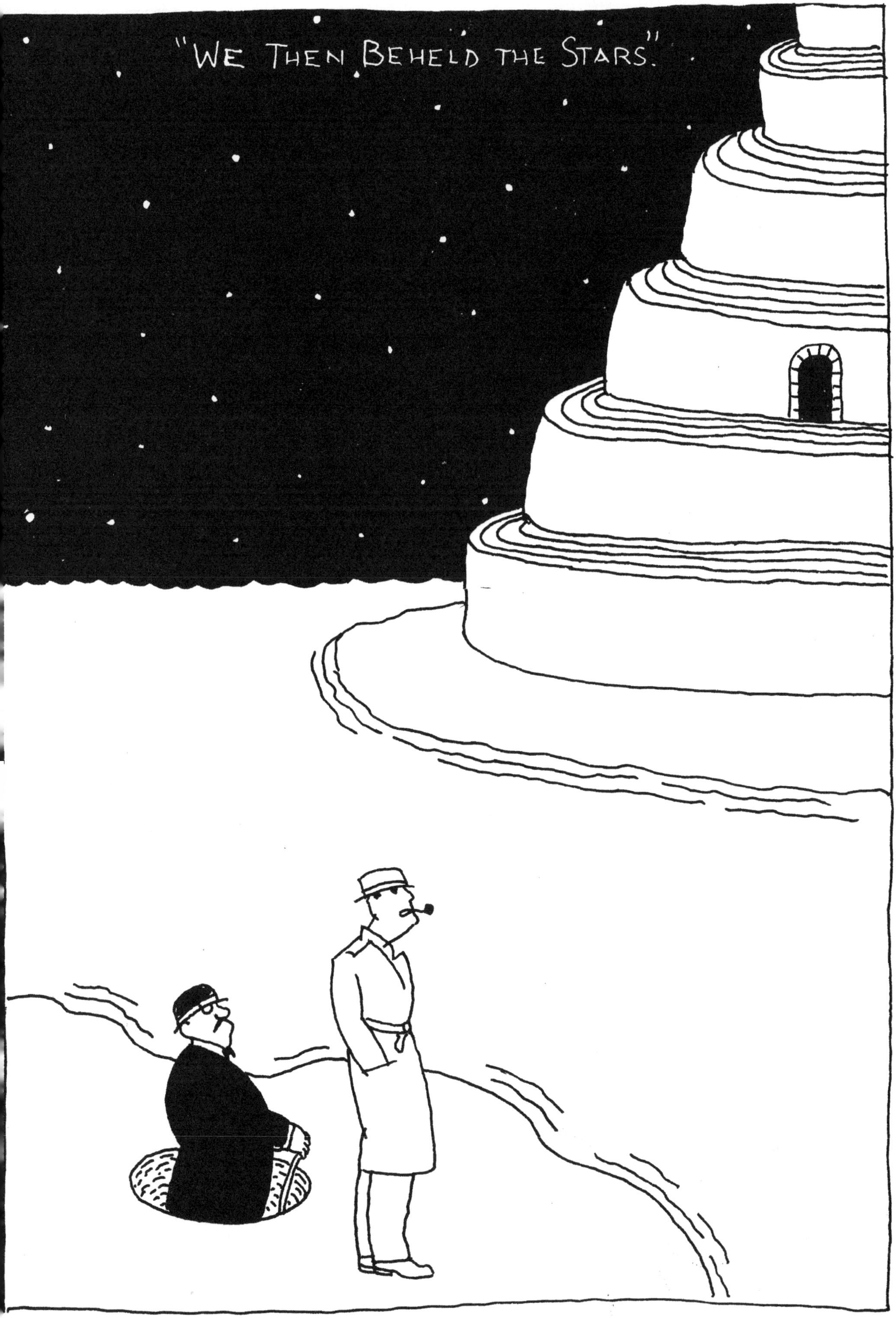
"WE THEN BEHELD THE STARS."

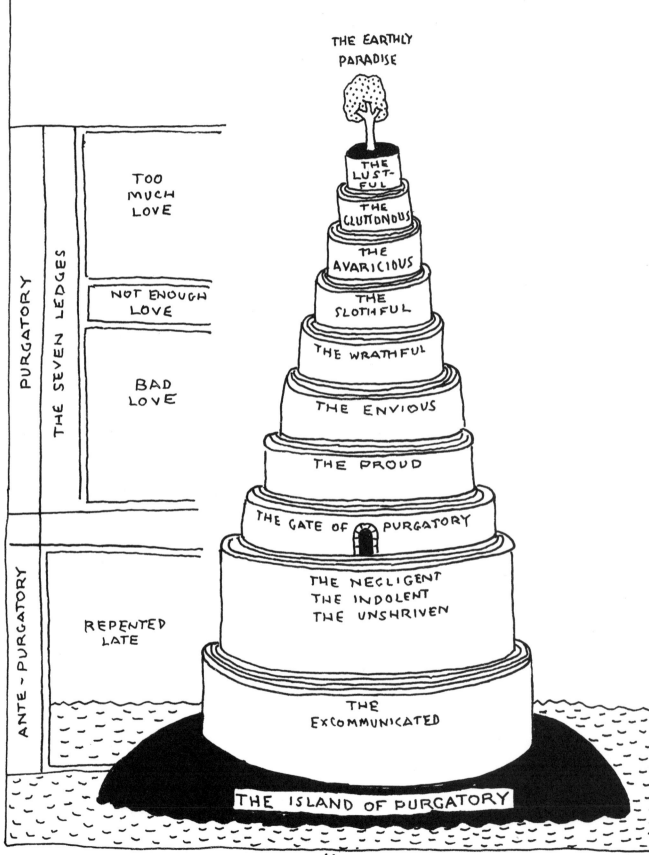

THE EARTHLY
PARADISE

TOO
MUCH
LOVE

NOT ENOUGH
LOVE

BAD
LOVE

THE SEVEN LEDGES

PURGATORY

THE
LUST-
FUL

THE
GLUTTONOUS

THE
AVARICIOUS

THE
SLOTHFUL

THE WRATHFUL

THE ENVIOUS

THE PROUD

THE GATE OF PURGATORY

THE NEGLIGENT
THE INDOLENT
THE UNSHRIVEN

REPENTED
LATE

ANTE - PURGATORY

THE
EXCOMMUNICATED

THE ISLAND OF PURGATORY

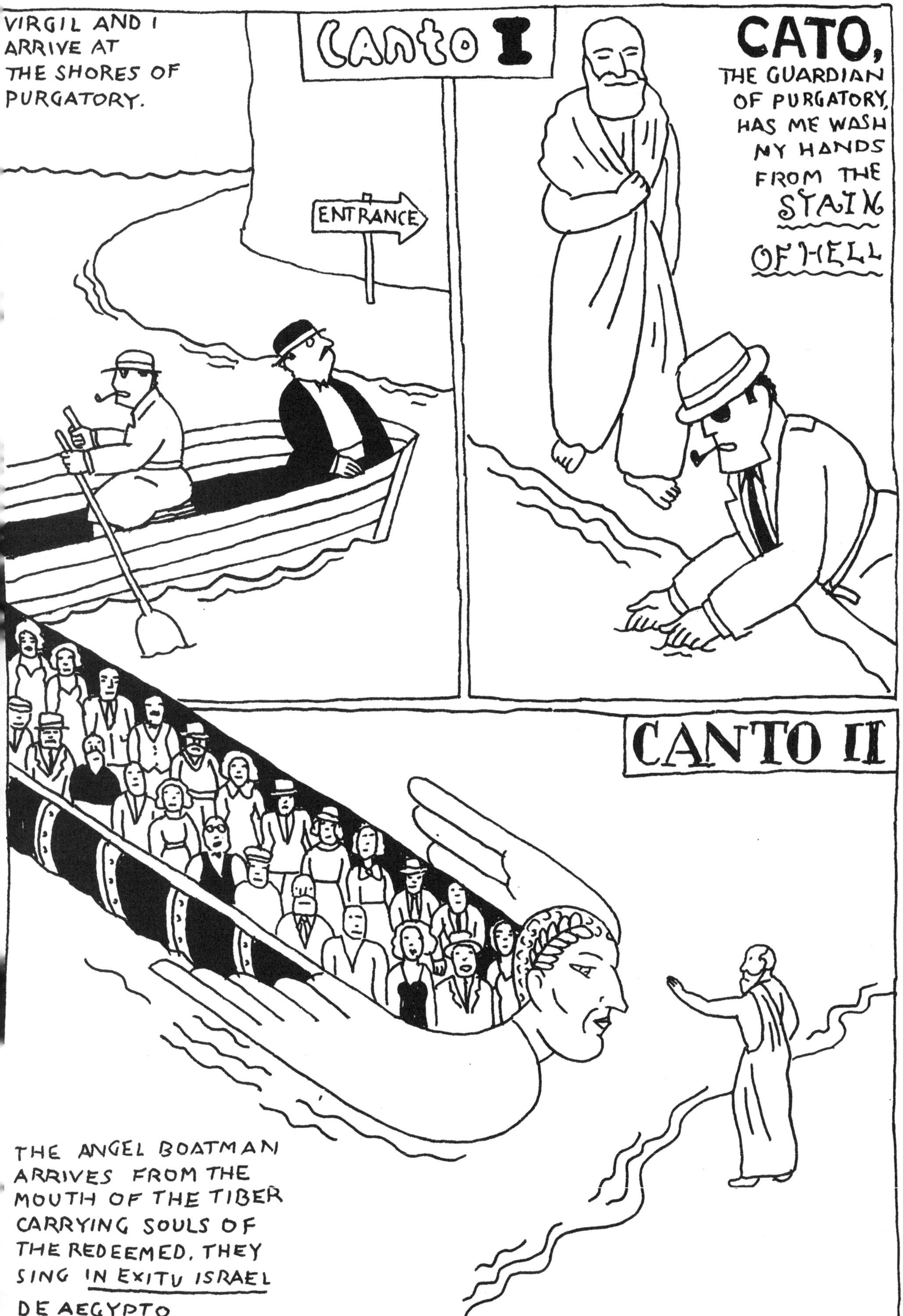
VIRGIL AND I ARRIVE AT THE SHORES OF PURGATORY.
CANTO I
ENTRANCE
CATO, THE GUARDIAN OF PURGATORY, HAS ME WASH MY HANDS FROM THE STAIN OF HELL
CANTO II
THE ANGEL BOATMAN ARRIVES FROM THE MOUTH OF THE TIBER CARRYING SOULS OF THE REDEEMED. THEY SING IN EXITU ISRAEL DE AEGYPTO.

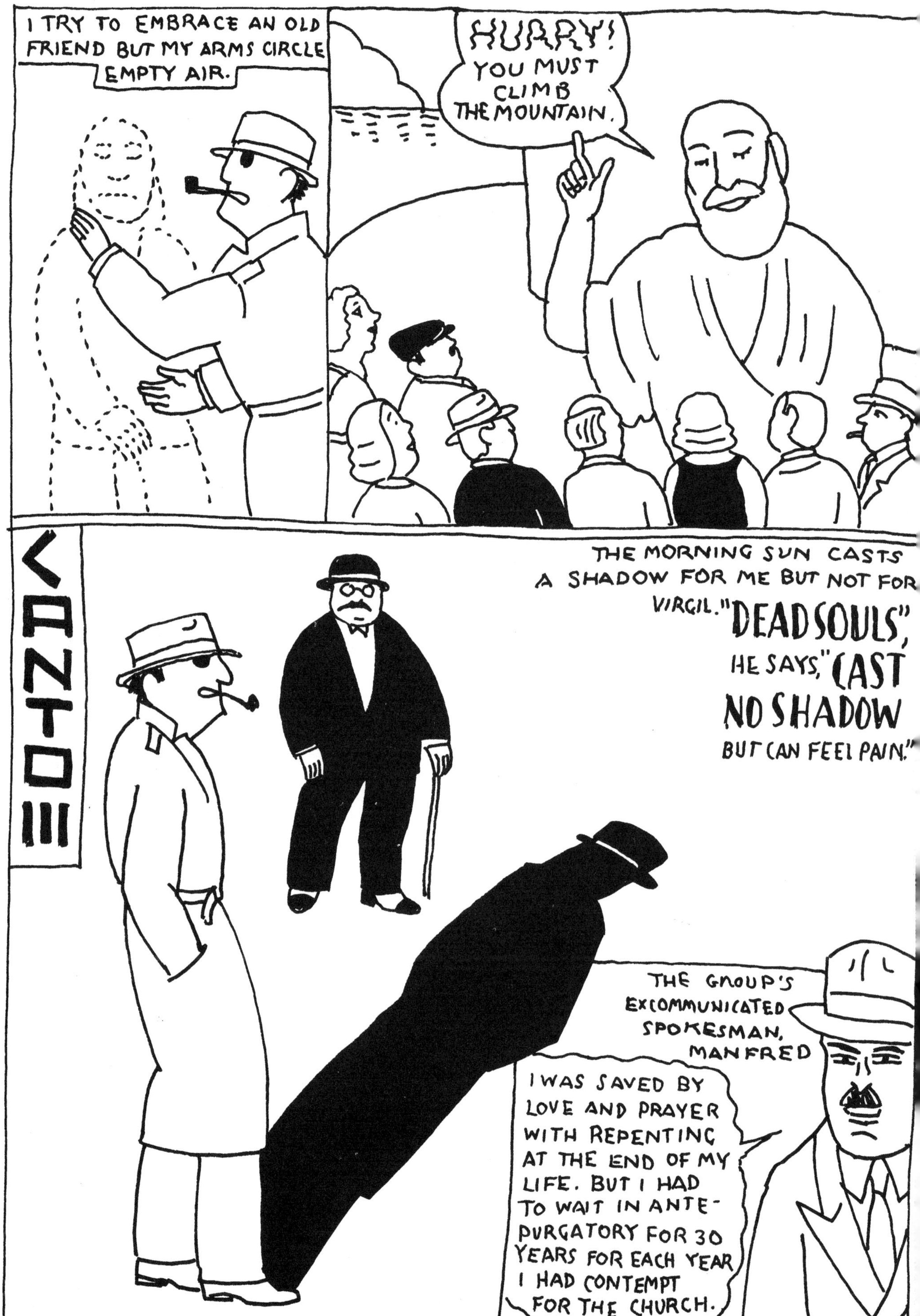
I TRY TO EMBRACE AN OLD FRIEND BUT MY ARMS CIRCLE EMPTY AIR.
HURRY! YOU MUST CLIMB THE MOUNTAIN.
CANTO III
THE MORNING SUN CASTS A SHADOW FOR ME BUT NOT FOR VIRGIL. "DEAD SOULS", HE SAYS, "CAST NO SHADOW BUT CAN FEEL PAIN."
THE GROUP'S EXCOMMUNICATED SPOKESMAN, MANFRED
I WAS SAVED BY LOVE AND PRAYER WITH REPENTING AT THE END OF MY LIFE. BUT I HAD TO WAIT IN ANTE-PURGATORY FOR 30 YEARS FOR EACH YEAR I HAD CONTEMPT FOR THE CHURCH.

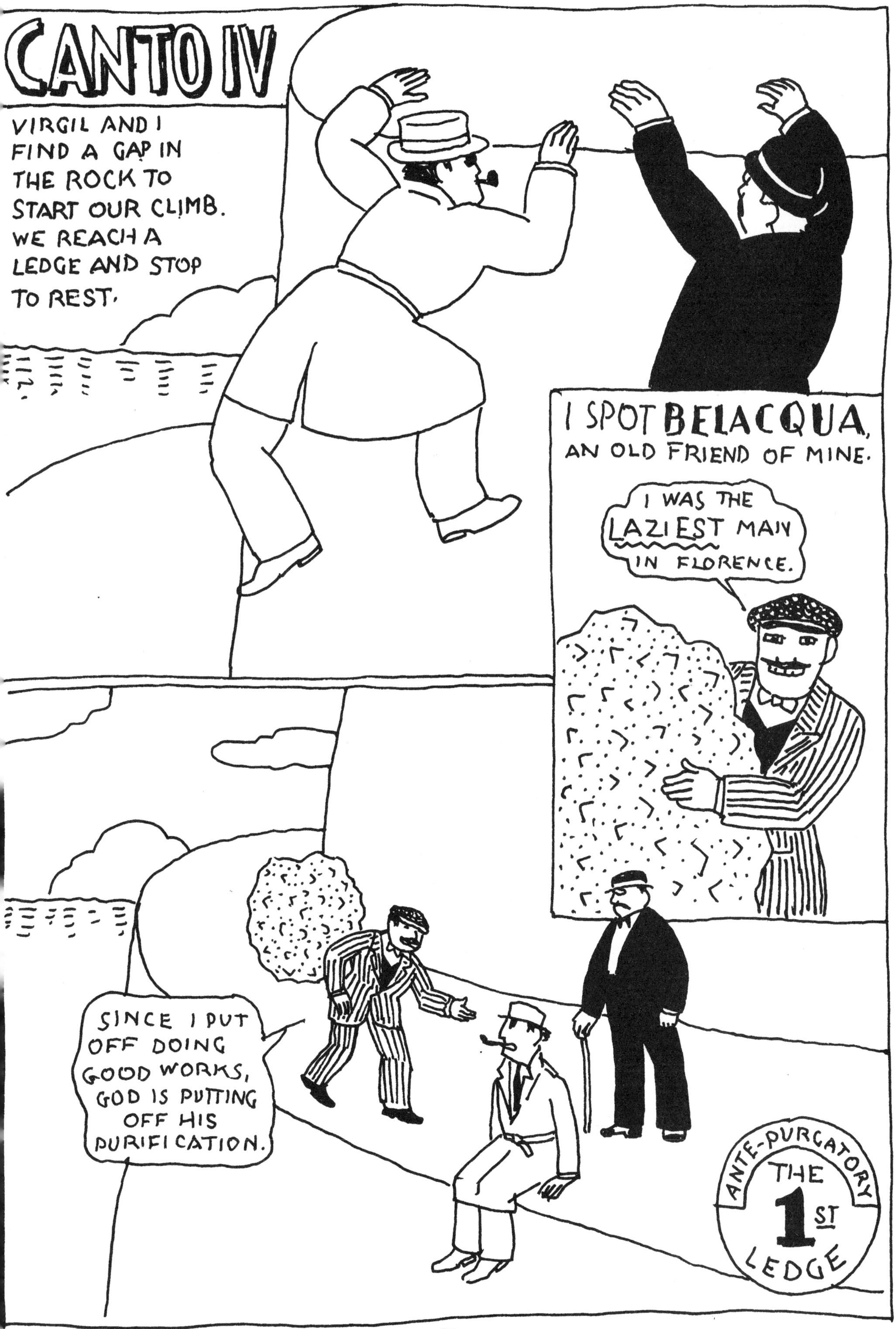
CANTO IV
VIRGIL AND I FIND A GAP IN THE ROCK TO START OUR CLIMB. WE REACH A LEDGE AND STOP TO REST.
I SPOT BELACQUA, AN OLD FRIEND OF MINE.
I WAS THE LAZIEST MAN IN FLORENCE.
SINCE I PUT OFF DOING GOOD WORKS, GOD IS PUTTING OFF HIS PURIFICATION.
ANTE-PURGATORY THE 1ST LEDGE

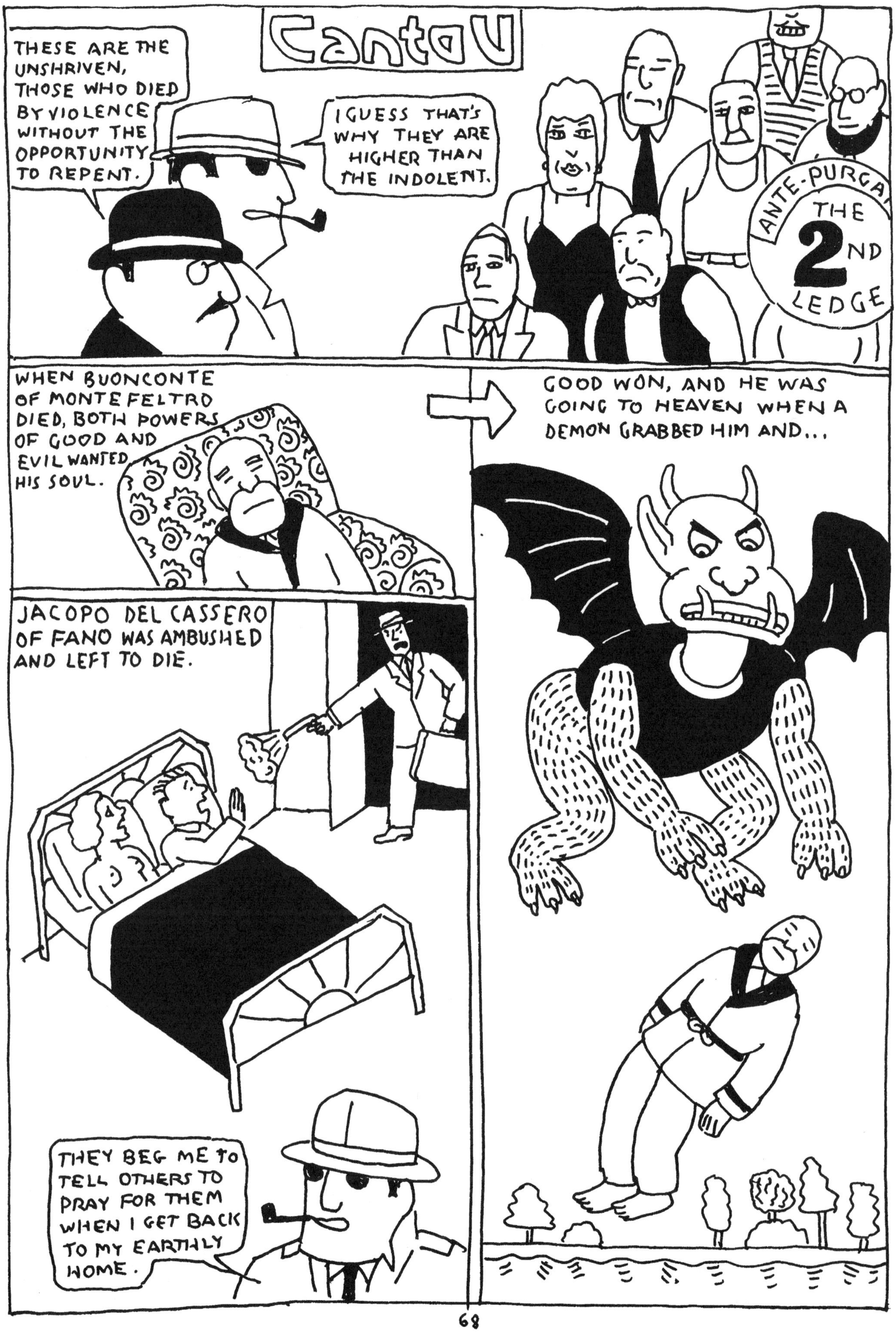
Canto V
THESE ARE THE UNSHRIVEN, THOSE WHO DIED BY VIOLENCE WITHOUT THE OPPORTUNITY TO REPENT.
I GUESS THAT'S WHY THEY ARE HIGHER THAN THE INDOLENT.
ANTE-PURGA
THE 2ND LEDGE
WHEN BUONCONTE OF MONTEFELTRO DIED, BOTH POWERS OF GOOD AND EVIL WANTED HIS SOUL.
GOOD WON, AND HE WAS GOING TO HEAVEN WHEN A DEMON GRABBED HIM AND...
JACOPO DEL CASSERO OF FANO WAS AMBUSHED AND LEFT TO DIE.
THEY BEG ME TO TELL OTHERS TO PRAY FOR THEM WHEN I GET BACK TO MY EARTHLY HOME.

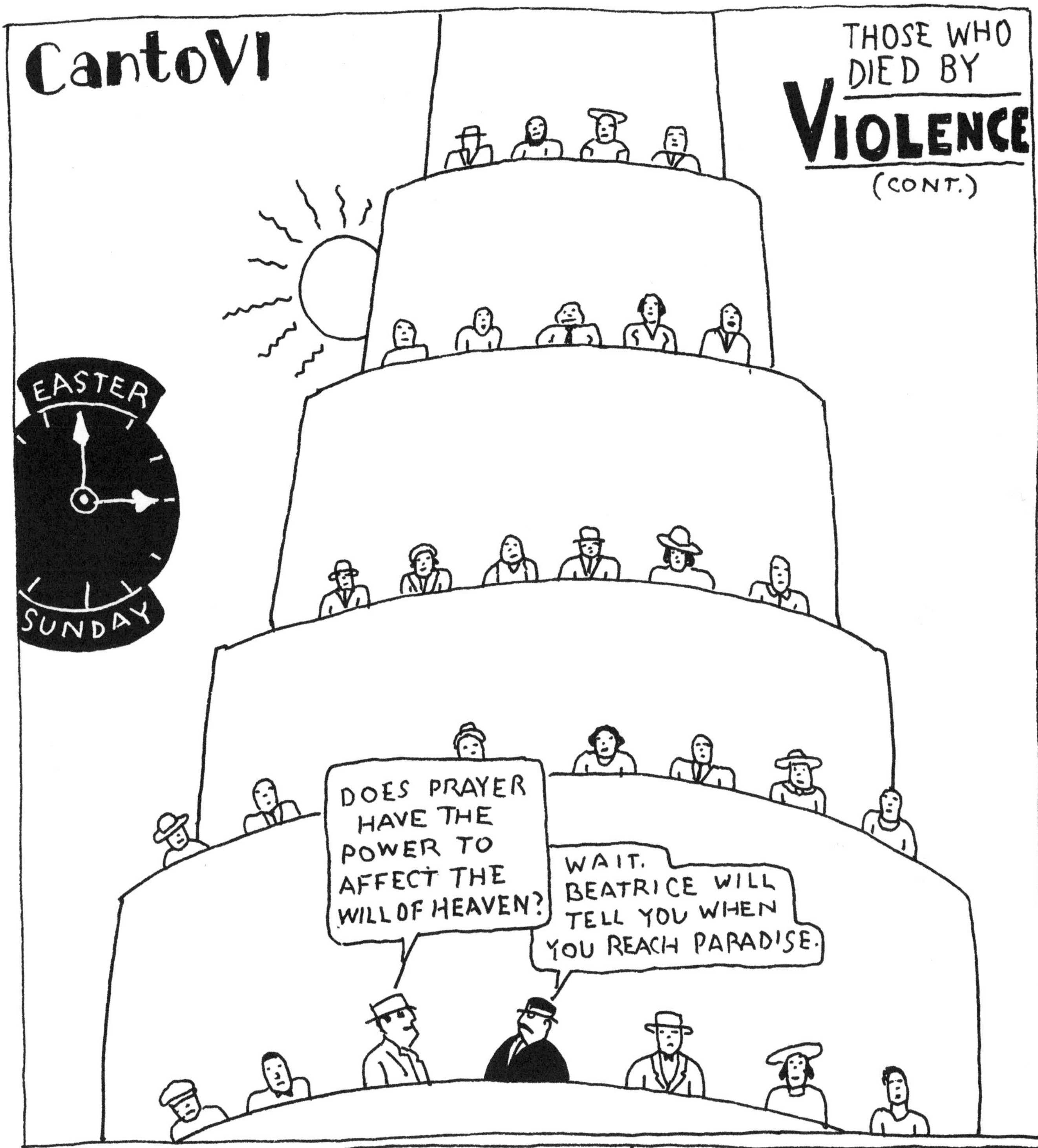
Canto VI
THOSE WHO DIED BY VIOLENCE (CONT.)
EASTER SUNDAY
DOES PRAYER HAVE THE POWER TO AFFECT THE WILL OF HEAVEN?
WAIT. BEATRICE WILL TELL YOU WHEN YOU REACH PARADISE.
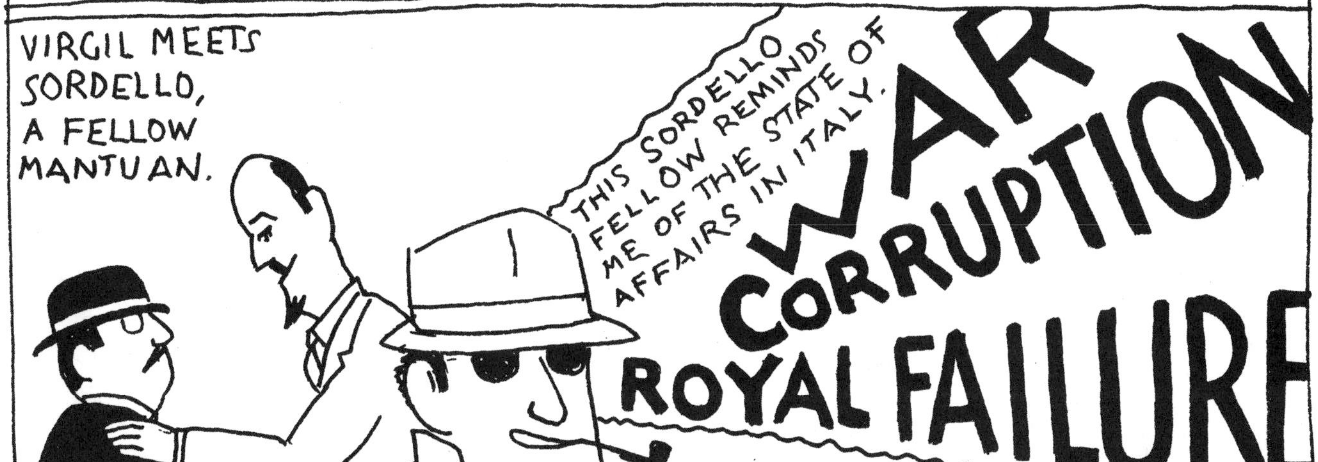
VIRGIL MEETS SORDELLO, A FELLOW MANTUAN.
THIS SORDELLO FELLOW REMINDS ME OF THE STATE OF AFFAIRS IN ITALY.
WAR
CORRUPTION
ROYAL FAILURE

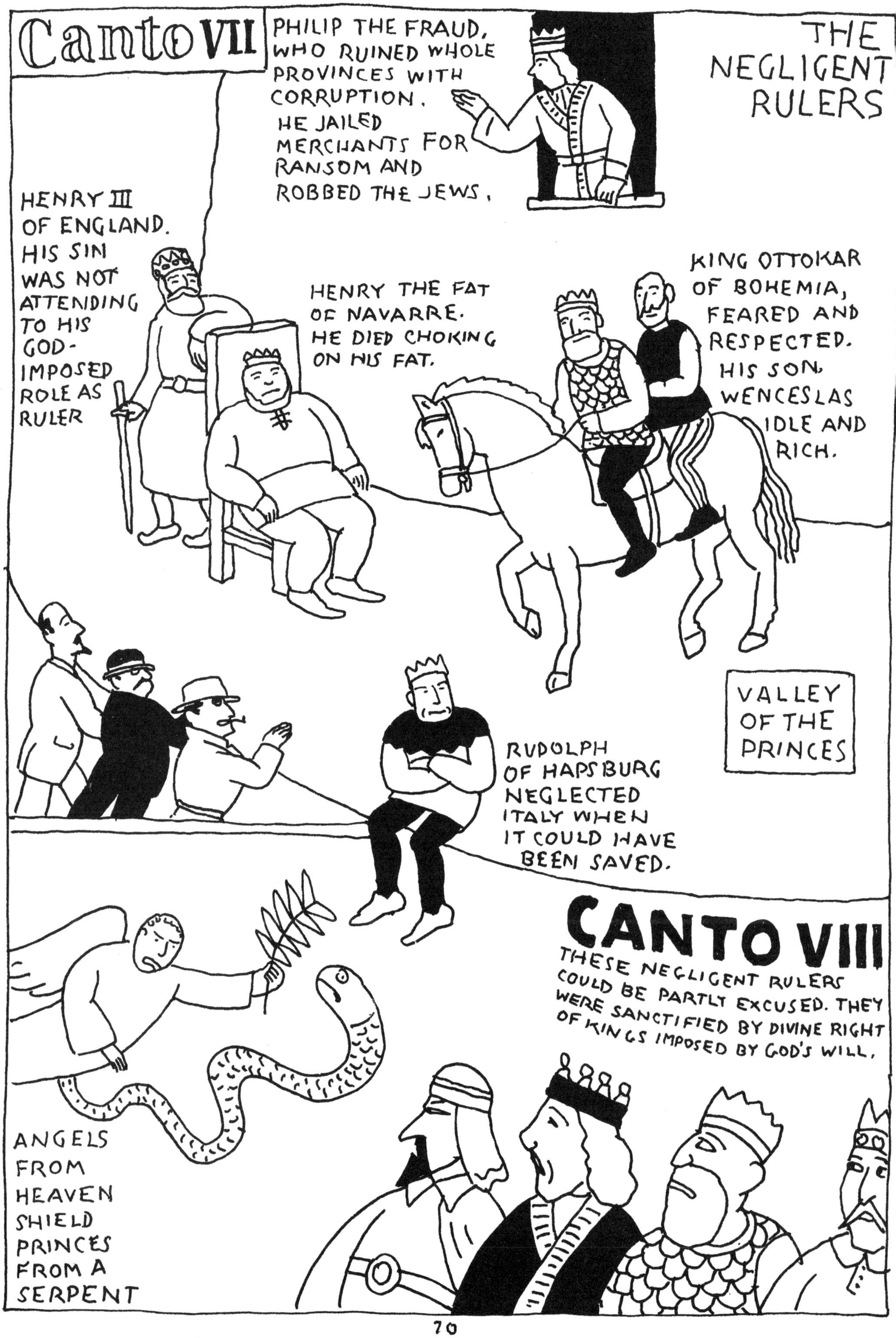

Canto VII
THE NEGLIGENT RULERS
PHILIP THE FRAUD, WHO RUINED WHOLE PROVINCES WITH CORRUPTION. HE JAILED MERCHANTS FOR RANSOM AND ROBBED THE JEWS.
HENRY III OF ENGLAND. HIS SIN WAS NOT ATTENDING TO HIS GOD-IMPOSED ROLE AS RULER
HENRY THE FAT OF NAVARRE. HE DIED CHOKING ON HIS FAT.
KING OTTOKAR OF BOHEMIA, FEARED AND RESPECTED. HIS SON, WENCESLAS IDLE AND RICH.
VALLEY OF THE PRINCES
RUDOLPH OF HAPSBURG NEGLECTED ITALY WHEN IT COULD HAVE BEEN SAVED.
CANTO VIII
THESE NEGLIGENT RULERS COULD BE PARTLY EXCUSED. THEY WERE SANCTIFIED BY DIVINE RIGHT OF KINGS IMPOSED BY GOD'S WILL.
ANGELS FROM HEAVEN SHIELD PRINCES FROM A SERPENT

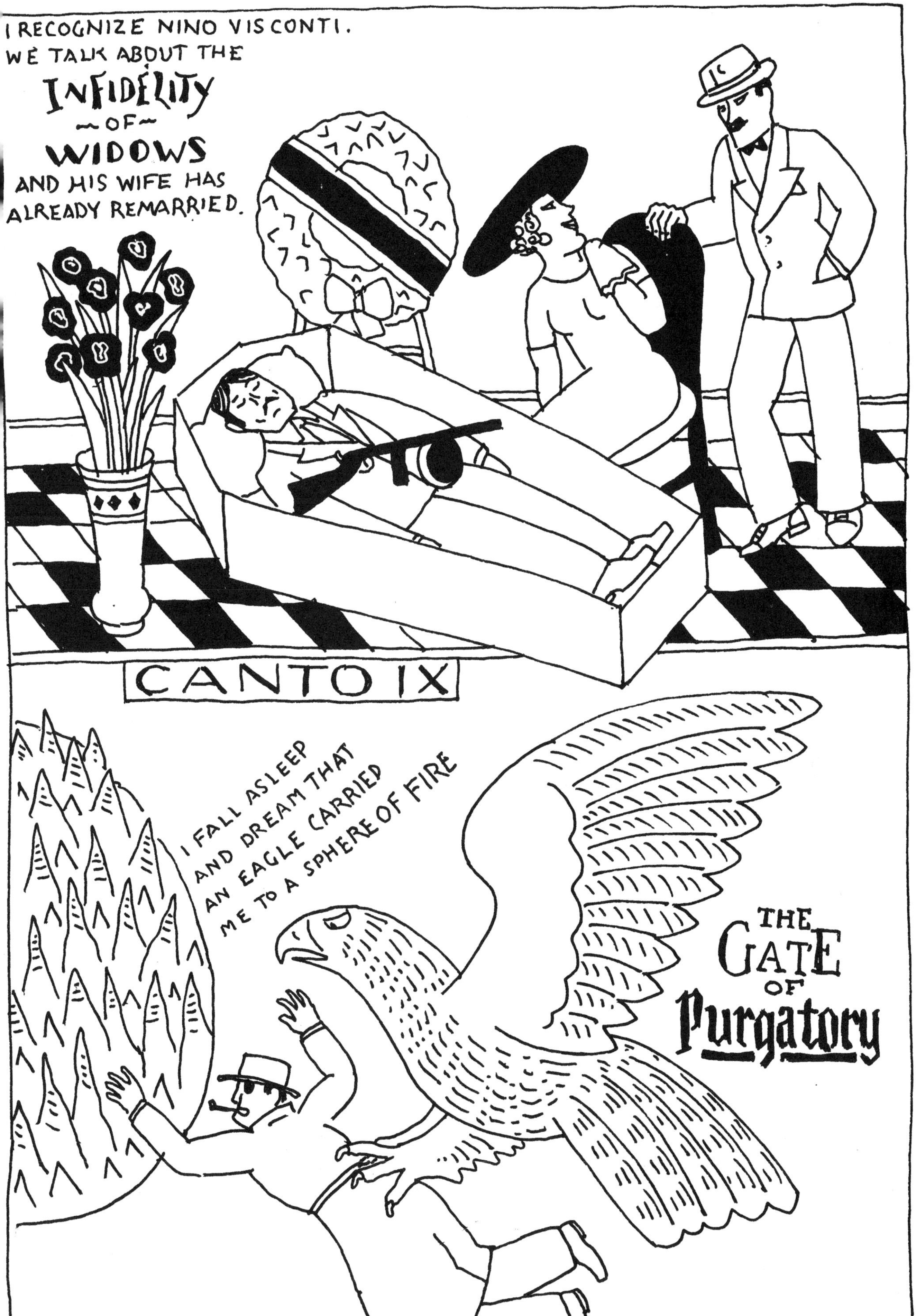
I RECOGNIZE NINO VISCONTI. WE TALK ABOUT THE
INFIDÉLITY ~OF~ WIDOWS
AND HIS WIFE HAS ALREADY REMARRIED.
CANTO IX
I FALL ASLEEP AND DREAM THAT AN EAGLE CARRIED ME TO A SPHERE OF FIRE
THE GATE OF Purgatory

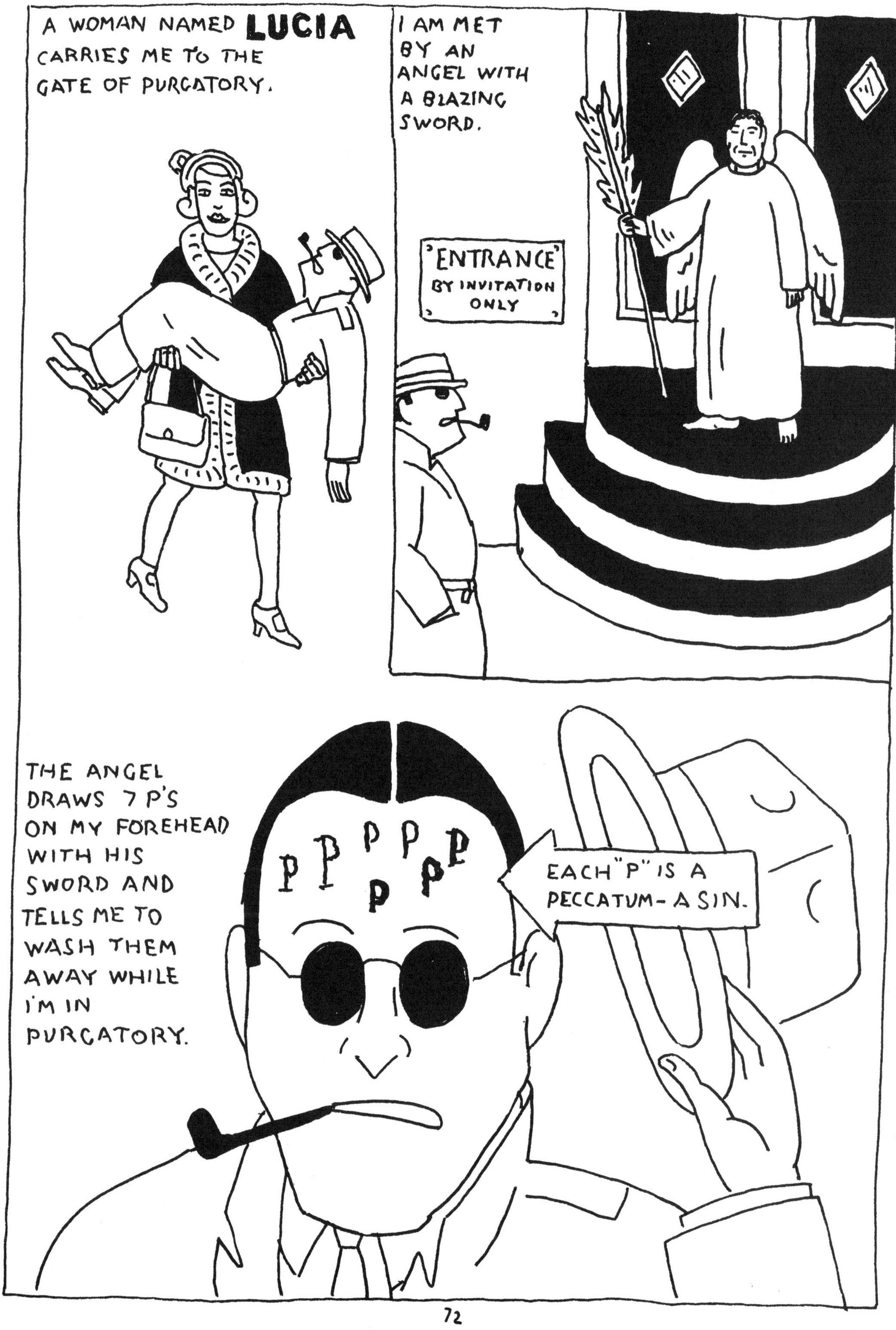
A WOMAN NAMED LUCIA CARRIES ME TO THE GATE OF PURGATORY.
I AM MET BY AN ANGEL WITH A BLAZING SWORD.
"ENTRANCE" BY INVITATION ONLY
THE ANGEL DRAWS 7 P'S ON MY FOREHEAD WITH HIS SWORD AND TELLS ME TO WASH THEM AWAY WHILE I'M IN PURGATORY.
P P P P P P P
EACH "P" IS A PECCATUM - A SIN.

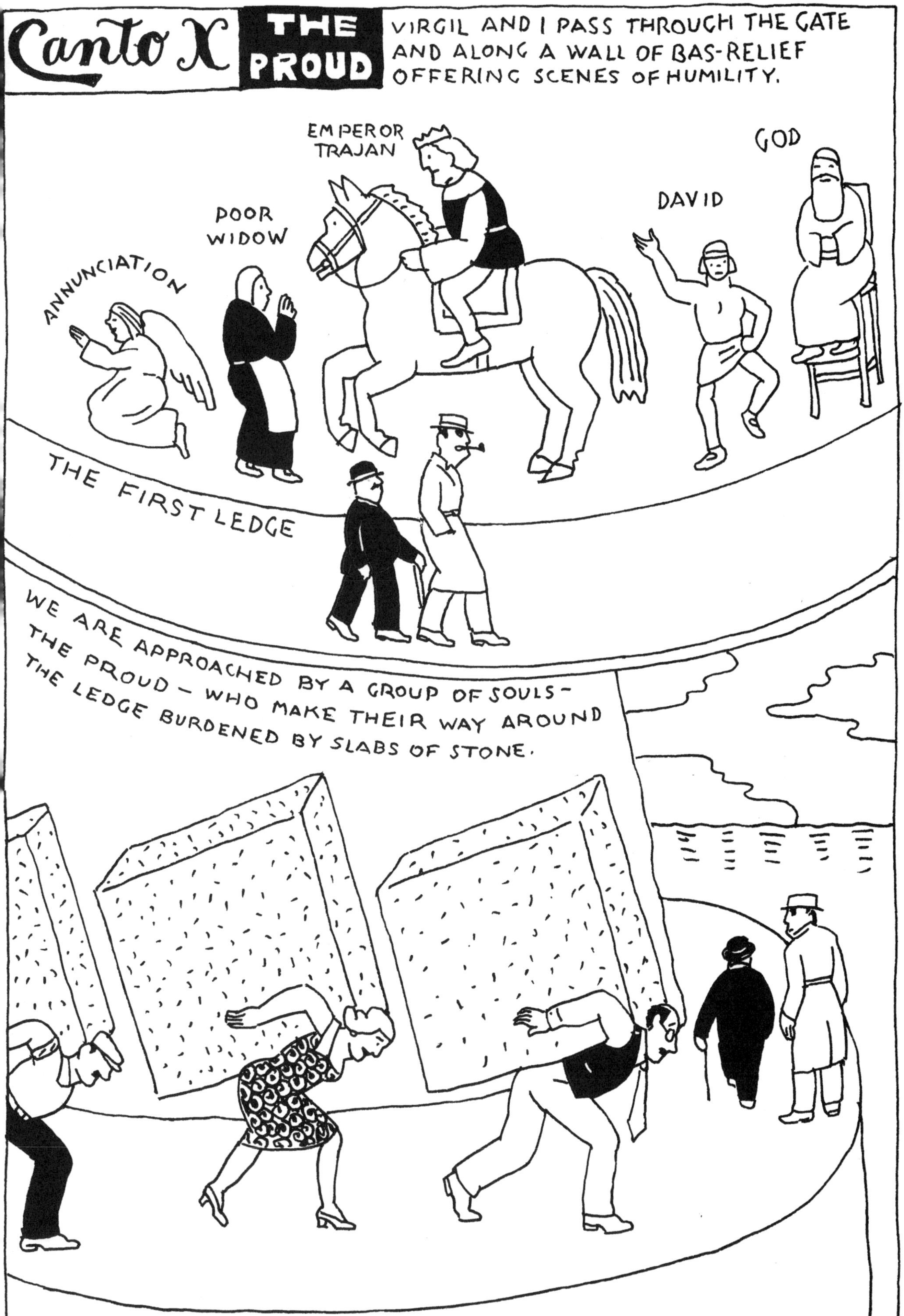
Canto X
THE PROUD
VIRGIL AND I PASS THROUGH THE GATE AND ALONG A WALL OF BAS-RELIEF OFFERING SCENES OF HUMILITY.
EMPEROR TRAJAN
GOD
POOR WIDOW
DAVID
ANNUNCIATION
THE FIRST LEDGE
WE ARE APPROACHED BY A GROUP OF SOULS - THE PROUD - WHO MAKE THEIR WAY AROUND THE LEDGE BURDENED BY SLABS OF STONE.

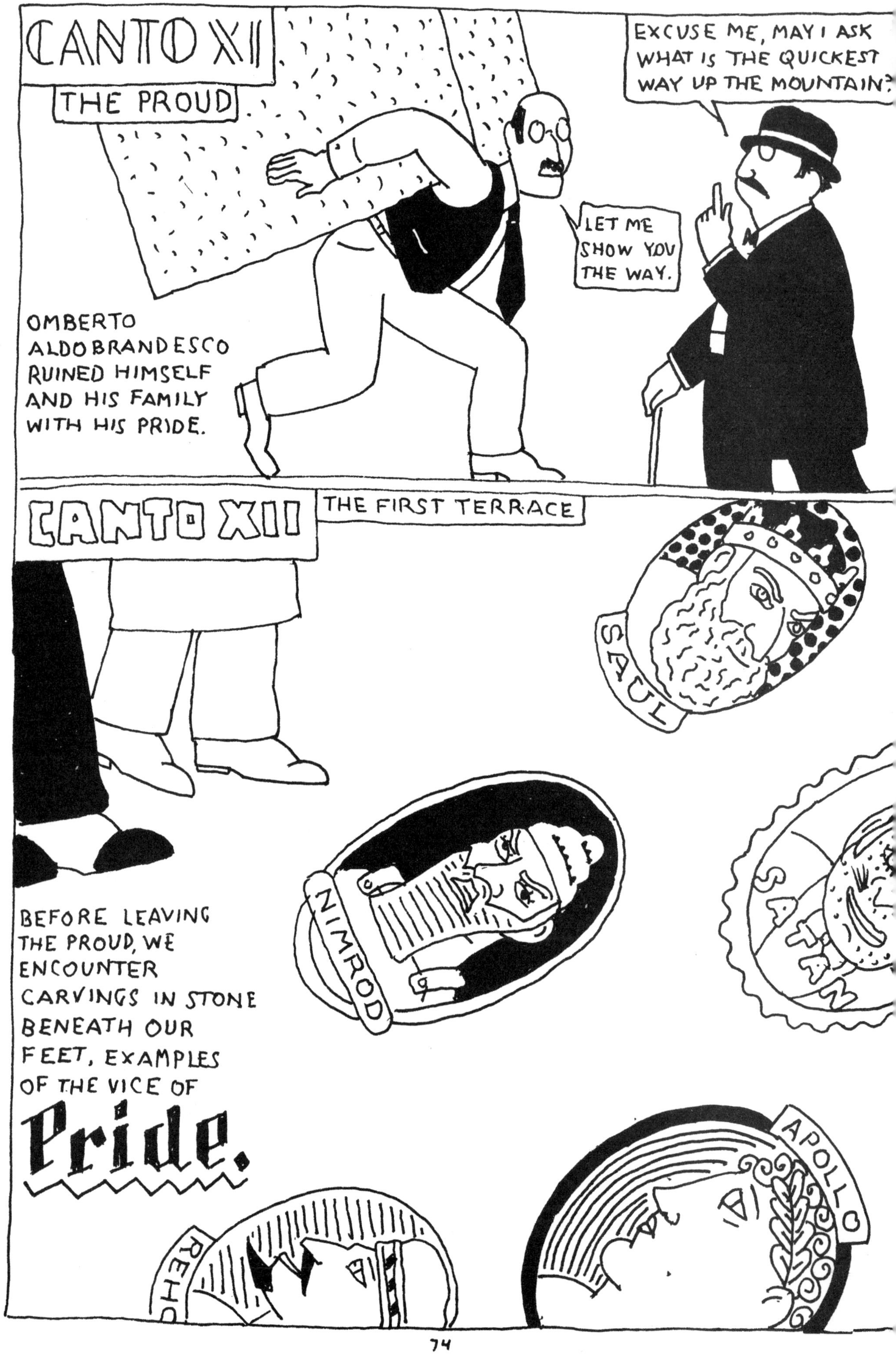
CANTO XI
THE PROUD
EXCUSE ME, MAY I ASK WHAT IS THE QUICKEST WAY UP THE MOUNTAIN?
LET ME SHOW YOU THE WAY.
OMBERTO ALDOBRANDESCO RUINED HIMSELF AND HIS FAMILY WITH HIS PRIDE.
CANTO XII
THE FIRST TERRACE
SAUL
BEFORE LEAVING THE PROUD, WE ENCOUNTER CARVINGS IN STONE BENEATH OUR FEET, EXAMPLES OF THE VICE OF
Pride.
NIMROD
SATAN
APOLLO

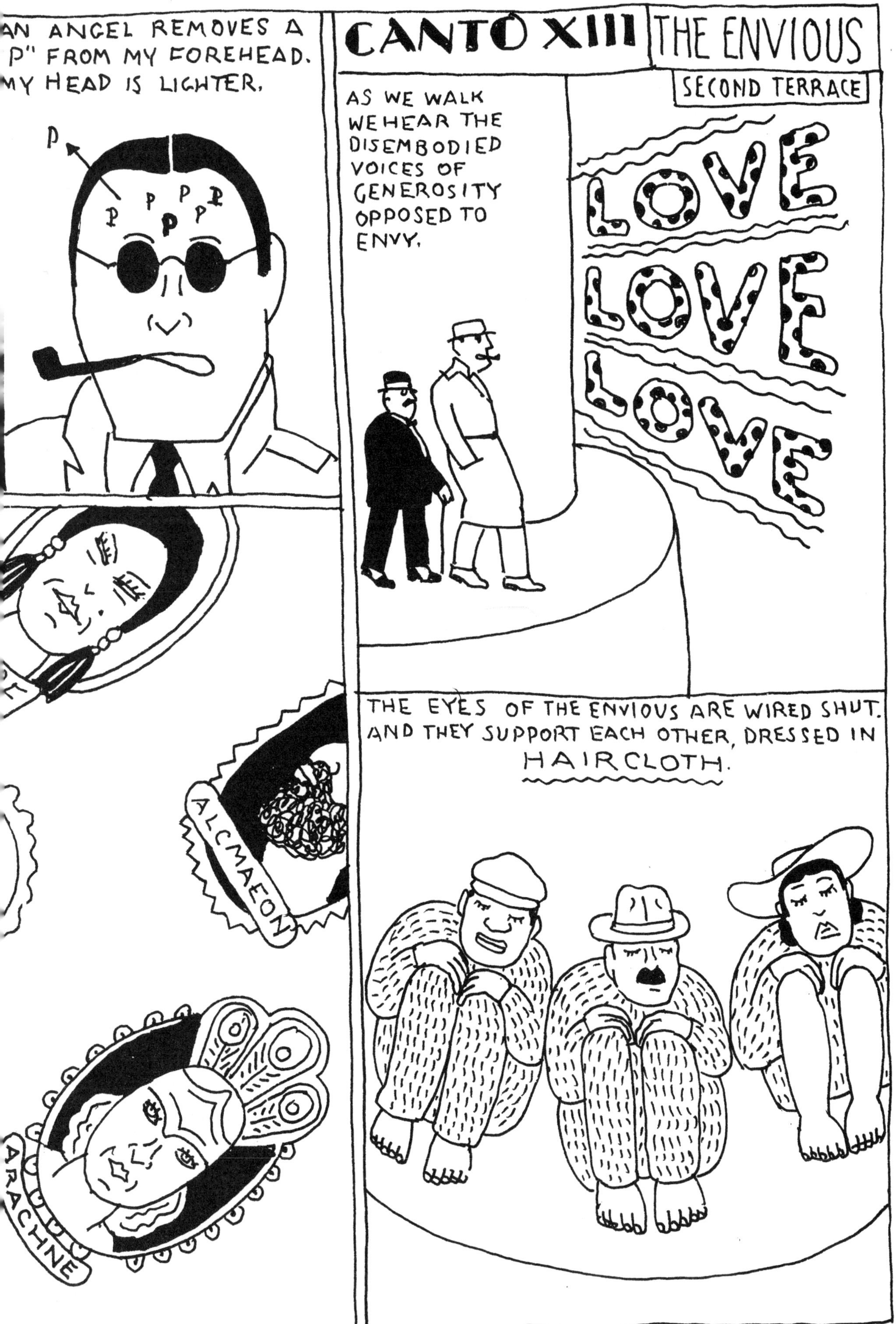
AN ANGEL REMOVES A
"P" FROM MY FOREHEAD.
MY HEAD IS LIGHTER.
P
CANTO XIII
THE ENVIOUS
SECOND TERRACE
AS WE WALK WE HEAR THE DISEMBODIED VOICES OF GENEROSITY OPPOSED TO ENVY.
LOVE
LOVE
LOVE
ALCMAEON
ARACHNE
THE EYES OF THE ENVIOUS ARE WIRED SHUT. AND THEY SUPPORT EACH OTHER, DRESSED IN HAIRCLOTH.

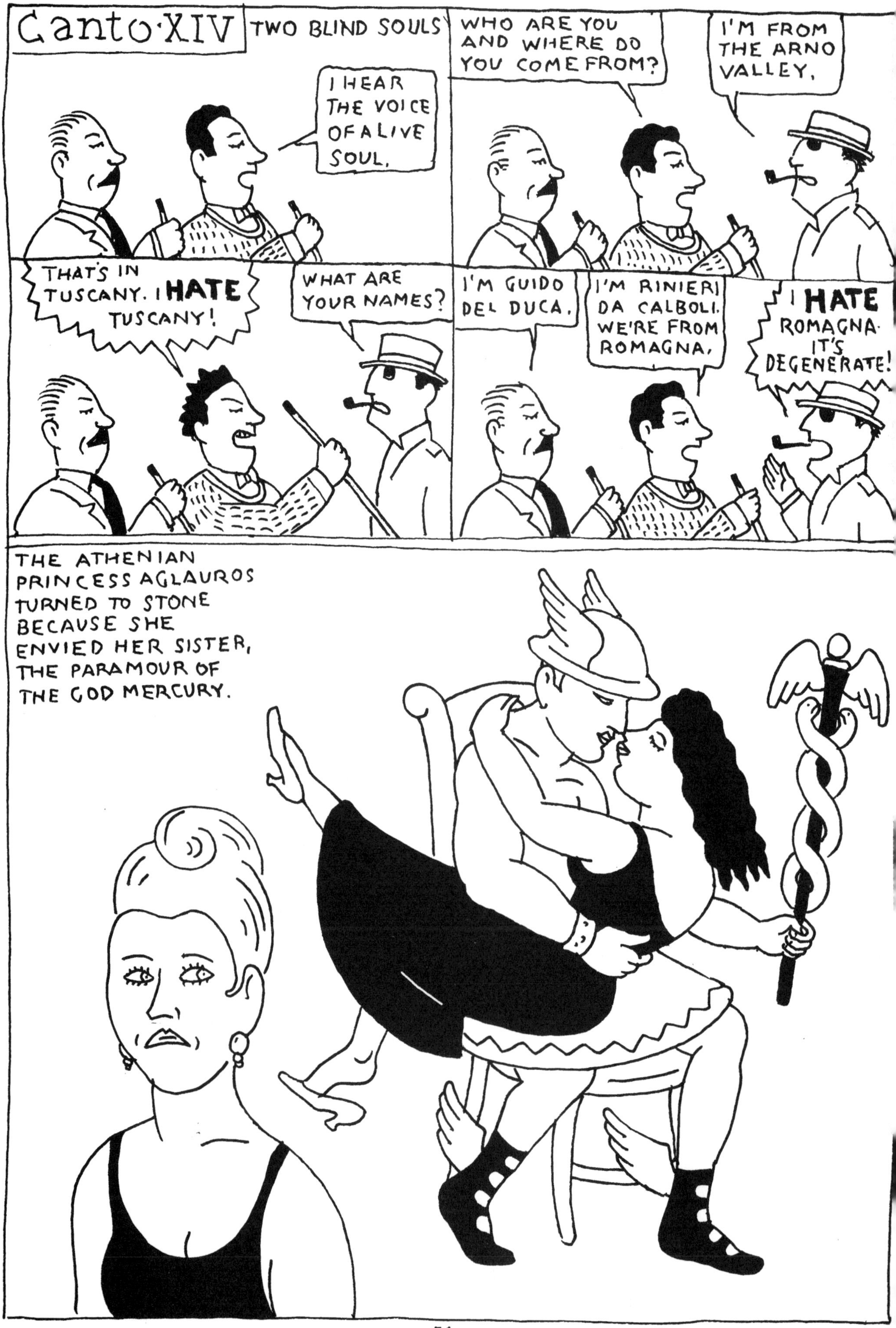
Canto·XIV
TWO BLIND SOULS
I HEAR THE VOICE OF A LIVE SOUL.
WHO ARE YOU AND WHERE DO YOU COME FROM?
I'M FROM THE ARNO VALLEY.
THAT'S IN TUSCANY. I **HATE** TUSCANY!
WHAT ARE YOUR NAMES?
I'M GUIDO DEL DUCA.
I'M RINIERI DA CALBOLI. WE'RE FROM ROMAGNA.
I **HATE** ROMAGNA. IT'S DEGENERATE!
THE ATHENIAN PRINCESS AGLAUROS TURNED TO STONE BECAUSE SHE ENVIED HER SISTER, THE PARAMOUR OF THE GOD MERCURY.

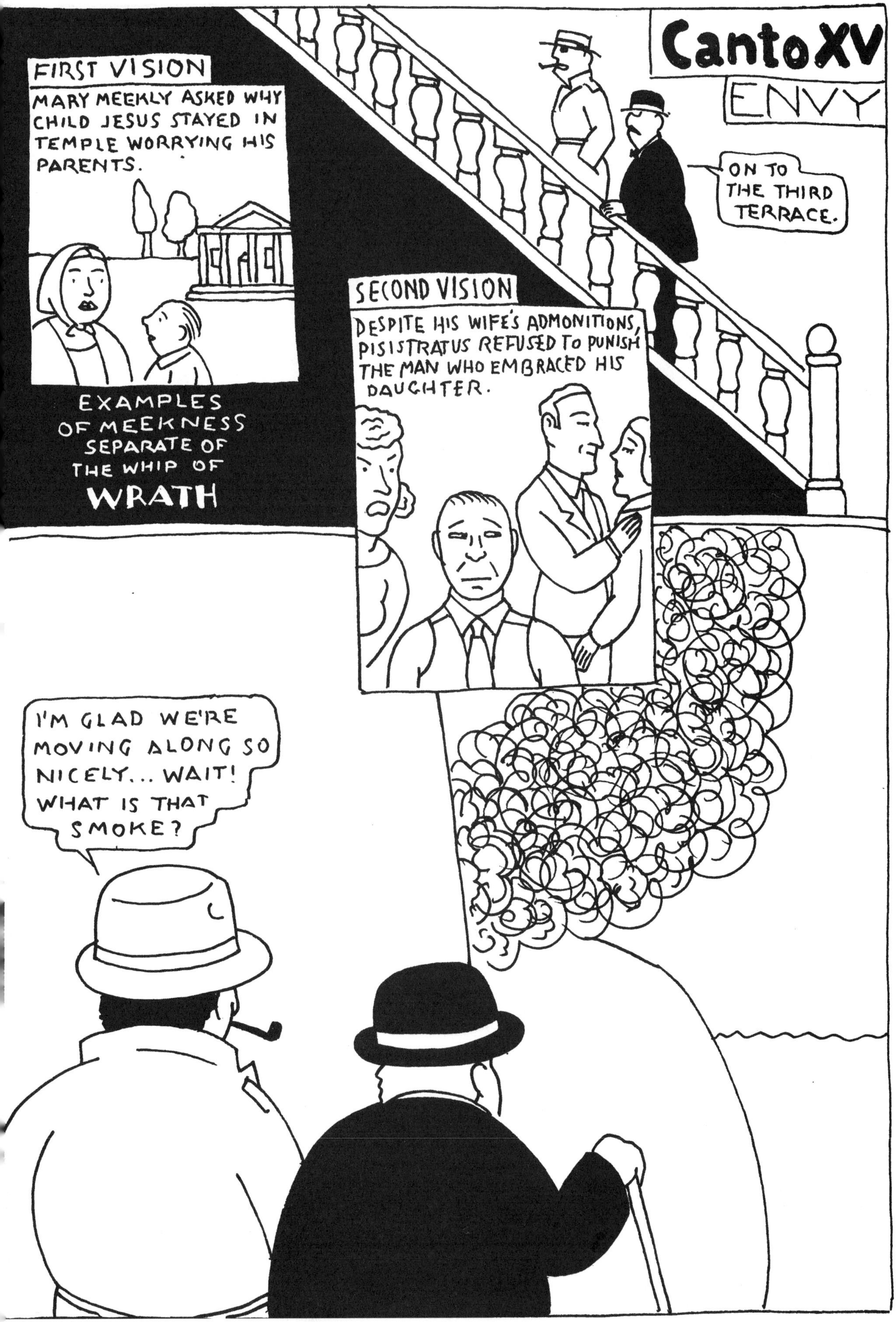
Canto XV
ENVY
FIRST VISION
MARY MEEKLY ASKED WHY CHILD JESUS STAYED IN TEMPLE WORRYING HIS PARENTS.
ON TO THE THIRD TERRACE.
SECOND VISION
DESPITE HIS WIFE'S ADMONITIONS, PISISTRATUS REFUSED TO PUNISH THE MAN WHO EMBRACED HIS DAUGHTER.
EXAMPLES OF MEEKNESS SEPARATE OF THE WHIP OF WRATH
I'M GLAD WE'RE MOVING ALONG SO NICELY... WAIT! WHAT IS THAT SMOKE?

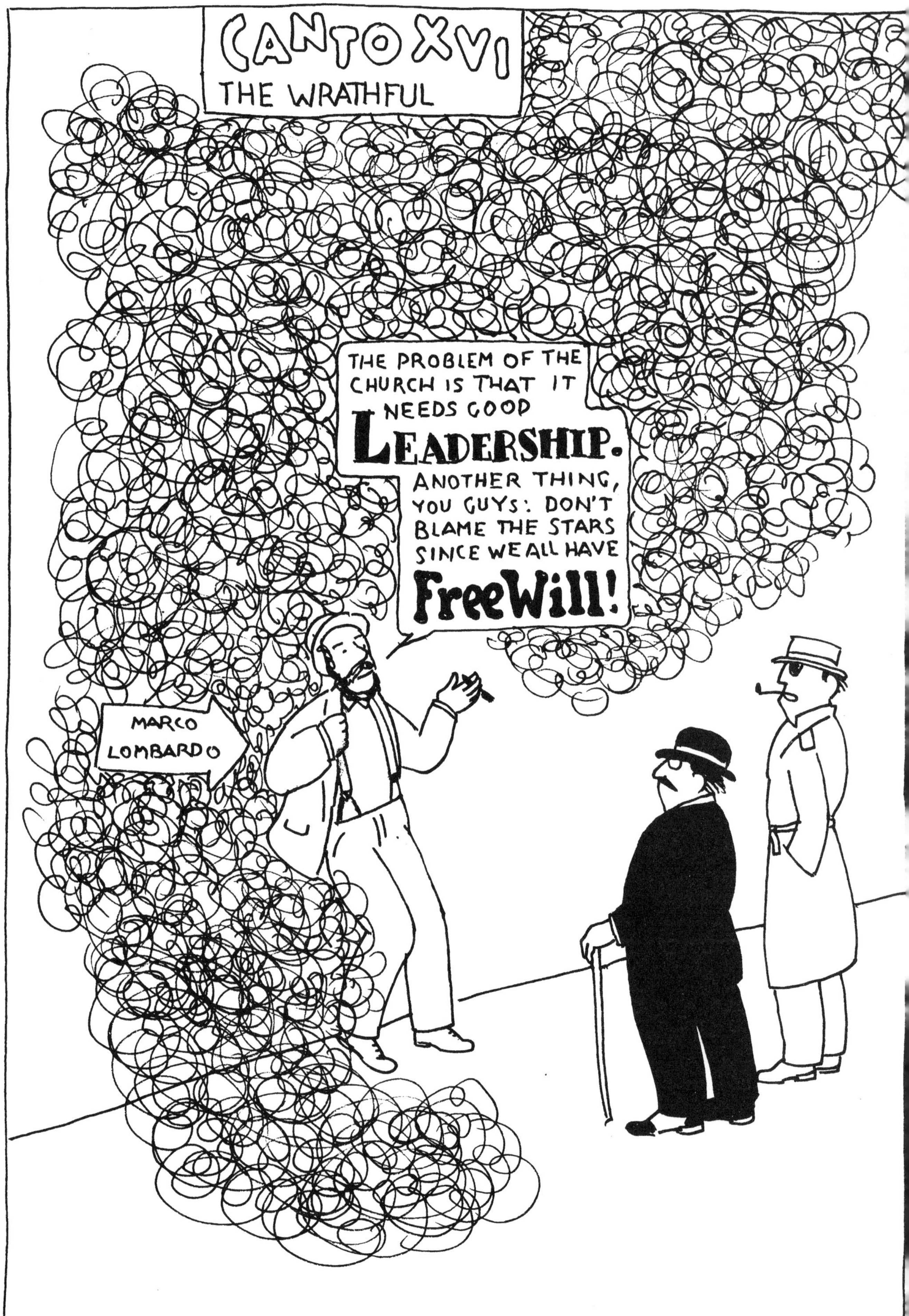
CANTO XVI
THE WRATHFUL
THE PROBLEM OF THE CHURCH IS THAT IT NEEDS GOOD LEADERSHIP. ANOTHER THING, YOU GUYS: DON'T BLAME THE STARS SINCE WE ALL HAVE FreeWill!
MARCO LOMBARDO

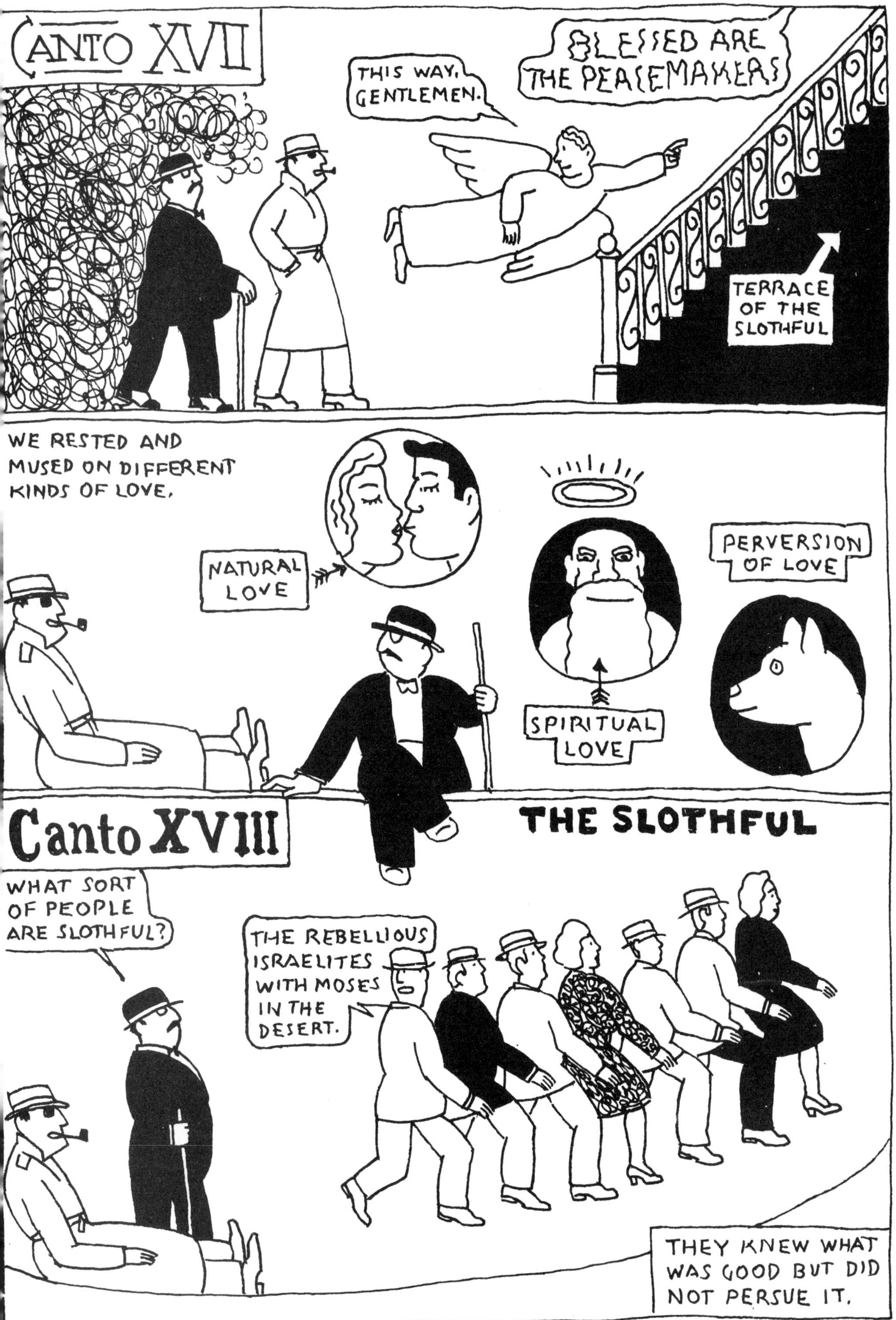
CANTO XVII
THIS WAY, GENTLEMEN.
BLESSED ARE THE PEACEMAKERS
TERRACE OF THE SLOTHFUL
WE RESTED AND MUSED ON DIFFERENT KINDS OF LOVE.
NATURAL LOVE
SPIRITUAL LOVE
PERVERSION OF LOVE
Canto XVIII
THE SLOTHFUL
WHAT SORT OF PEOPLE ARE SLOTHFUL?
THE REBELLIOUS ISRAELITES WITH MOSES IN THE DESERT.
THEY KNEW WHAT WAS GOOD BUT DID NOT PERSUE IT.

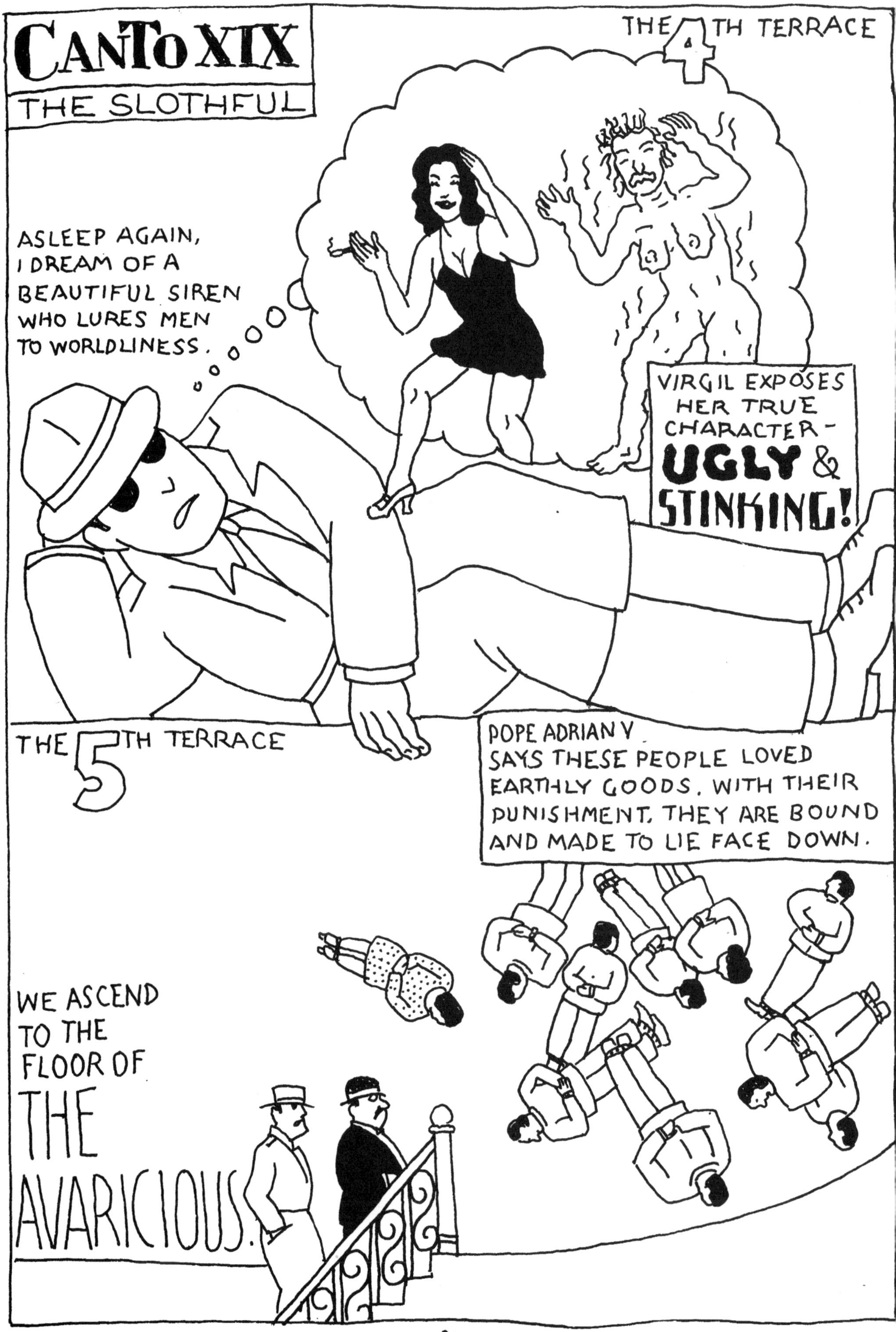
CANTO XIX
THE SLOTHFUL
THE 4TH TERRACE
ASLEEP AGAIN, I DREAM OF A BEAUTIFUL SIREN WHO LURES MEN TO WORLDLINESS.
VIRGIL EXPOSES HER TRUE CHARACTER - UGLY & STINKING!
THE 5TH TERRACE
POPE ADRIAN V SAYS THESE PEOPLE LOVED EARTHLY GOODS. WITH THEIR PUNISHMENT, THEY ARE BOUND AND MADE TO LIE FACE DOWN.
WE ASCEND TO THE FLOOR OF THE AVARICIOUS.

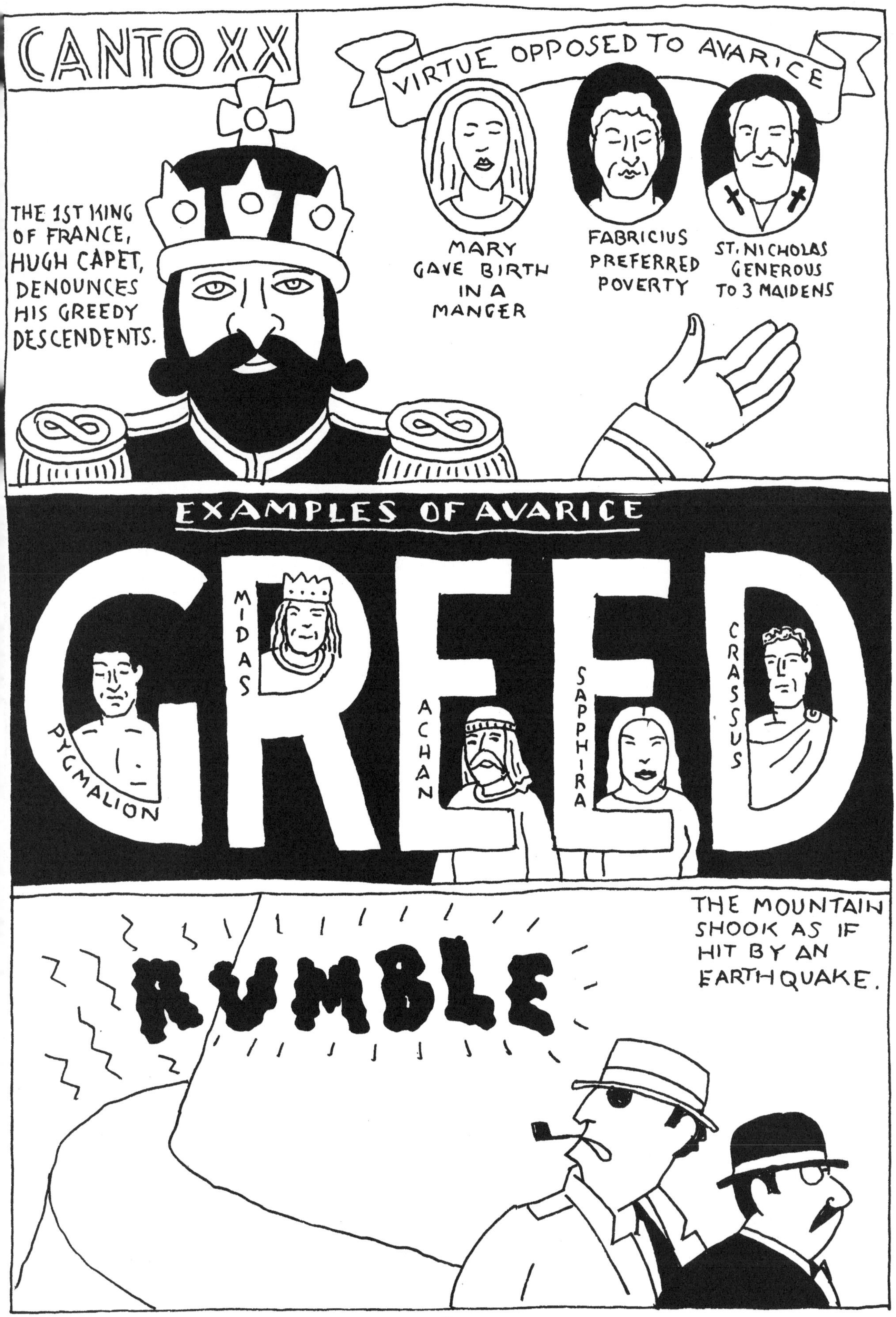
CANTO XX
VIRTUE OPPOSED TO AVARICE
THE 1ST KING OF FRANCE, HUGH CAPET, DENOUNCES HIS GREEDY DESCENDENTS.
MARY GAVE BIRTH IN A MANGER
FABRICIUS PREFERRED POVERTY
ST. NICHOLAS GENEROUS TO 3 MAIDENS
EXAMPLES OF AVARICE
GREED
PYGMALION
MIDAS
ACHAN
SAPPHIRA
CRASSUS
THE MOUNTAIN SHOOK AS IF HIT BY AN EARTHQUAKE.
RUMBLE

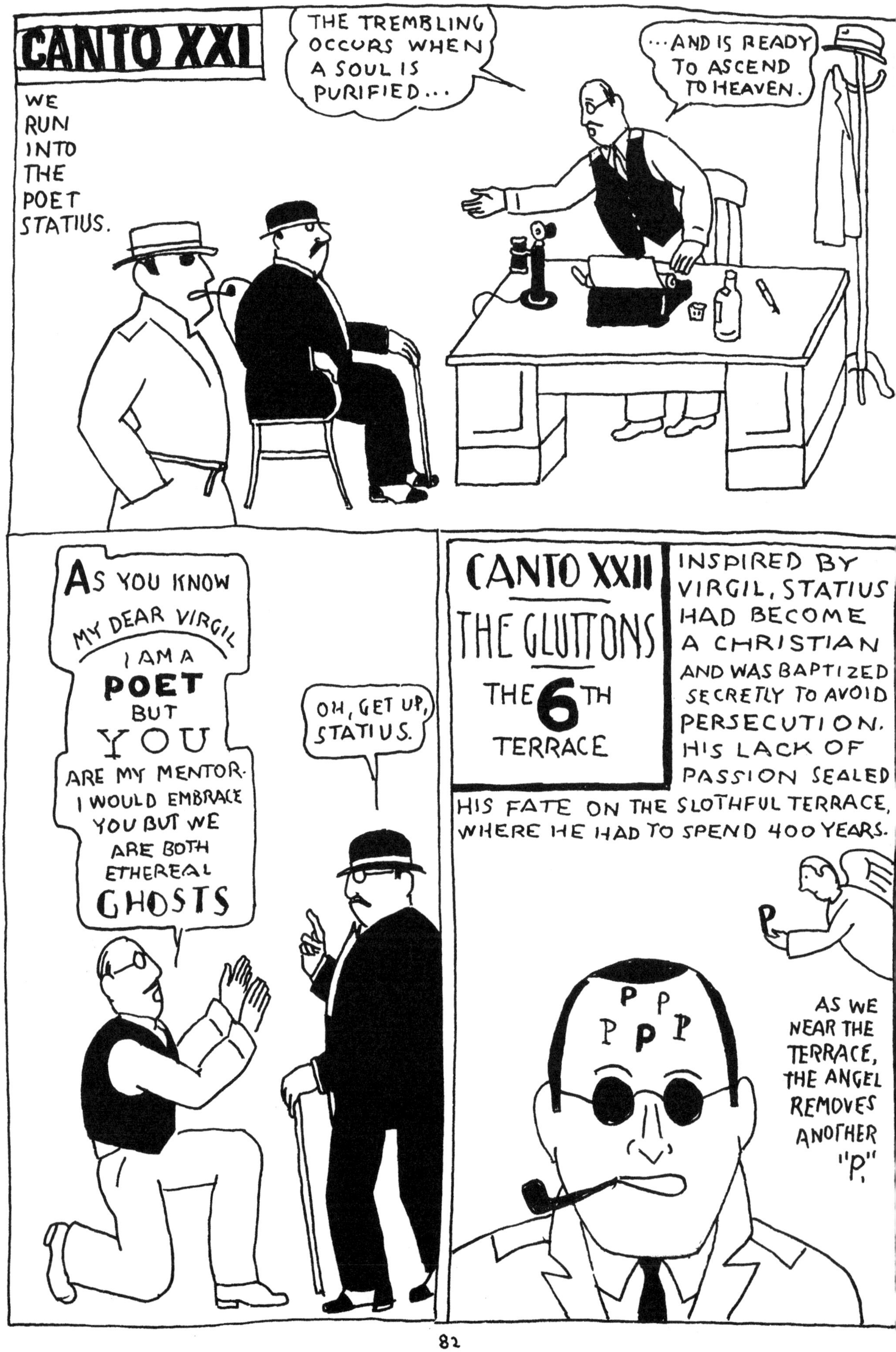
CANTO XXI
WE RUN INTO THE POET STATIUS.
THE TREMBLING OCCURS WHEN A SOUL IS PURIFIED...
...AND IS READY TO ASCEND TO HEAVEN.
AS YOU KNOW MY DEAR VIRGIL I AM A POET BUT YOU ARE MY MENTOR. I WOULD EMBRACE YOU BUT WE ARE BOTH ETHEREAL GHOSTS
OH, GET UP, STATIUS.
CANTO XXII
THE GLUTTONS
THE 6TH TERRACE
INSPIRED BY VIRGIL, STATIUS HAD BECOME A CHRISTIAN AND WAS BAPTIZED SECRETLY TO AVOID PERSECUTION. HIS LACK OF PASSION SEALED HIS FATE ON THE SLOTHFUL TERRACE, WHERE HE HAD TO SPEND 400 YEARS.
P
P P P P P
AS WE NEAR THE TERRACE, THE ANGEL REMOVES ANOTHER "P."

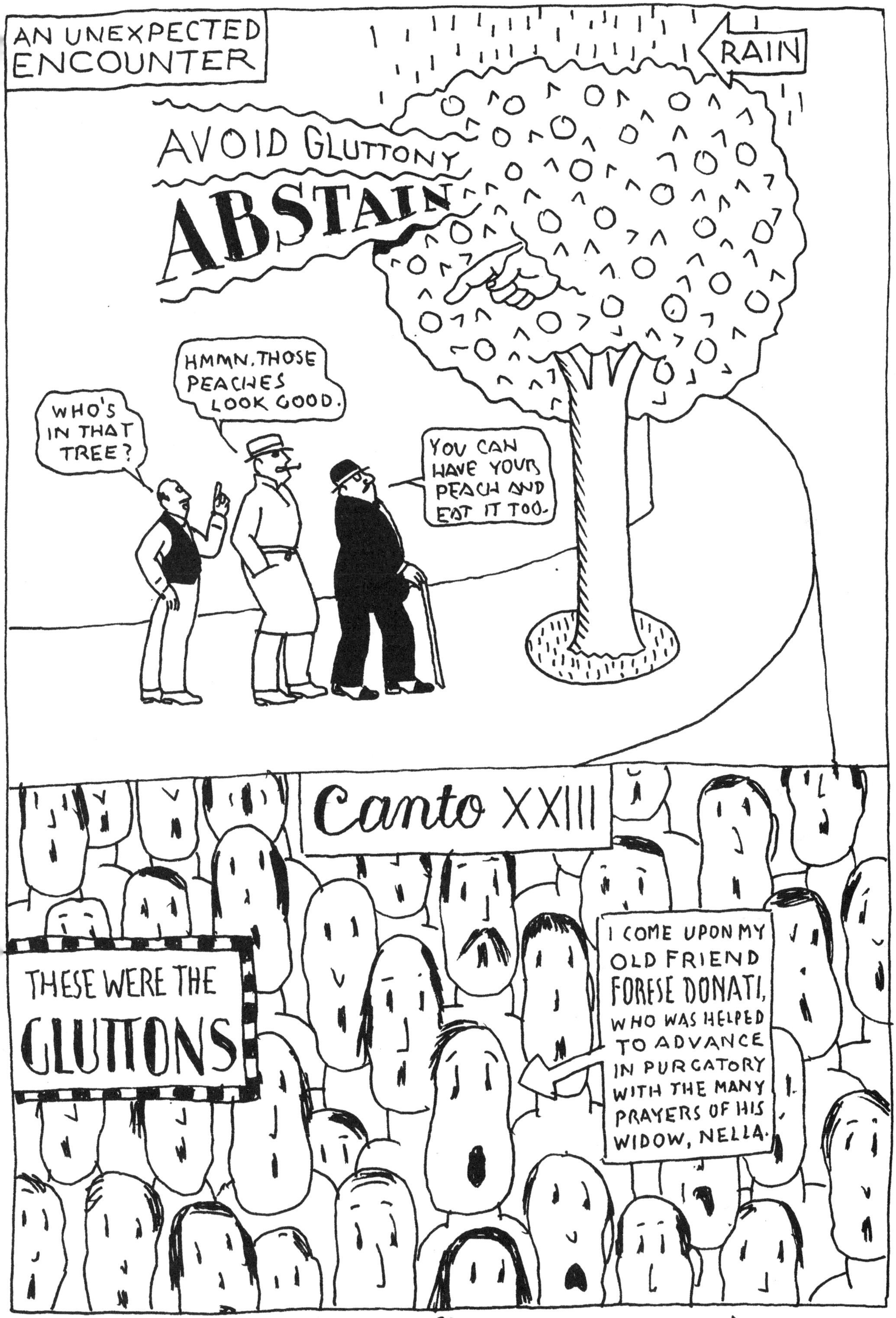
AN UNEXPECTED ENCOUNTER
RAIN
AVOID GLUTTONY
ABSTAIN
WHO'S IN THAT TREE?
HMMN, THOSE PEACHES LOOK GOOD.
YOU CAN HAVE YOUR PEACH AND EAT IT TOO.
Canto XXIII
THESE WERE THE GLUTTONS
I COME UPON MY OLD FRIEND FORESE DONATI, WHO WAS HELPED TO ADVANCE IN PURGATORY WITH THE MANY PRAYERS OF HIS WIDOW, NELLA.

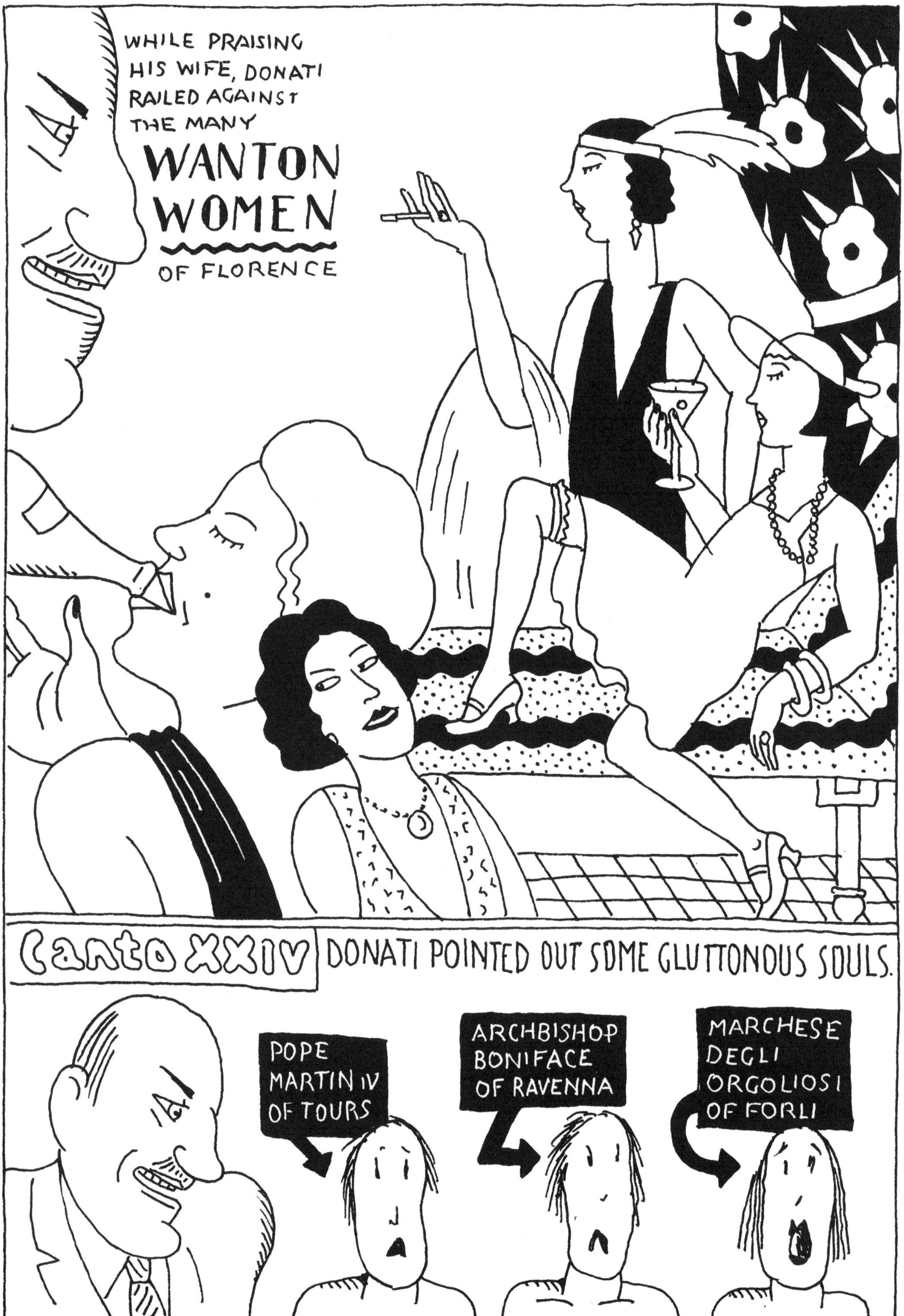
WHILE PRAISING HIS WIFE, DONATI RAILED AGAINST THE MANY
WANTON WOMEN
OF FLORENCE
Canto XXIV
DONATI POINTED OUT SOME GLUTTONOUS SOULS.
POPE MARTIN IV OF TOURS
ARCHBISHOP BONIFACE OF RAVENNA
MARCHESE DEGLI ORGOLIOSI OF FORLI

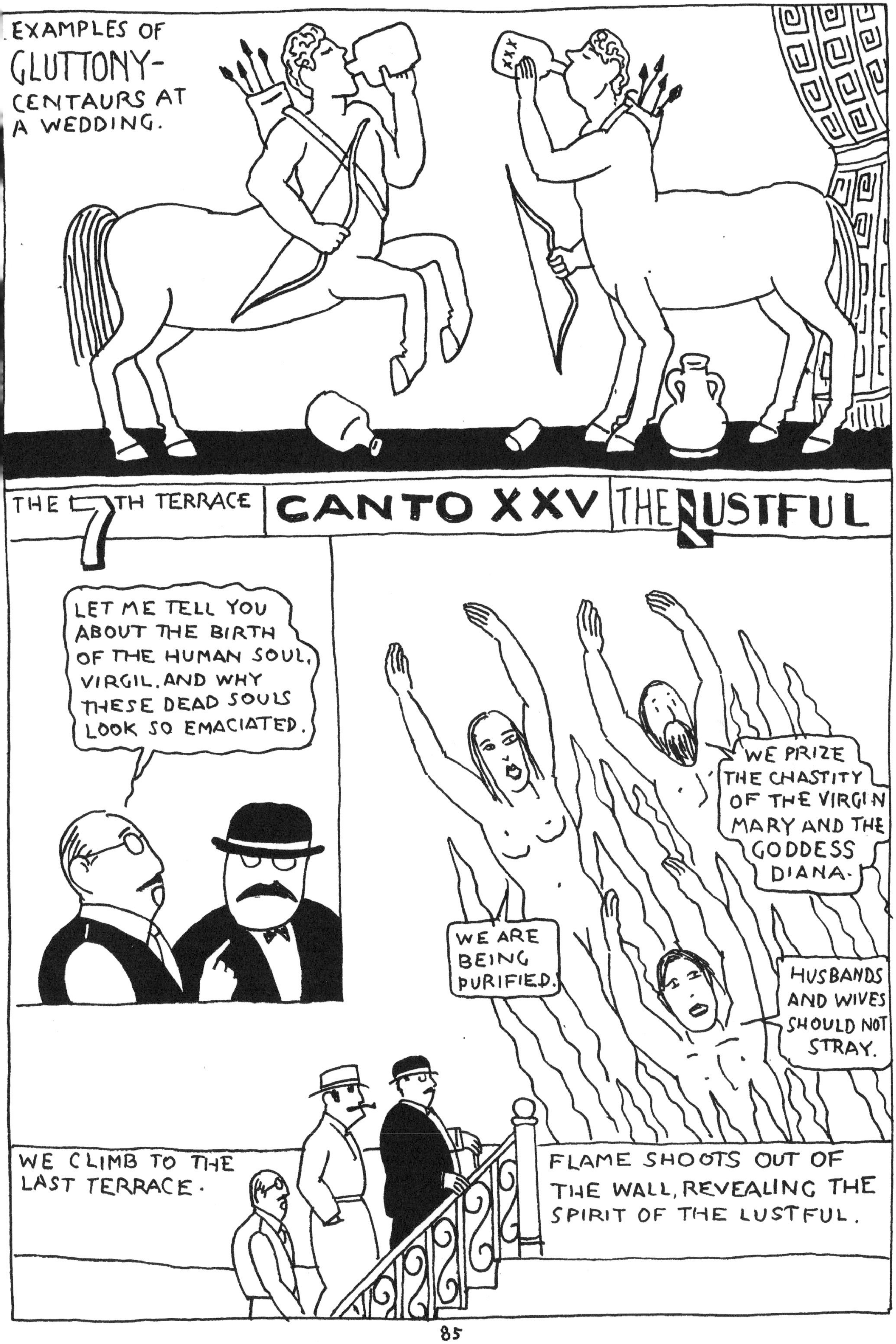
EXAMPLES OF GLUTTONY- CENTAURS AT A WEDDING.
XXX
THE 7TH TERRACE
CANTO XXV
THE LUSTFUL
LET ME TELL YOU ABOUT THE BIRTH OF THE HUMAN SOUL, VIRGIL, AND WHY THESE DEAD SOULS LOOK SO EMACIATED.
WE PRIZE THE CHASTITY OF THE VIRGIN MARY AND THE GODDESS DIANA.
WE ARE BEING PURIFIED.
HUSBANDS AND WIVES SHOULD NOT STRAY.
WE CLIMB TO THE LAST TERRACE.
FLAME SHOOTS OUT OF THE WALL, REVEALING THE SPIRIT OF THE LUSTFUL.

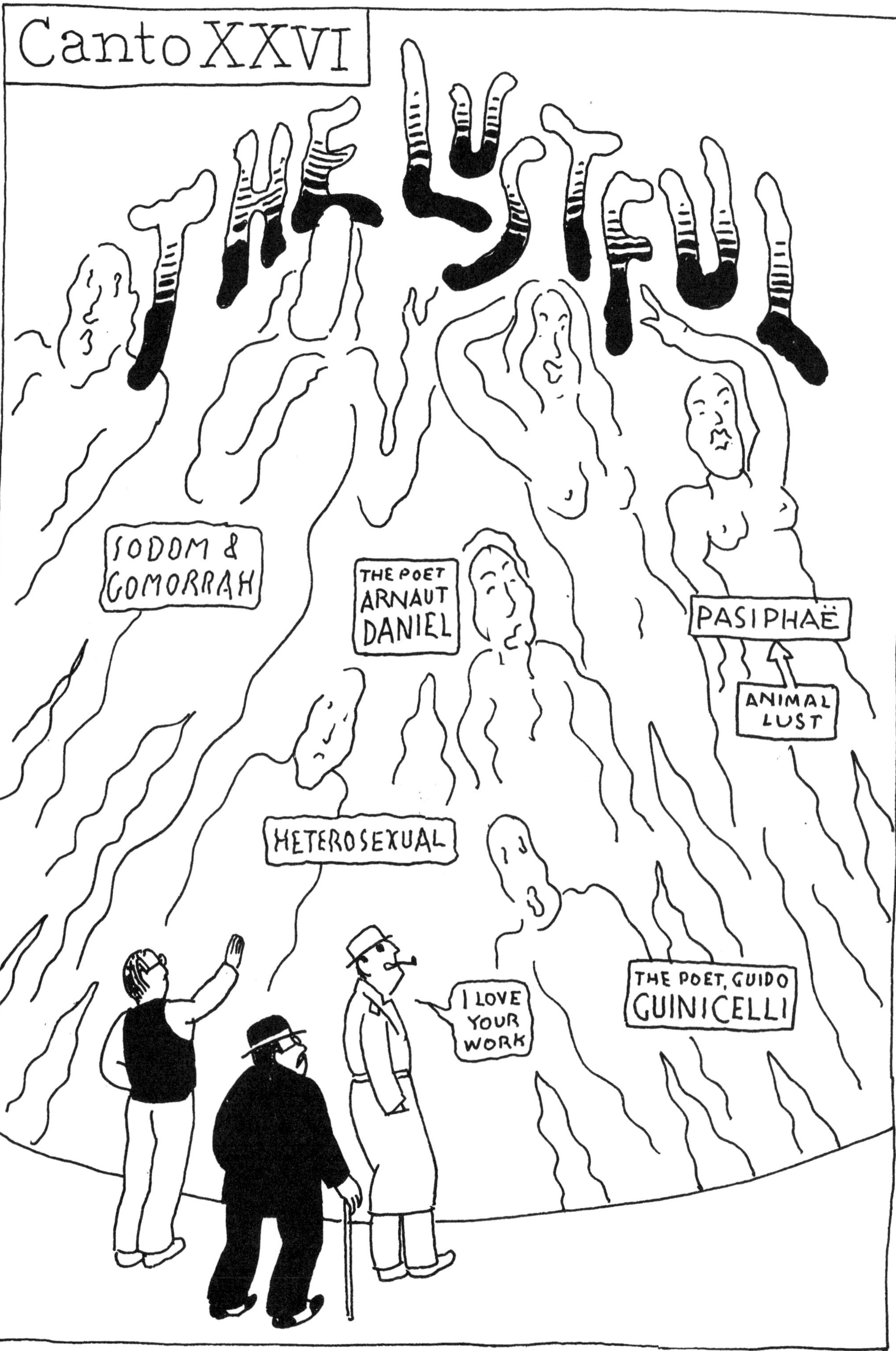
Canto XXVI
THE LUSTFUL
SODOM & GOMORRAH
THE POET ARNAUT DANIEL
PASIPHAË
ANIMAL LUST
HETEROSEXUAL
I LOVE YOUR WORK
THE POET, GUIDO GUINICELLI

CANTO XXVII | FROM THE LUSTFUL TERRACE TO EARTHLY PARADISE

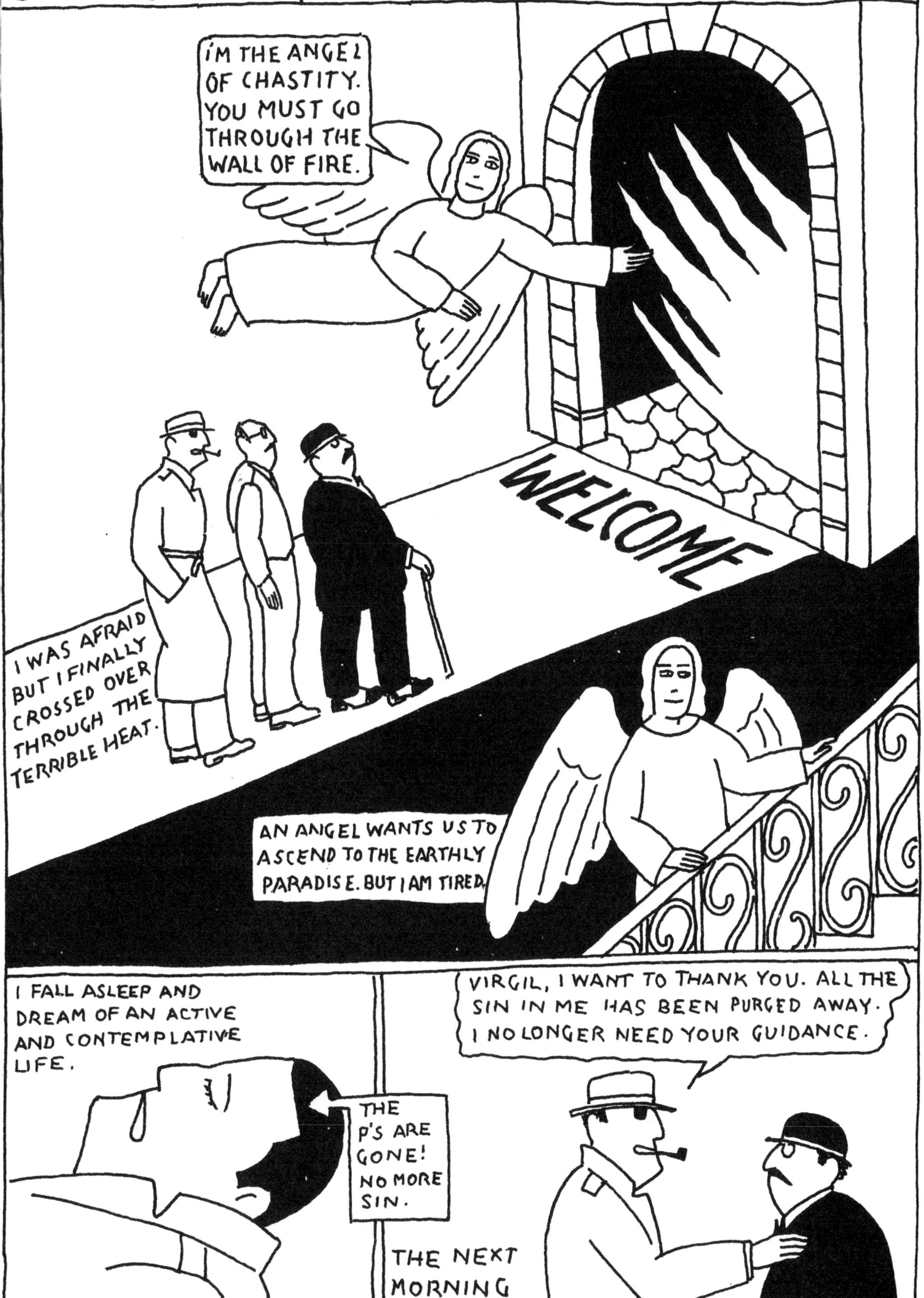

I'M THE ANGEL OF CHASTITY. YOU MUST GO THROUGH THE WALL OF FIRE.
WELCOME
I WAS AFRAID BUT I FINALLY CROSSED OVER THROUGH THE TERRIBLE HEAT.
AN ANGEL WANTS US TO ASCEND TO THE EARTHLY PARADISE. BUT I AM TIRED.
I FALL ASLEEP AND DREAM OF AN ACTIVE AND CONTEMPLATIVE LIFE.
THE P'S ARE GONE! NO MORE SIN.
THE NEXT MORNING
VIRGIL, I WANT TO THANK YOU. ALL THE SIN IN ME HAS BEEN PURGED AWAY. I NO LONGER NEED YOUR GUIDANCE.

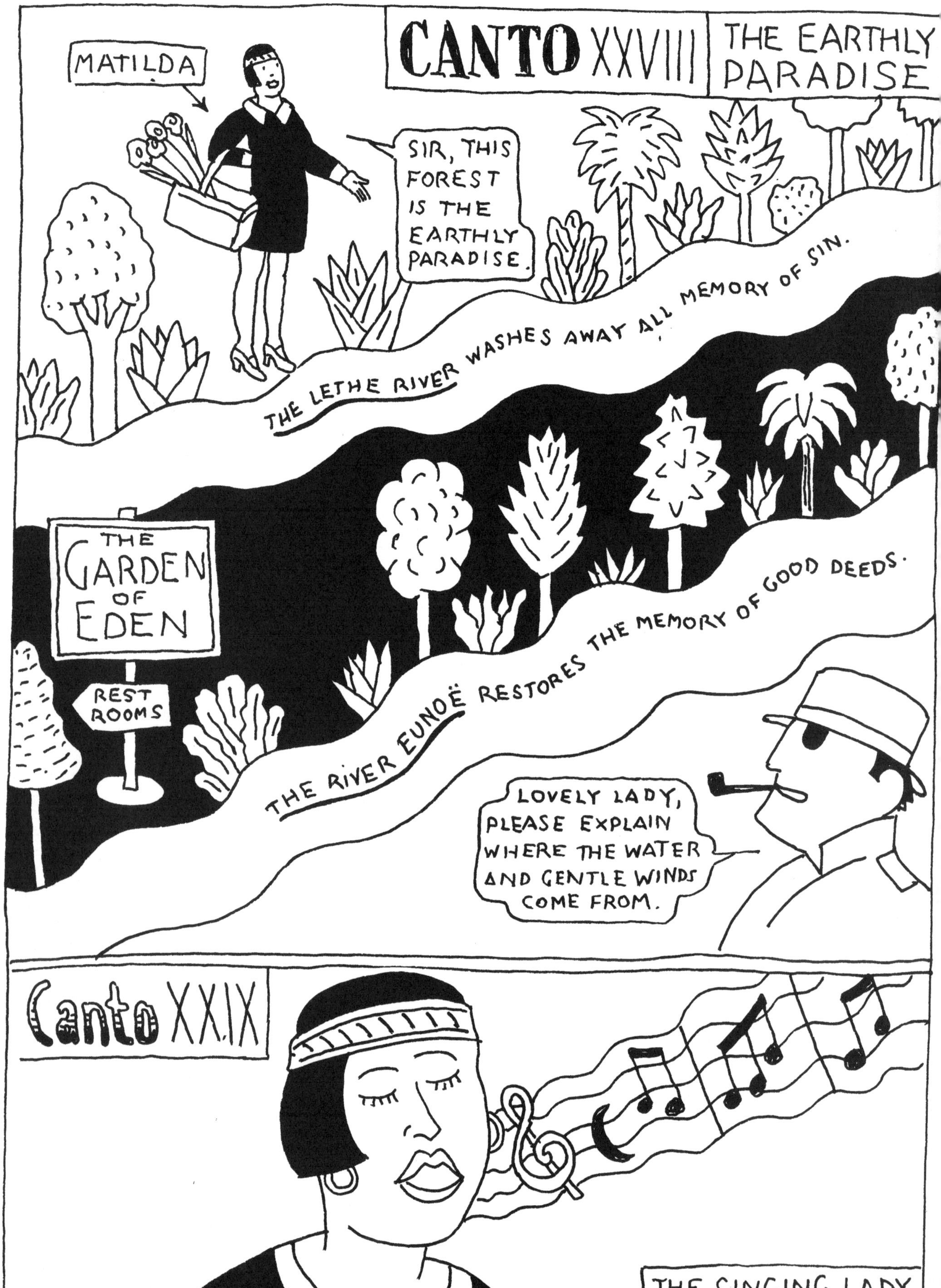
CANTO XXVIII
THE EARTHLY PARADISE
MATILDA
SIR, THIS FOREST IS THE EARTHLY PARADISE.
THE LETHE RIVER WASHES AWAY ALL MEMORY OF SIN.
THE GARDEN OF EDEN
REST ROOMS
THE RIVER EUNOË RESTORES THE MEMORY OF GOOD DEEDS.
LOVELY LADY, PLEASE EXPLAIN WHERE THE WATER AND GENTLE WINDS COME FROM.
Canto XXIX
THE SINGING LADY ASKS ME TO FOLLOW HER UPSTREAM.

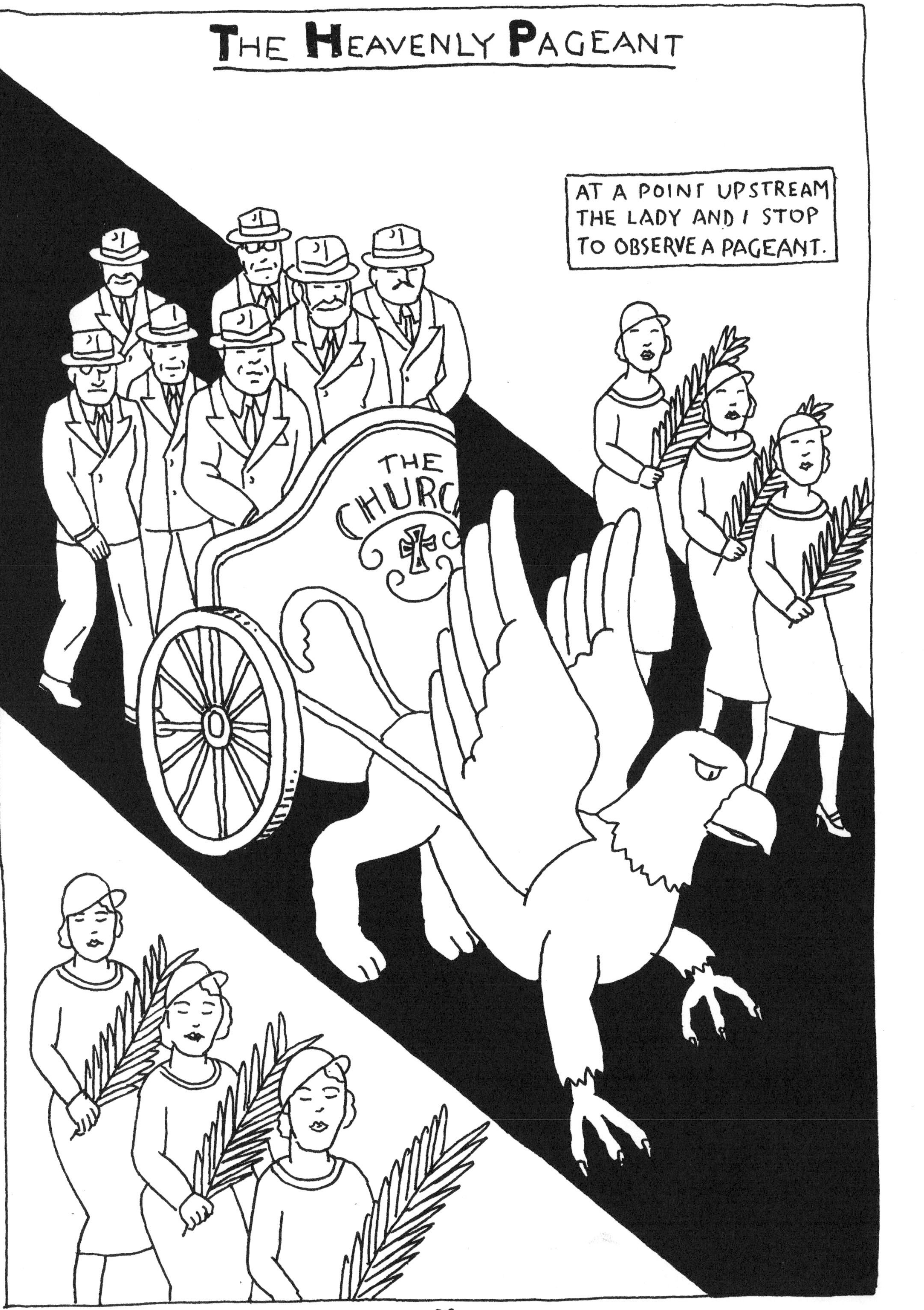
THE HEAVENLY PAGEANT
AT A POINT UPSTREAM THE LADY AND I STOP TO OBSERVE A PAGEANT.
THE CHURCH

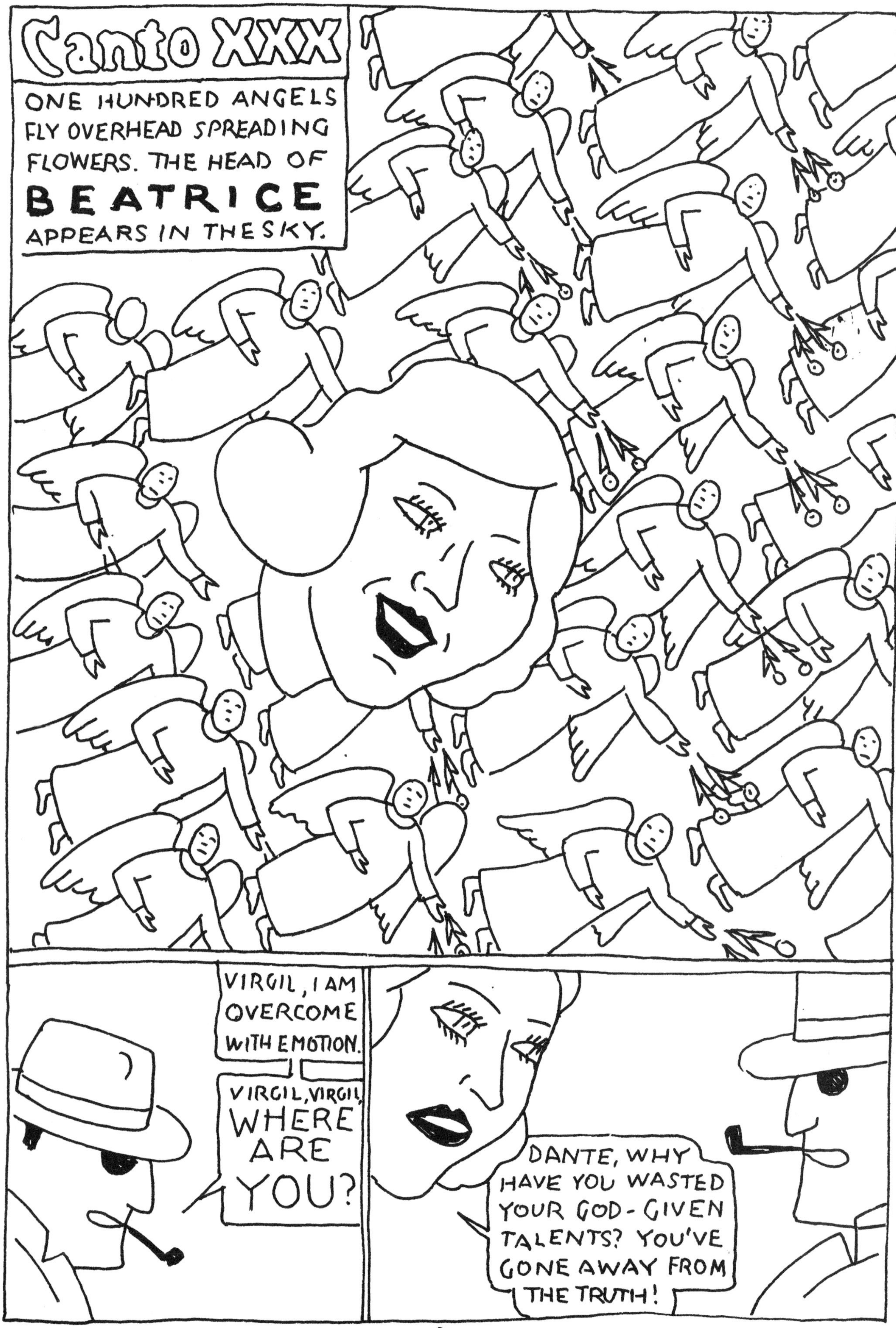
Canto XXX
ONE HUNDRED ANGELS FLY OVERHEAD SPREADING FLOWERS. THE HEAD OF BEATRICE APPEARS IN THE SKY.
VIRGIL, I AM OVERCOME WITH EMOTION.
VIRGIL, VIRGIL, WHERE ARE YOU?
DANTE, WHY HAVE YOU WASTED YOUR GOD-GIVEN TALENTS? YOU'VE GONE AWAY FROM THE TRUTH!

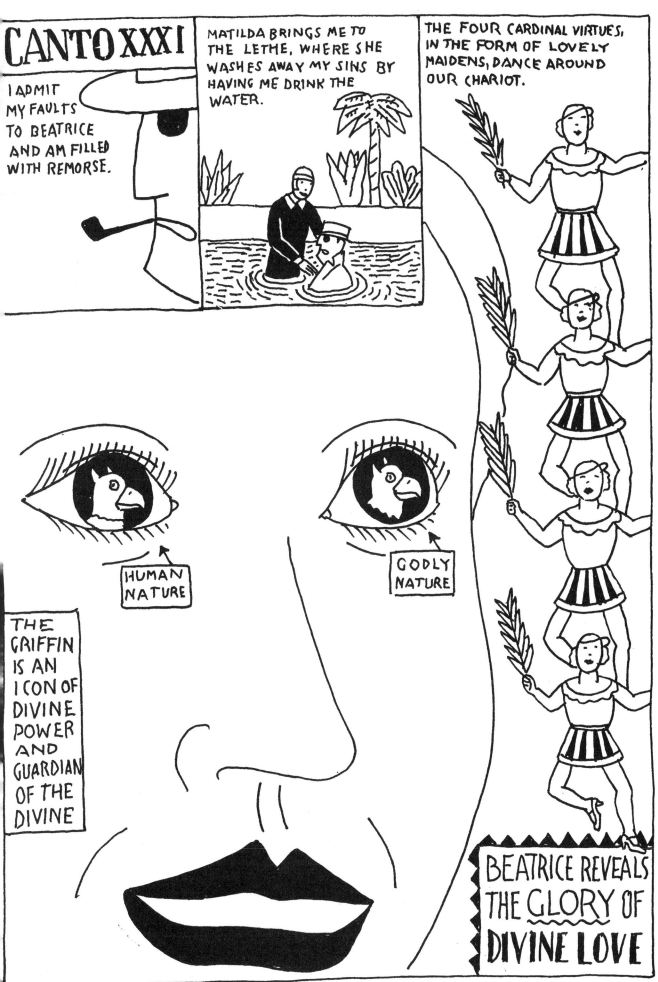

CANTO XXXI

I ADMIT MY FAULTS TO BEATRICE AND AM FILLED WITH REMORSE.

MATILDA BRINGS ME TO THE LETHE, WHERE SHE WASHES AWAY MY SINS BY HAVING ME DRINK THE WATER.

THE FOUR CARDINAL VIRTUES, IN THE FORM OF LOVELY MAIDENS, DANCE AROUND OUR CHARIOT.

HUMAN NATURE

GODLY NATURE

THE GRIFFIN IS AN ICON OF DIVINE POWER AND GUARDIAN OF THE DIVINE

BEATRICE REVEALS THE GLORY OF DIVINE LOVE

CANTO XXXII

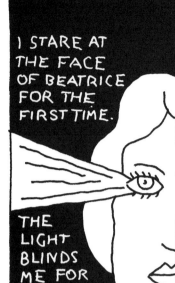

I STARE AT THE FACE OF BEATRICE FOR THE FIRST TIME.

THE LIGHT BLINDS ME FOR AWHILE.

STATIUS AND I COME UPON THE TREE OF KNOWLEDGE. IT IS BARE.

THE GRIFFIN POKES THE TREE. IT GROWS LEAVES AND BLOSSOMS.

AN **Eagle** **FOX** AND **DRAGON** ATTACK THE TREE — THE CORRUPT CHURCH ALLEGORY

THE ROMAN EMPIRE

HERESY

SATAN

THE HARLOT GIRL FRIEND OF A GIANT HAS A ROVING EYE. HE BEATS HER.

THE CORRUPTED PAPACY

THE FRENCH MONARCHY

THE CHARIOT GROWS FEATHERS AND SEVEN HEADS.

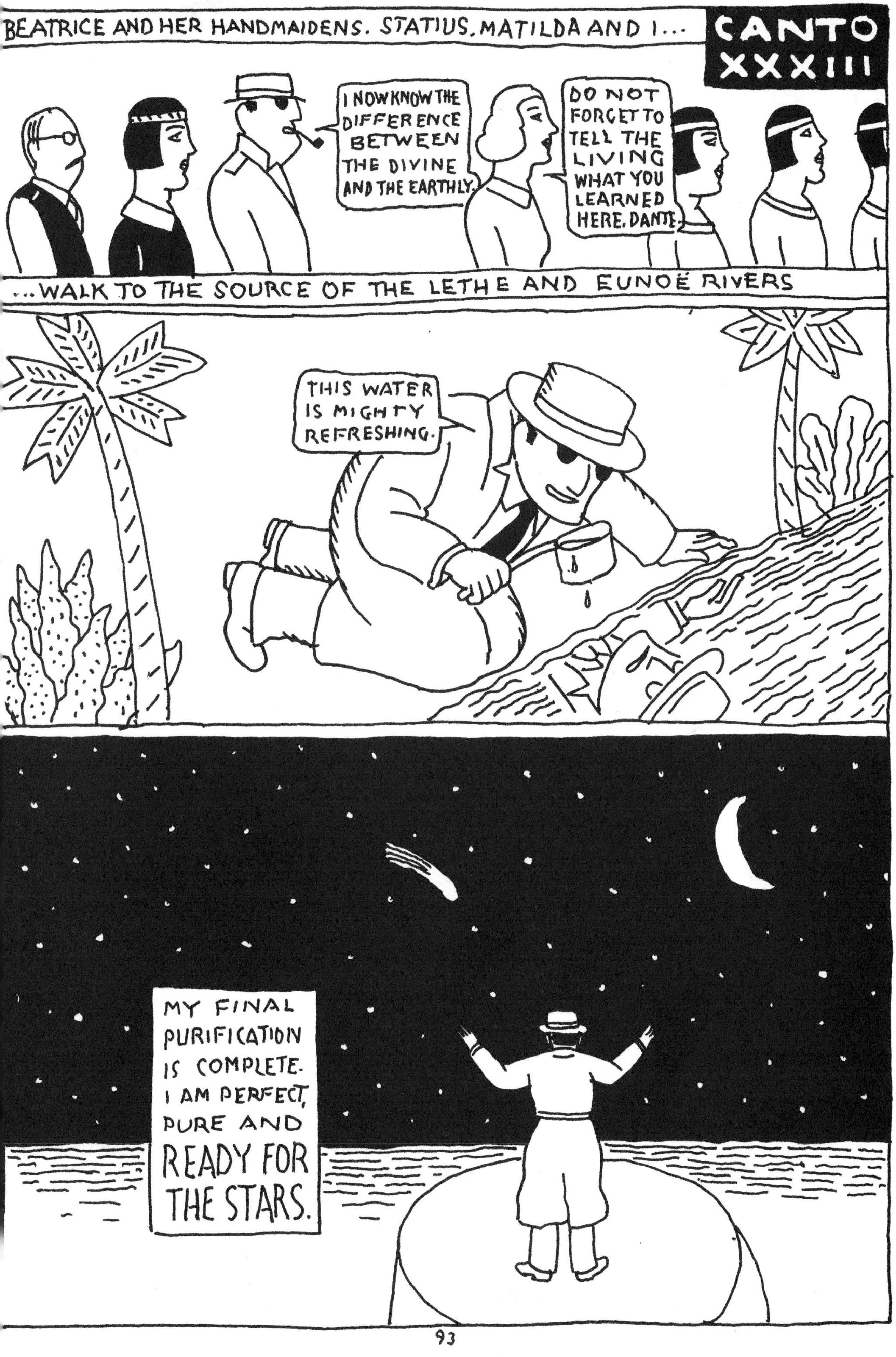

BEATRICE AND HER HANDMAIDENS. STATIUS, MATILDA AND I...
CANTO XXXIII
I NOW KNOW THE DIFFERENCE BETWEEN THE DIVINE AND THE EARTHLY.
DO NOT FORGET TO TELL THE LIVING WHAT YOU LEARNED HERE, DANTE.
...WALK TO THE SOURCE OF THE LETHE AND EUNOË RIVERS
THIS WATER IS MIGHTY REFRESHING.
MY FINAL PURIFICATION IS COMPLETE. I AM PERFECT, PURE AND READY FOR THE STARS.

PARADISE

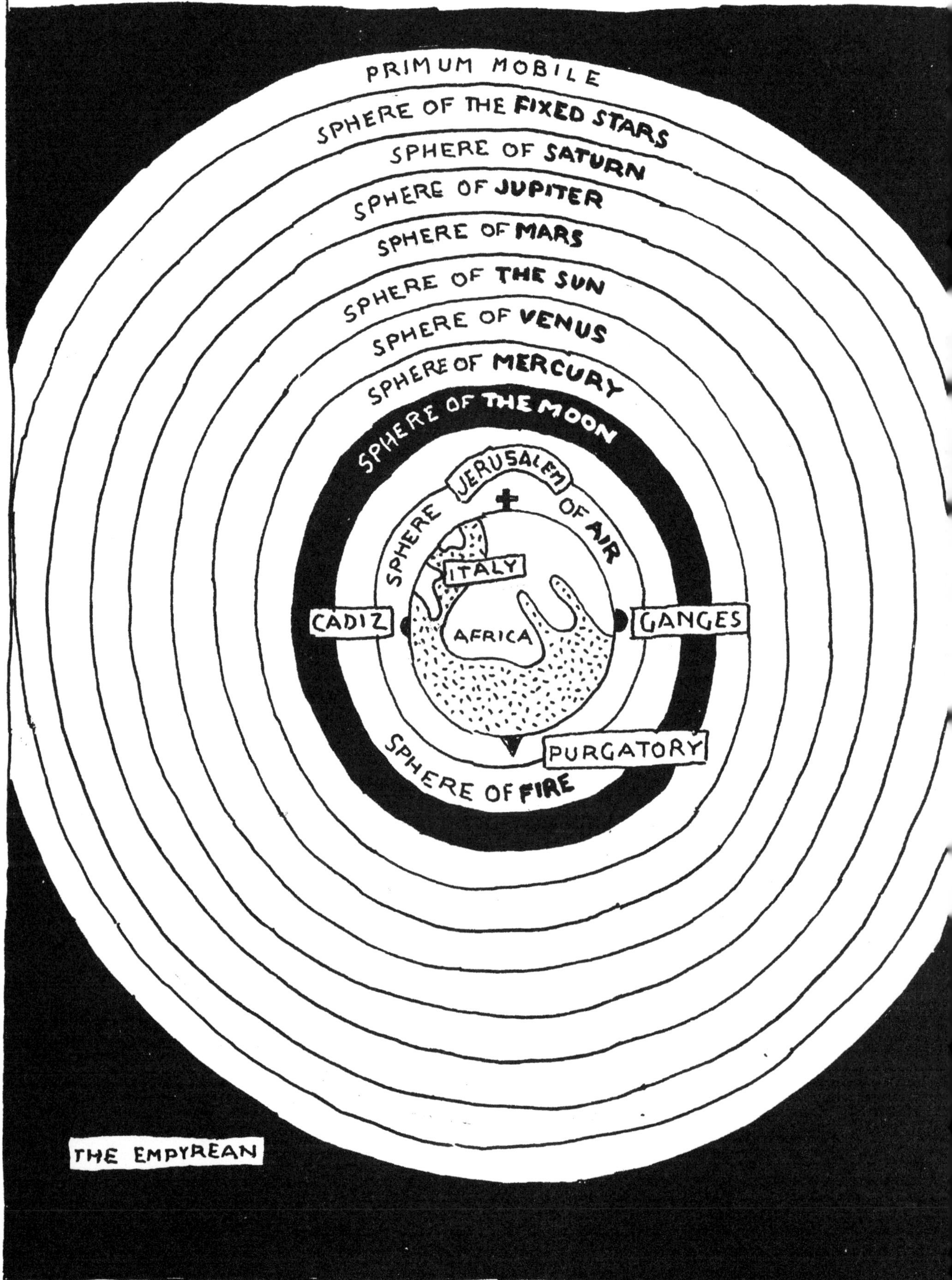
PRIMUM MOBILE
SPHERE OF THE FIXED STARS
SPHERE OF SATURN
SPHERE OF JUPITER
SPHERE OF MARS
SPHERE OF THE SUN
SPHERE OF VENUS
SPHERE OF MERCURY
SPHERE OF THE MOON
JERUSALEM
SPHERE OF AIR
ITALY
CADIZ
AFRICA
GANGES
PURGATORY
SPHERE OF FIRE
THE EMPYREAN

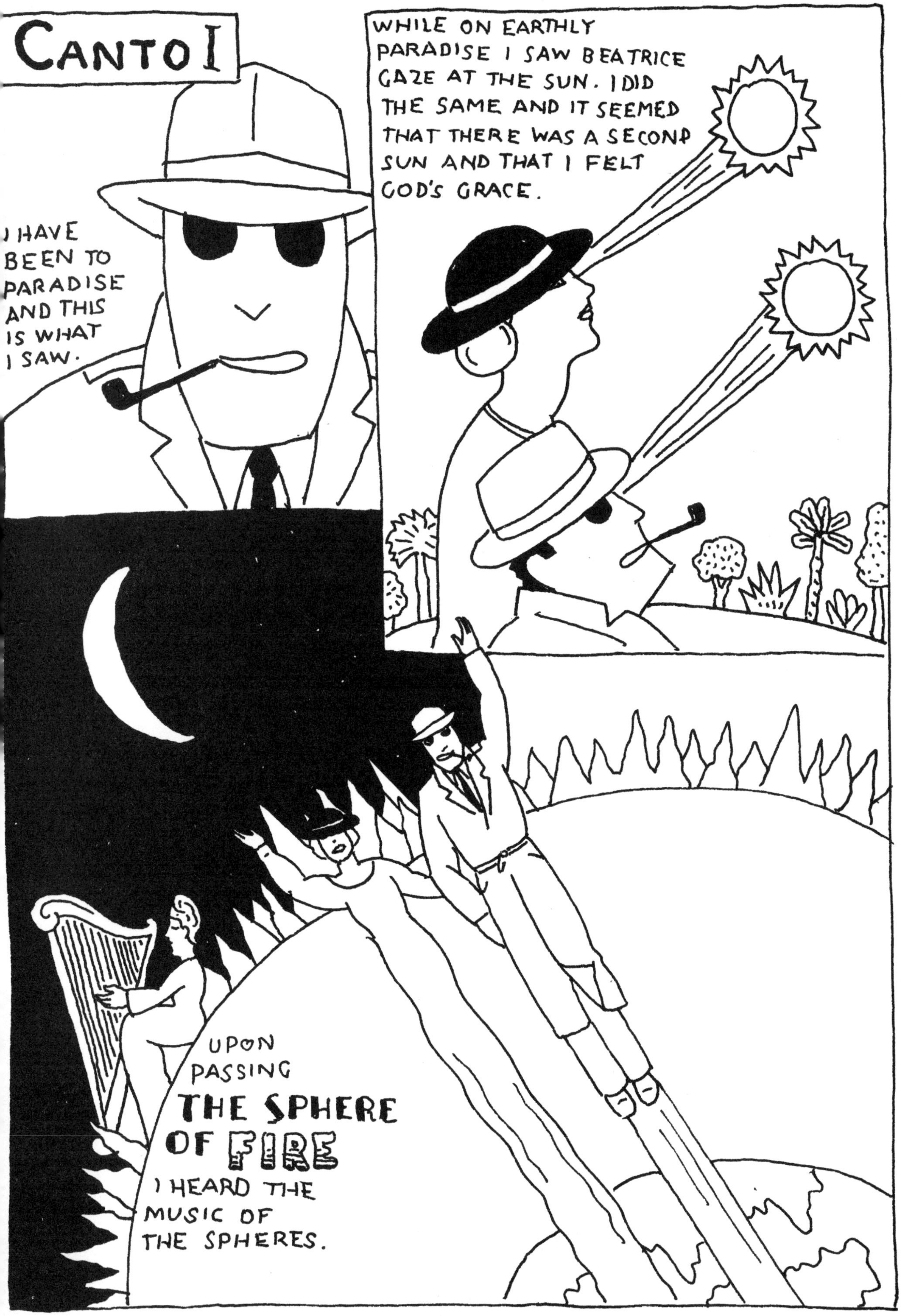

CANTO I
I HAVE BEEN TO PARADISE AND THIS IS WHAT I SAW.
WHILE ON EARTHLY PARADISE I SAW BEATRICE GAZE AT THE SUN. I DID THE SAME AND IT SEEMED THAT THERE WAS A SECOND SUN AND THAT I FELT GOD'S GRACE.
UPON PASSING THE SPHERE OF FIRE I HEARD THE MUSIC OF THE SPHERES.

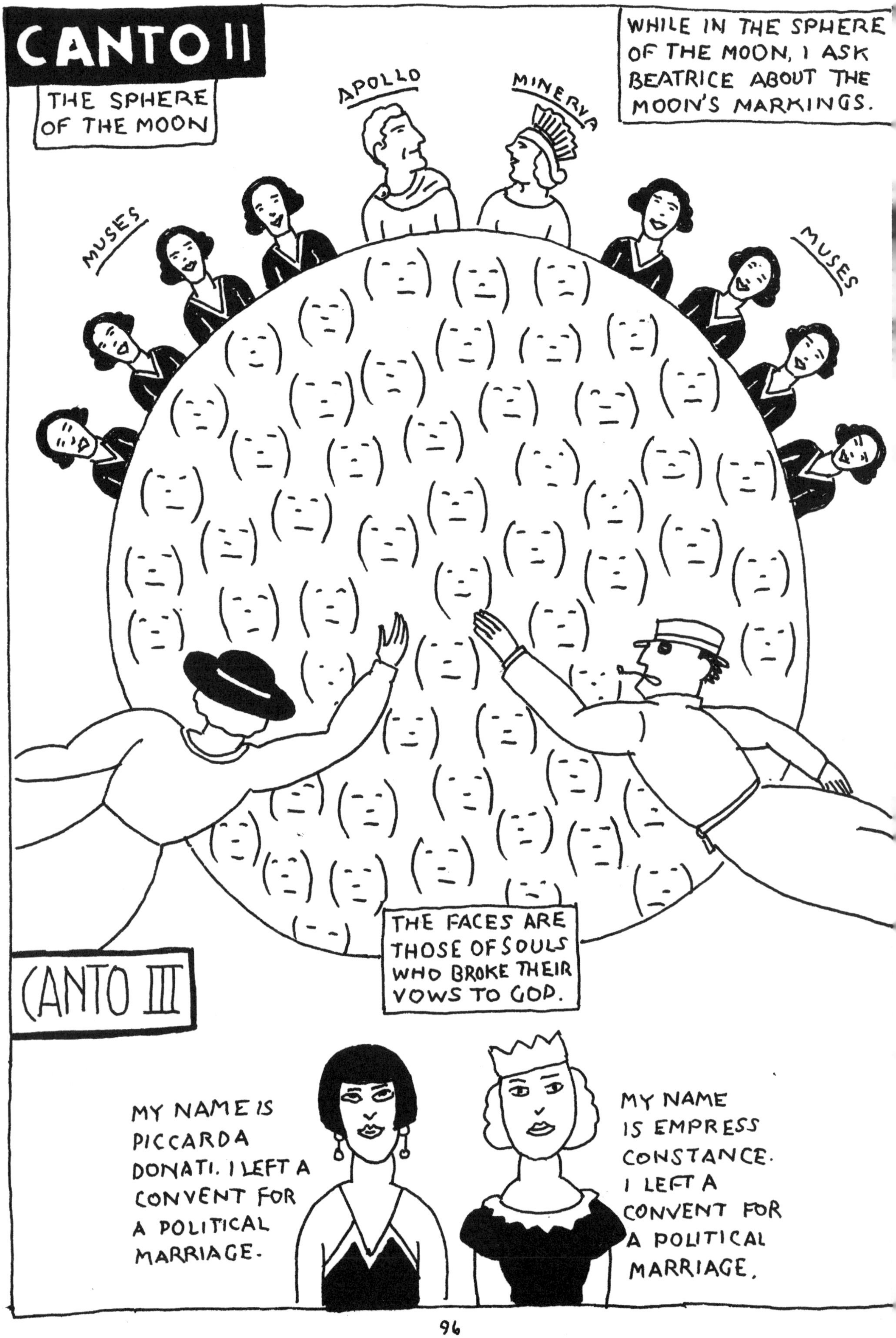
CANTO II
THE SPHERE OF THE MOON
APOLLO
MINERVA
WHILE IN THE SPHERE OF THE MOON, I ASK BEATRICE ABOUT THE MOON'S MARKINGS.
MUSES
MUSES
THE FACES ARE THOSE OF SOULS WHO BROKE THEIR VOWS TO GOD.
CANTO III
MY NAME IS PICCARDA DONATI. I LEFT A CONVENT FOR A POLITICAL MARRIAGE.
MY NAME IS EMPRESS CONSTANCE. I LEFT A CONVENT FOR A POLITICAL MARRIAGE.

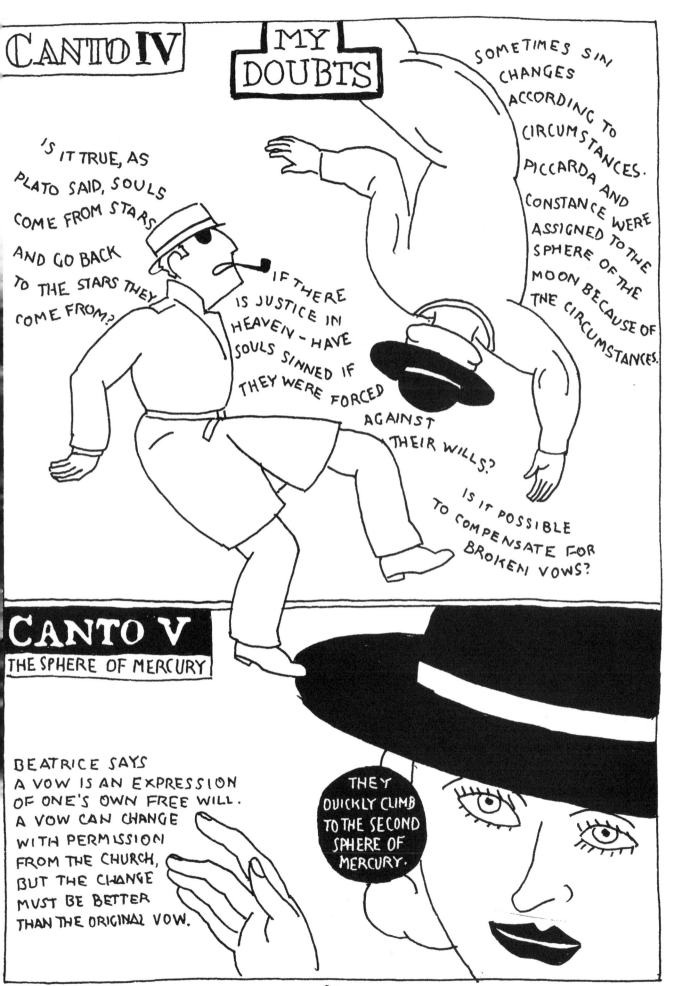

CANTO IV

MY DOUBTS

IS IT TRUE, AS PLATO SAID, SOULS COME FROM STARS AND GO BACK TO THE STARS THEY COME FROM?

IF THERE IS JUSTICE IN HEAVEN — HAVE SOULS SINNED IF THEY WERE FORCED AGAINST THEIR WILLS?

SOMETIMES SIN CHANGES ACCORDING TO CIRCUMSTANCES. PICCARDA AND CONSTANCE WERE ASSIGNED TO THE SPHERE OF THE MOON BECAUSE OF THE CIRCUMSTANCES.

IS IT POSSIBLE TO COMPENSATE FOR BROKEN VOWS?

CANTO V
THE SPHERE OF MERCURY

BEATRICE SAYS A VOW IS AN EXPRESSION OF ONE'S OWN FREE WILL. A VOW CAN CHANGE WITH PERMISSION FROM THE CHURCH, BUT THE CHANGE MUST BE BETTER THAN THE ORIGINAL VOW.

THEY QUICKLY CLIMB TO THE SECOND SPHERE OF MERCURY.

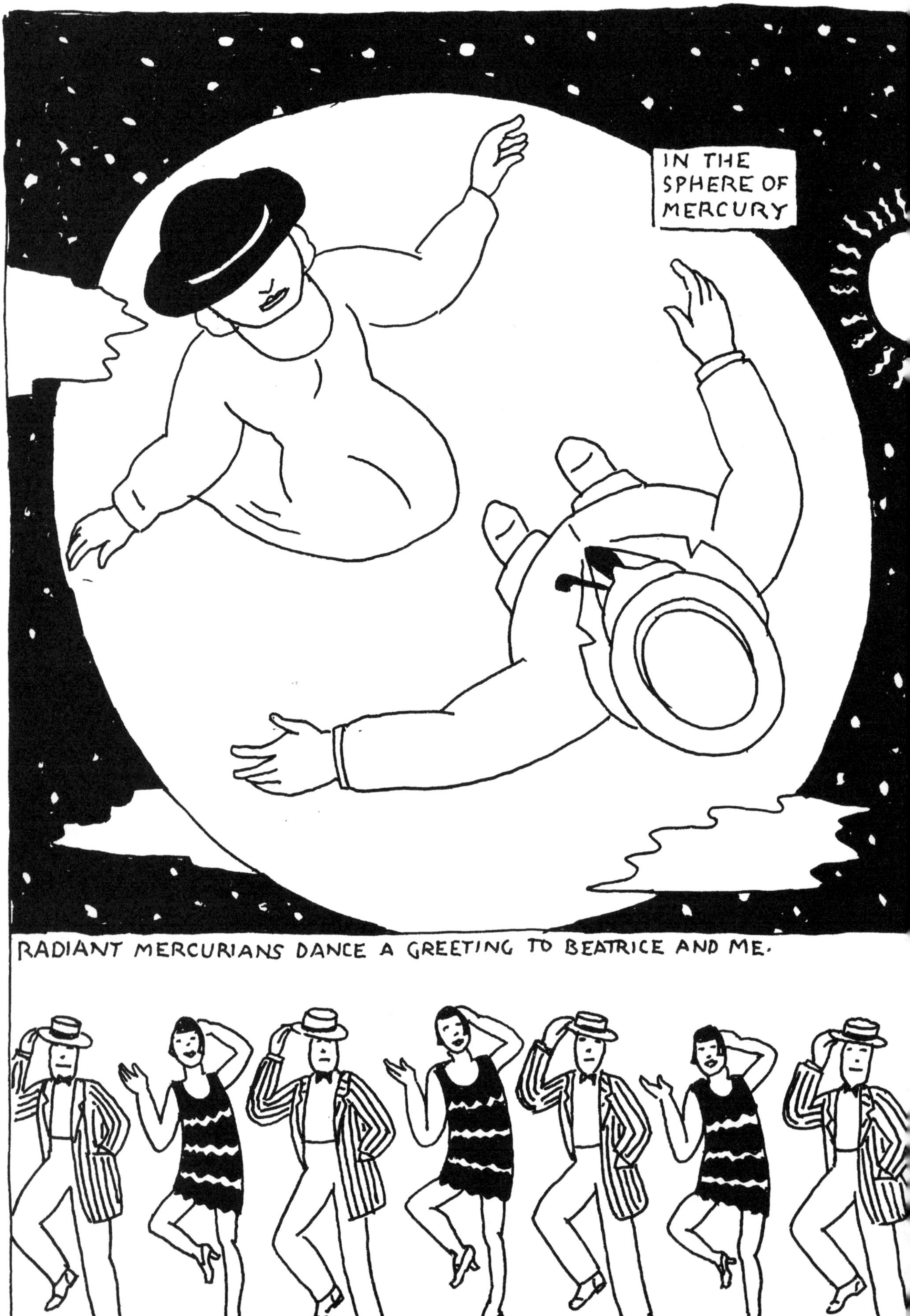
IN THE SPHERE OF MERCURY
RADIANT MERCURIANS DANCE A GREETING TO BEATRICE AND ME.

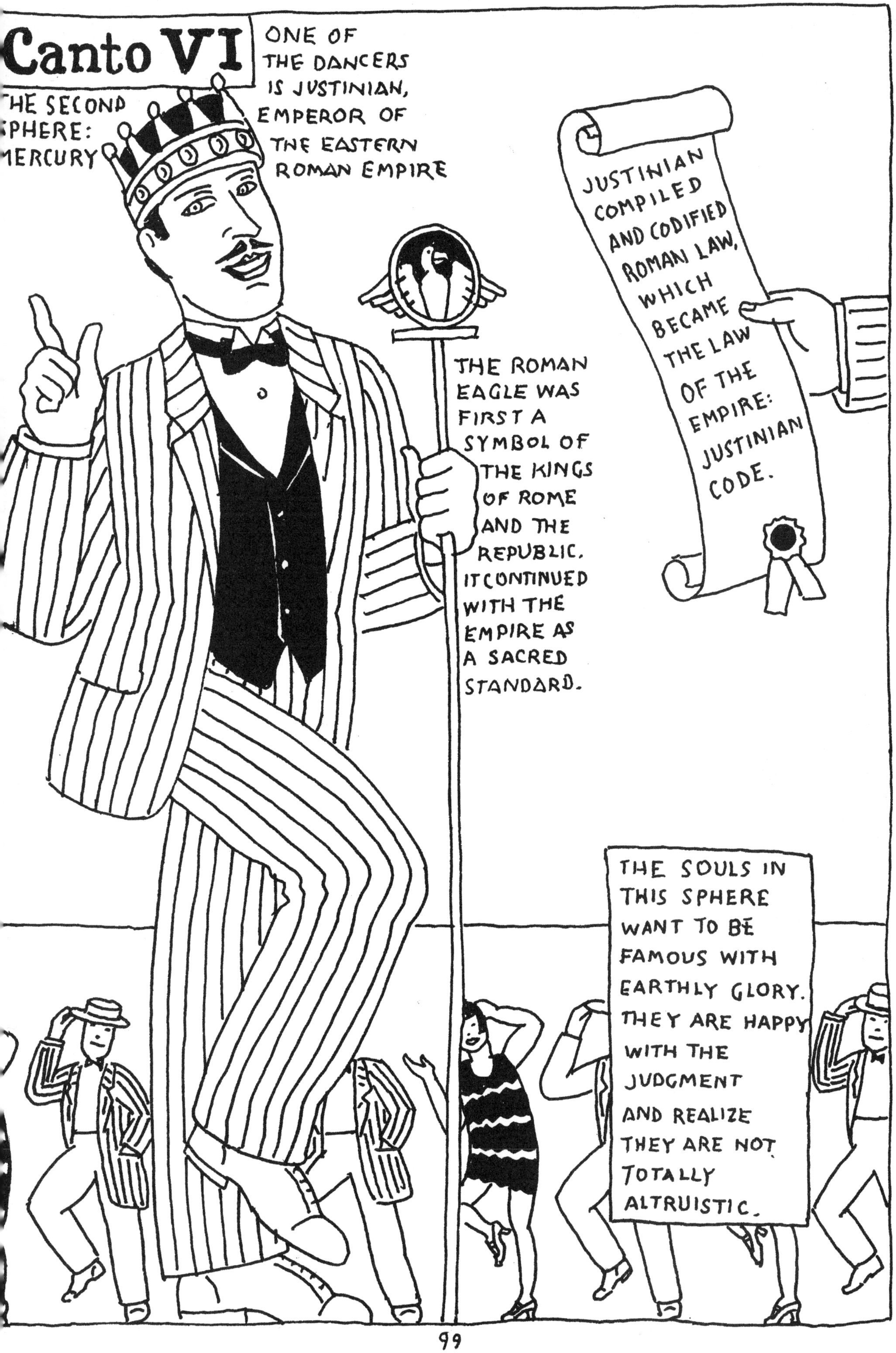
Canto VI
THE SECOND SPHERE: MERCURY
ONE OF THE DANCERS IS JUSTINIAN, EMPEROR OF THE EASTERN ROMAN EMPIRE
JUSTINIAN COMPILED AND CODIFIED ROMAN LAW, WHICH BECAME THE LAW OF THE EMPIRE: JUSTINIAN CODE.
THE ROMAN EAGLE WAS FIRST A SYMBOL OF THE KINGS OF ROME AND THE REPUBLIC. IT CONTINUED WITH THE EMPIRE AS A SACRED STANDARD.
THE SOULS IN THIS SPHERE WANT TO BE FAMOUS WITH EARTHLY GLORY. THEY ARE HAPPY WITH THE JUDGMENT AND REALIZE THEY ARE NOT TOTALLY ALTRUISTIC.

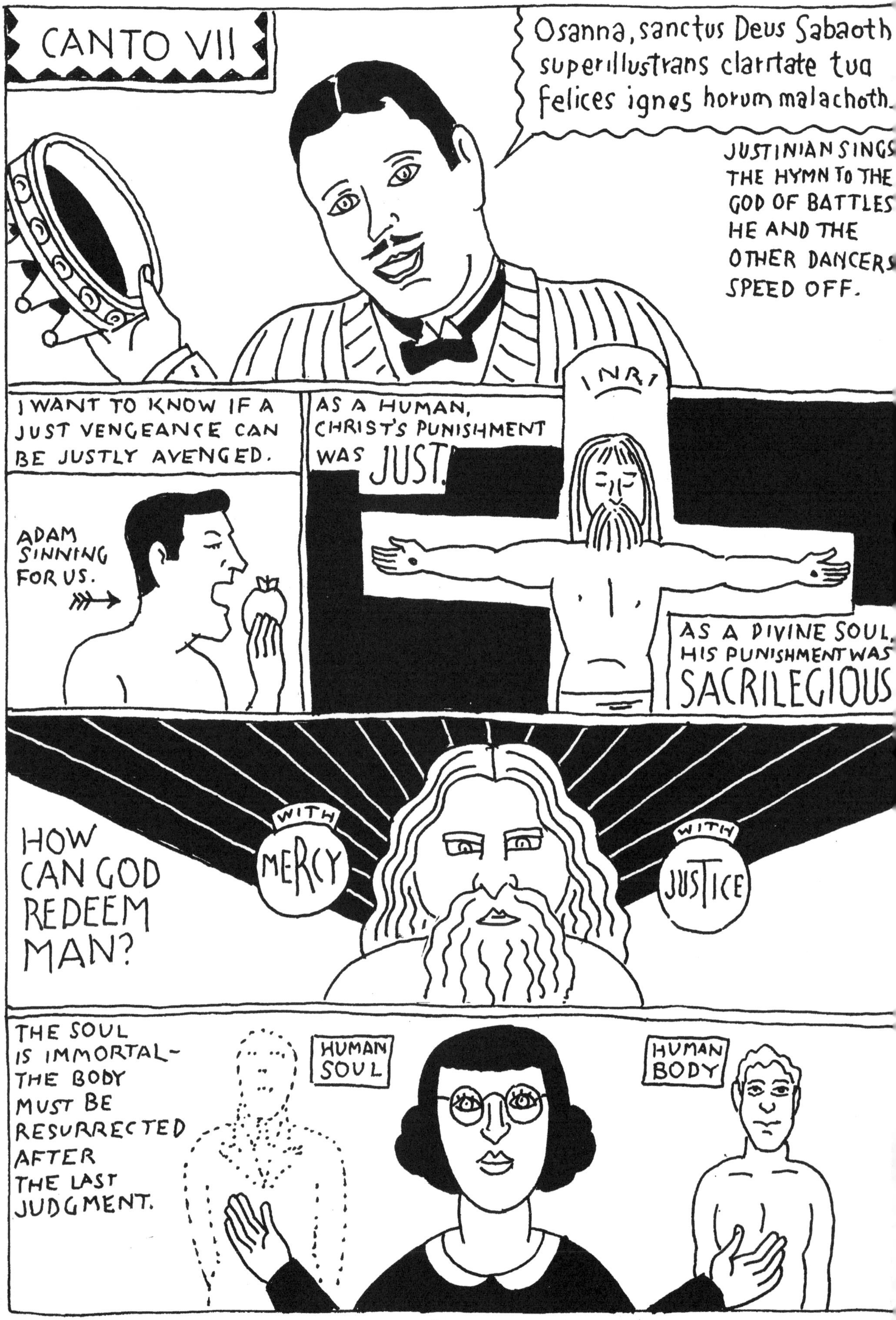
CANTO VII
Osanna, sanctus Deus Sabaoth superillustrans clarrtate tua felices ignes horum malachoth.
JUSTINIAN SINGS THE HYMN TO THE GOD OF BATTLES HE AND THE OTHER DANCERS SPEED OFF.
I WANT TO KNOW IF A JUST VENGEANCE CAN BE JUSTLY AVENGED.
ADAM SINNING FOR US.
AS A HUMAN, CHRIST'S PUNISHMENT WAS JUST.
INRI
AS A DIVINE SOUL, HIS PUNISHMENT WAS SACRILEGIOUS
HOW CAN GOD REDEEM MAN?
WITH MERCY
WITH JUSTICE
THE SOUL IS IMMORTAL - THE BODY MUST BE RESURRECTED AFTER THE LAST JUDGMENT.
HUMAN SOUL
HUMAN BODY

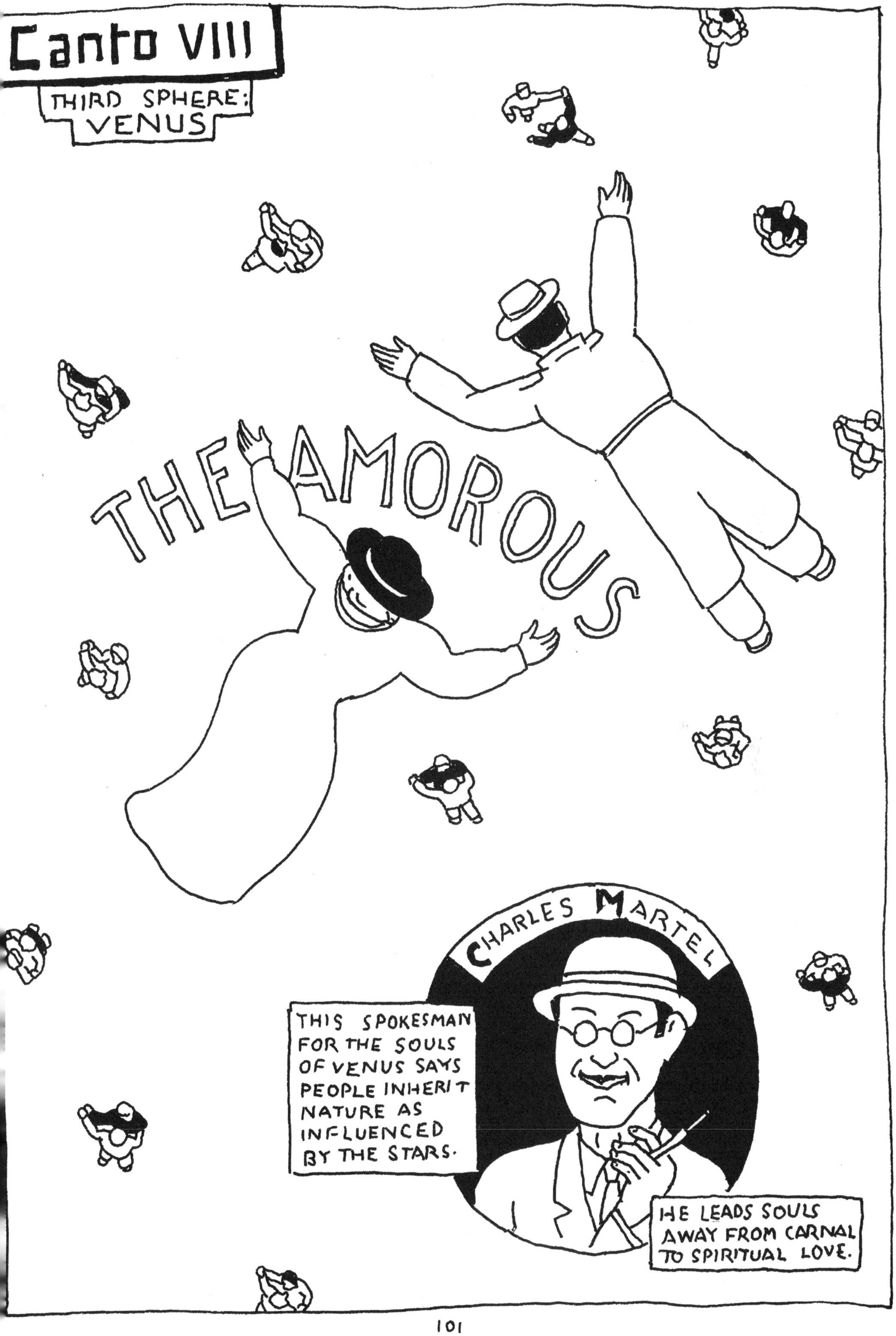
Canto VIII
THIRD SPHERE: VENUS
THE AMOROUS
CHARLES MARTEL
THIS SPOKESMAN FOR THE SOULS OF VENUS SAYS PEOPLE INHERIT NATURE AS INFLUENCED BY THE STARS.
HE LEADS SOULS AWAY FROM CARNAL TO SPIRITUAL LOVE.

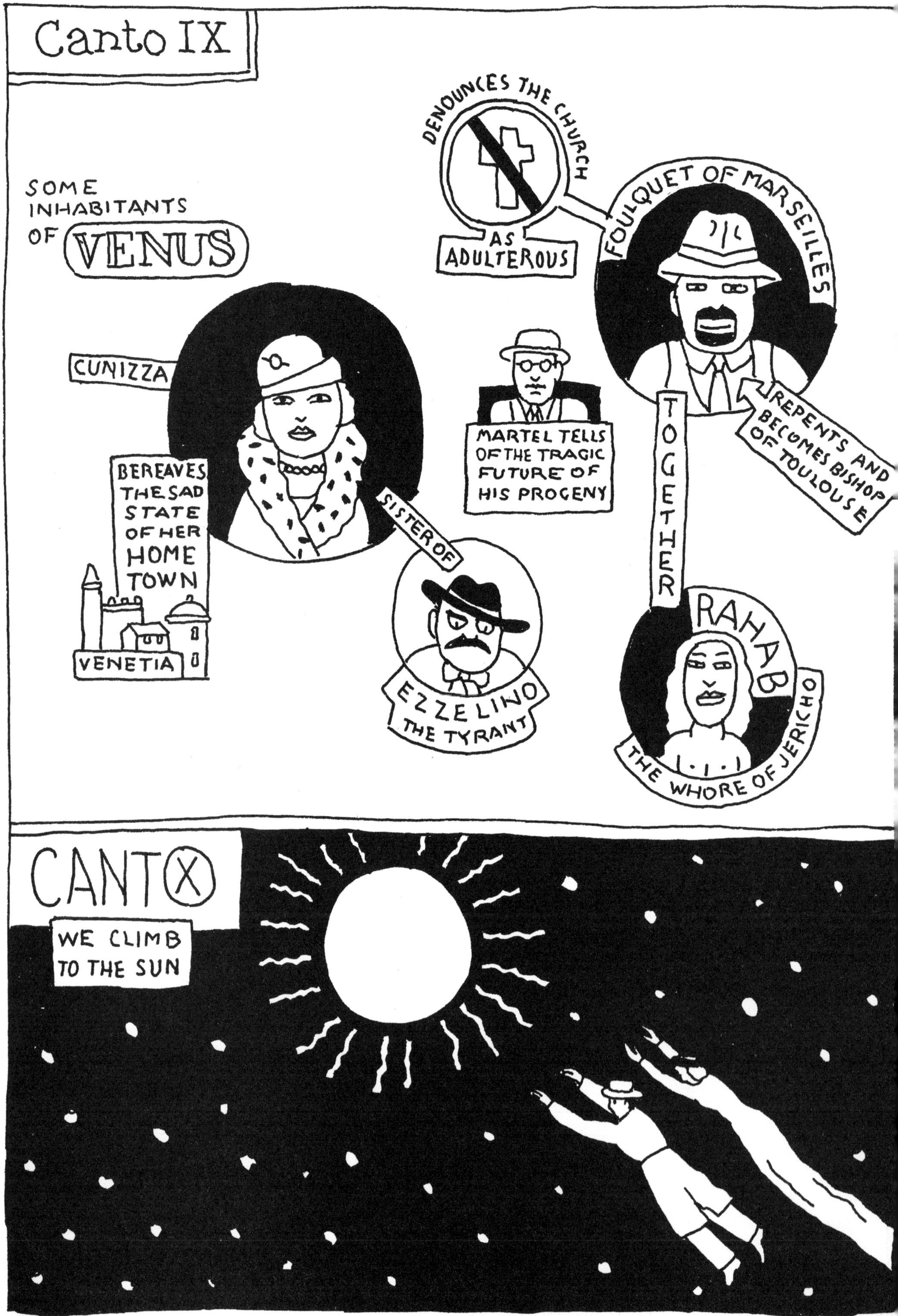
Canto IX
SOME INHABITANTS OF VENUS
DENOUNCES THE CHURCH AS ADULTEROUS
FOULQUET OF MARSEILLES
CUNIZZA
MARTEL TELLS OF THE TRAGIC FUTURE OF HIS PROGENY
TOGETHER
REPENTS AND BECOMES BISHOP OF TOULOUSE
BEREAVES THE SAD STATE OF HER HOME TOWN
VENETIA
SISTER OF
EZZELINO THE TYRANT
RAHAB
THE WHORE OF JERICHO
CANTO X
WE CLIMB TO THE SUN

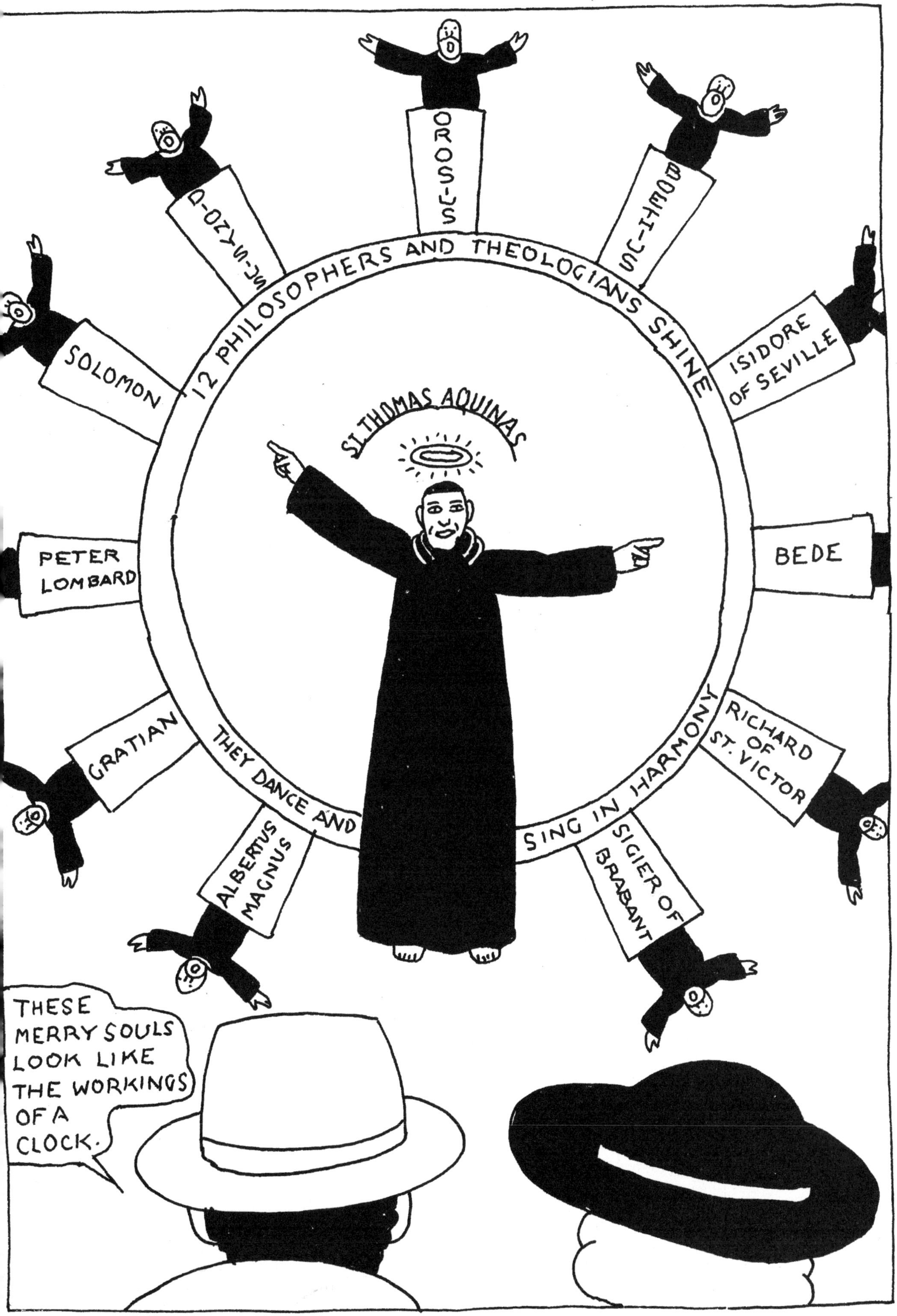

DIONYSIUS
OROSIUS
BOETHIUS
12 PHILOSOPHERS AND THEOLOGIANS SHINE
SOLOMON
ISIDORE OF SEVILLE
ST. THOMAS AQUINAS
PETER LOMBARD
BEDE
GRATIAN
THEY DANCE AND SING IN HARMONY
RICHARD OF ST. VICTOR
ALBERTUS MAGNUS
SIGIER OF BRABANT
THESE MERRY SOULS LOOK LIKE THE WORKINGS OF A CLOCK.

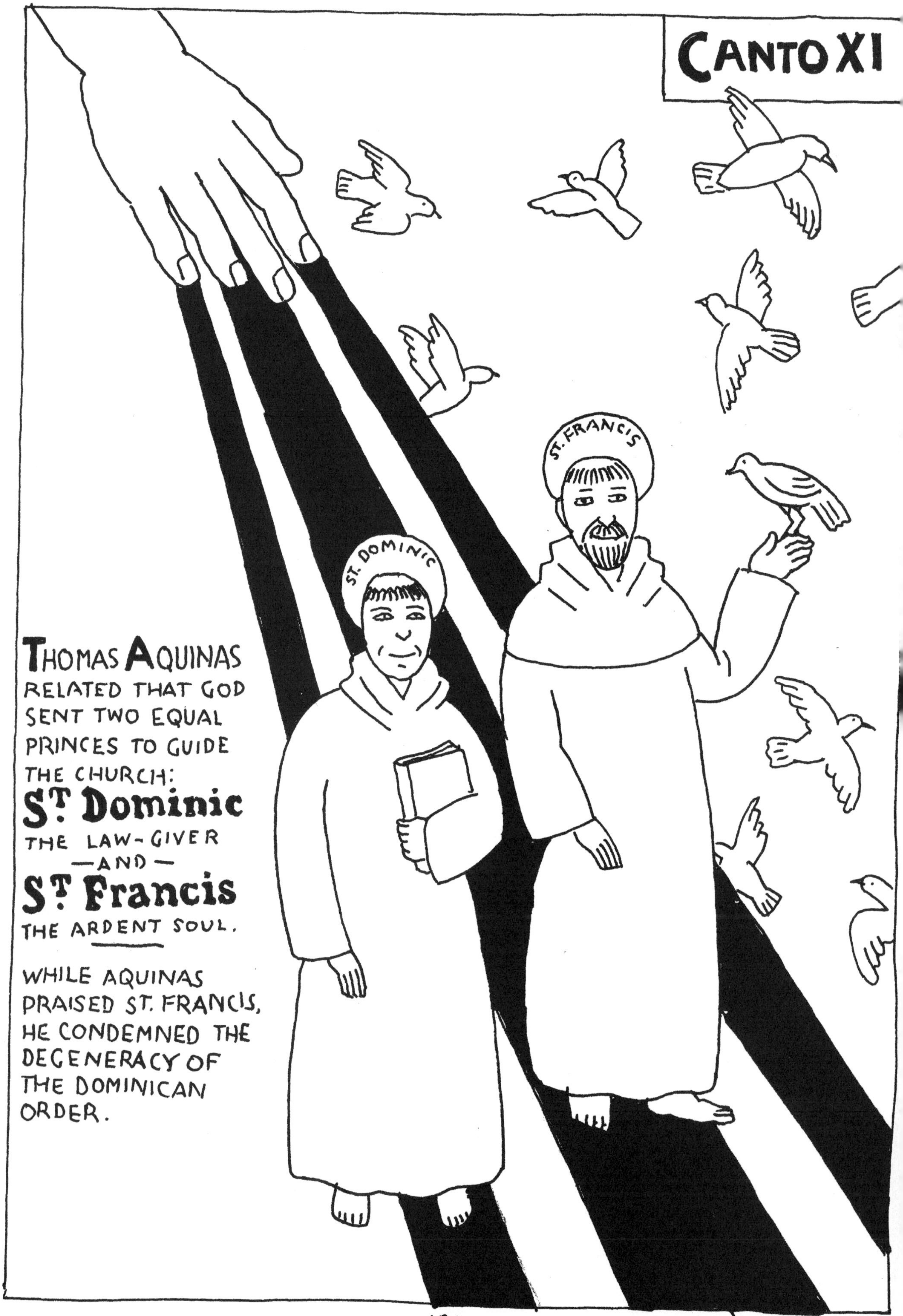
CANTO XI
ST. FRANCIS
ST. DOMINIC
THOMAS AQUINAS RELATED THAT GOD SENT TWO EQUAL PRINCES TO GUIDE THE CHURCH:
St. Dominic
THE LAW-GIVER
—AND—
St. Francis
THE ARDENT SOUL.
WHILE AQUINAS PRAISED ST. FRANCIS, HE CONDEMNED THE DEGENERACY OF THE DOMINICAN ORDER.

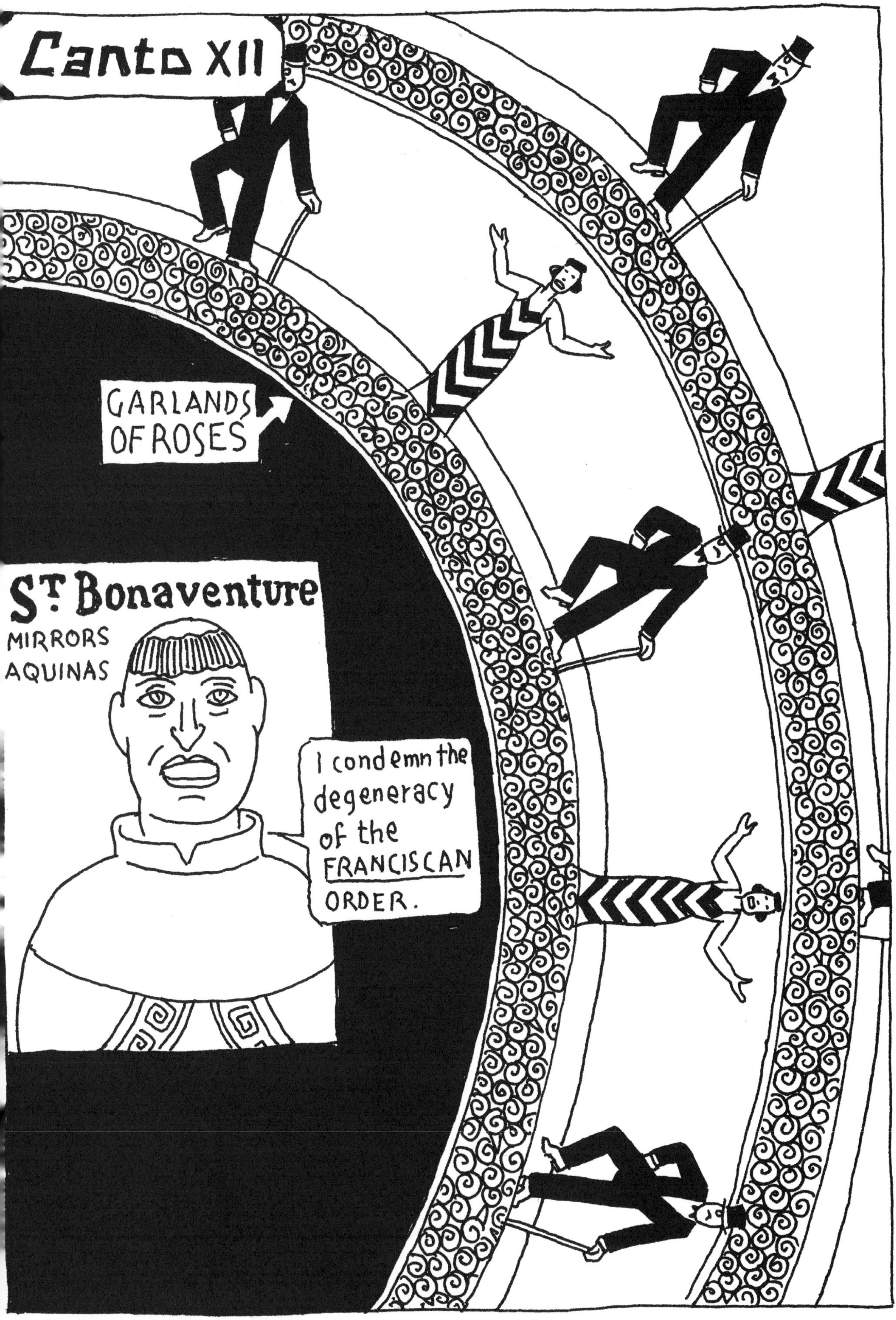
Canto XII
GARLANDS OF ROSES
St. Bonaventure
MIRRORS AQUINAS
I condemn the degeneracy of the FRANCISCAN ORDER.

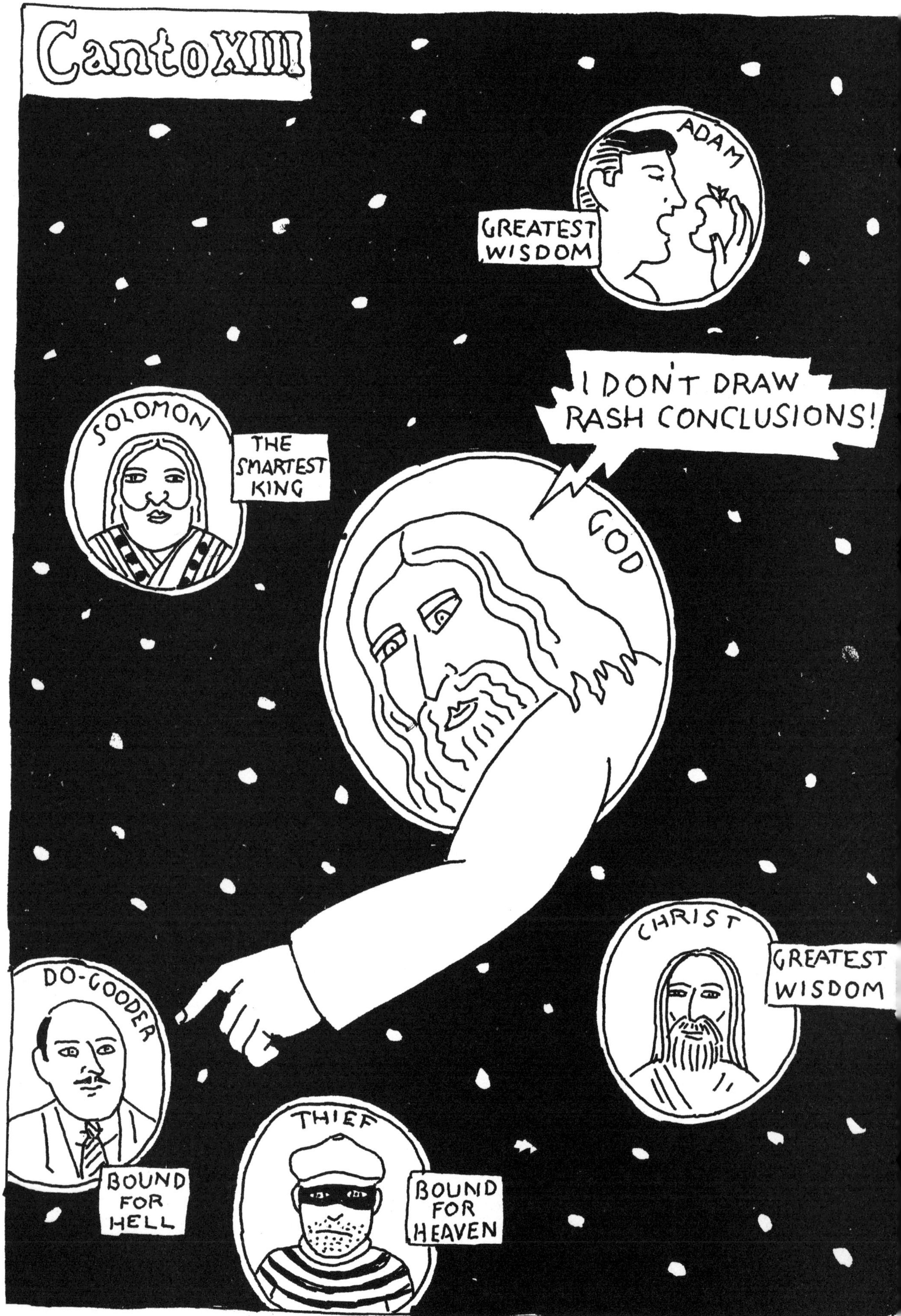
Canto XIII
ADAM
GREATEST WISDOM
SOLOMON
THE SMARTEST KING
GOD
I DON'T DRAW RASH CONCLUSIONS!
CHRIST
GREATEST WISDOM
DO-GOODER
BOUND FOR HELL
THIEF
BOUND FOR HEAVEN

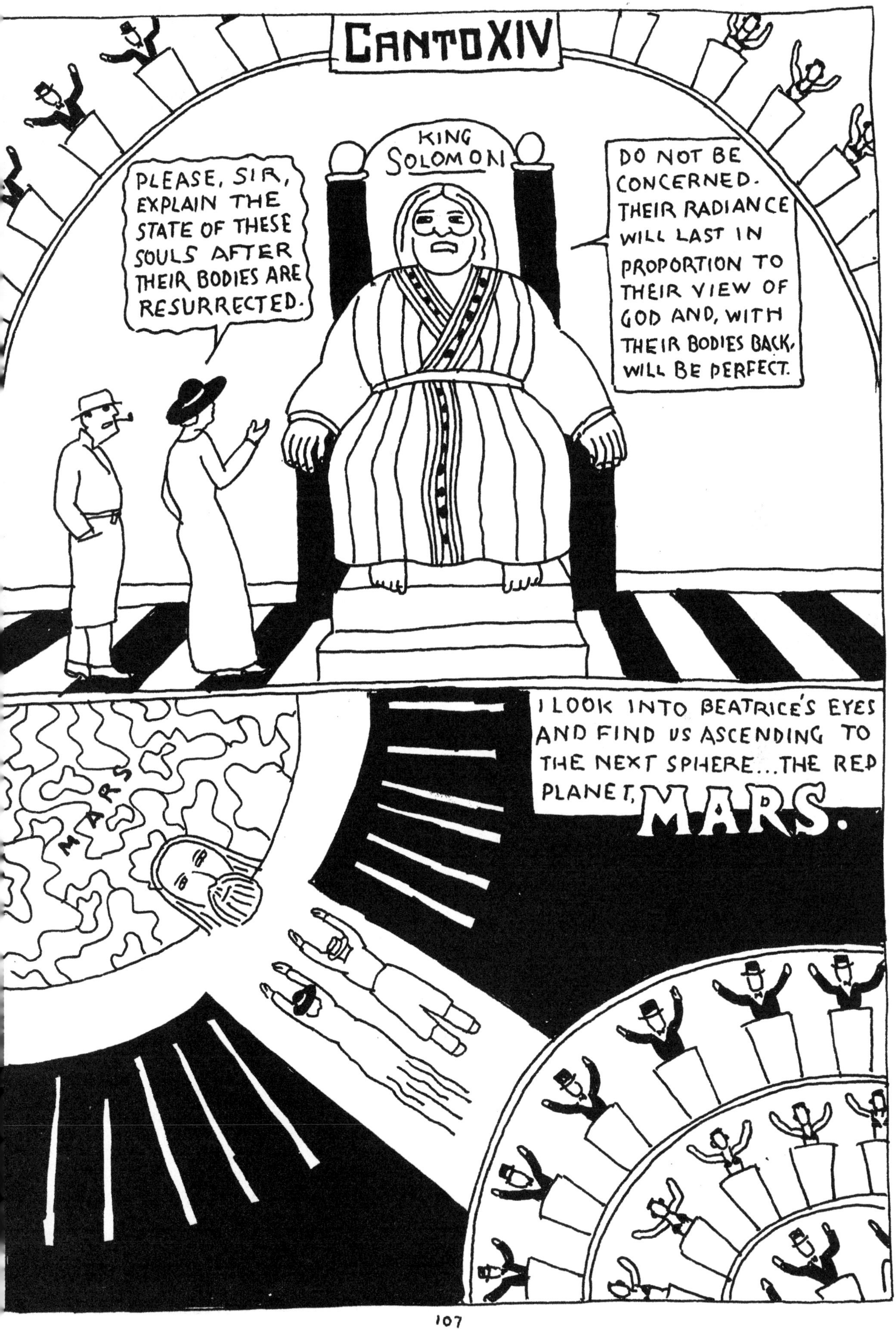
CANTO XIV
KING SOLOMON
PLEASE, SIR, EXPLAIN THE STATE OF THESE SOULS AFTER THEIR BODIES ARE RESURRECTED.
DO NOT BE CONCERNED. THEIR RADIANCE WILL LAST IN PROPORTION TO THEIR VIEW OF GOD AND, WITH THEIR BODIES BACK, WILL BE PERFECT.
MARS
I LOOK INTO BEATRICE'S EYES AND FIND US ASCENDING TO THE NEXT SPHERE... THE RED PLANET, MARS.

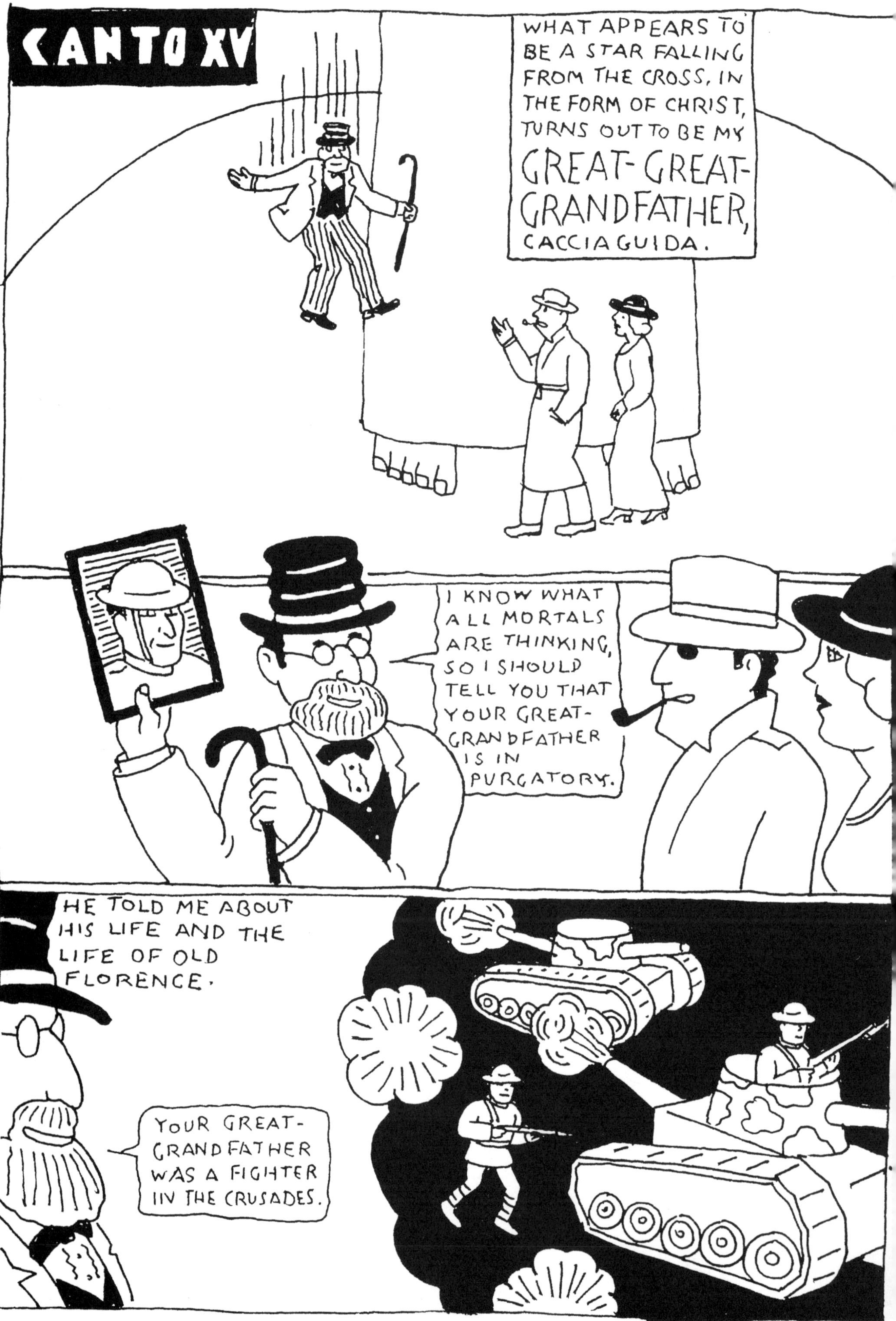
CANTO XV
WHAT APPEARS TO BE A STAR FALLING FROM THE CROSS, IN THE FORM OF CHRIST, TURNS OUT TO BE MY GREAT-GREAT-GRANDFATHER, CACCIAGUIDA.
I KNOW WHAT ALL MORTALS ARE THINKING, SO I SHOULD TELL YOU THAT YOUR GREAT-GRANDFATHER IS IN PURGATORY.
HE TOLD ME ABOUT HIS LIFE AND THE LIFE OF OLD FLORENCE.
YOUR GREAT-GRANDFATHER WAS A FIGHTER IIN THE CRUSADES.

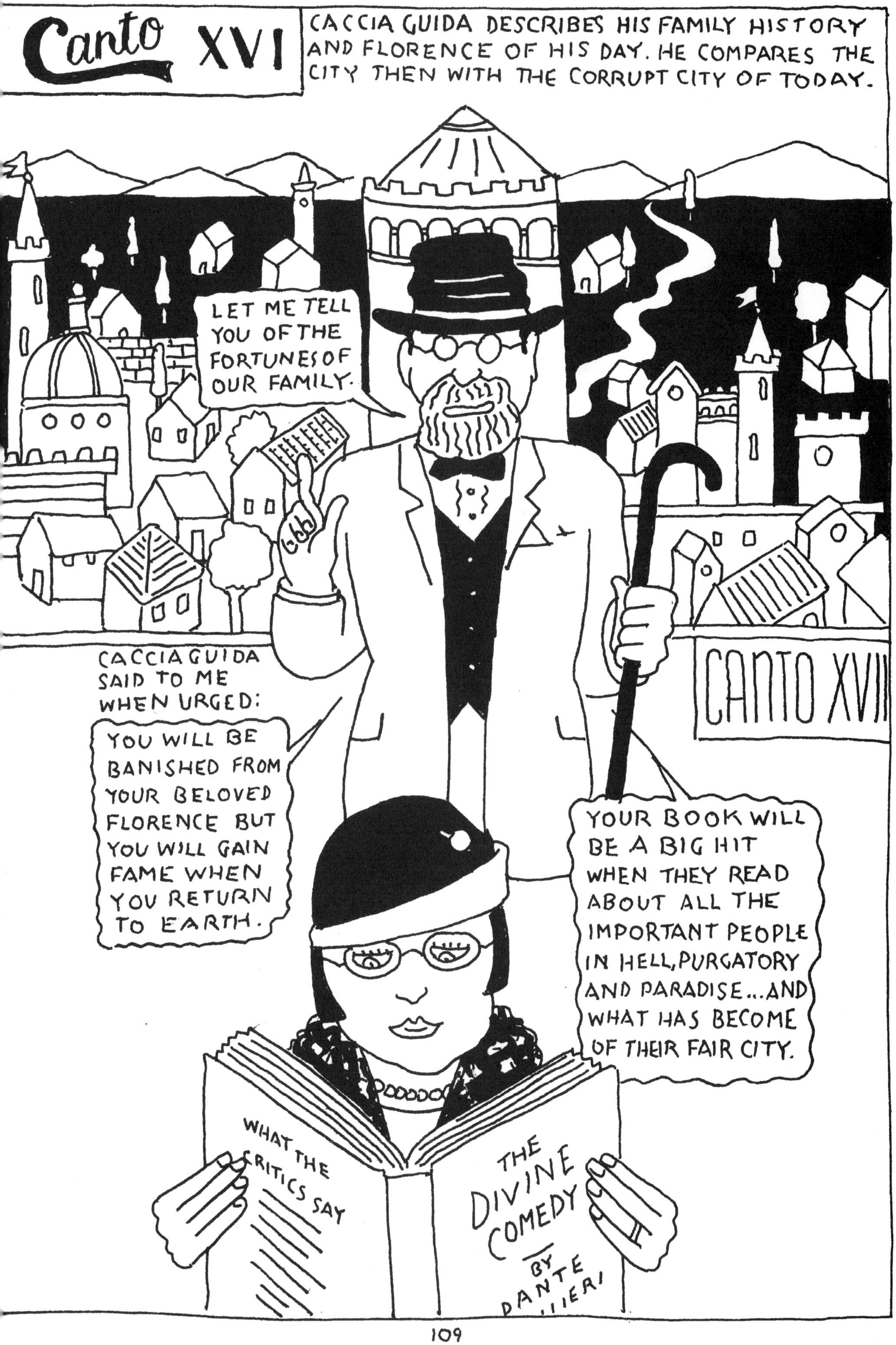

Canto XVI
CACCIA GUIDA DESCRIBES HIS FAMILY HISTORY AND FLORENCE OF HIS DAY. HE COMPARES THE CITY THEN WITH THE CORRUPT CITY OF TODAY.
LET ME TELL YOU OF THE FORTUNES OF OUR FAMILY.
CANTO XVII
CACCIAGUIDA SAID TO ME WHEN URGED:
YOU WILL BE BANISHED FROM YOUR BELOVED FLORENCE BUT YOU WILL GAIN FAME WHEN YOU RETURN TO EARTH.
YOUR BOOK WILL BE A BIG HIT WHEN THEY READ ABOUT ALL THE IMPORTANT PEOPLE IN HELL, PURGATORY AND PARADISE...AND WHAT HAS BECOME OF THEIR FAIR CITY.
WHAT THE CRITICS SAY
THE DIVINE COMEDY
BY DANTE

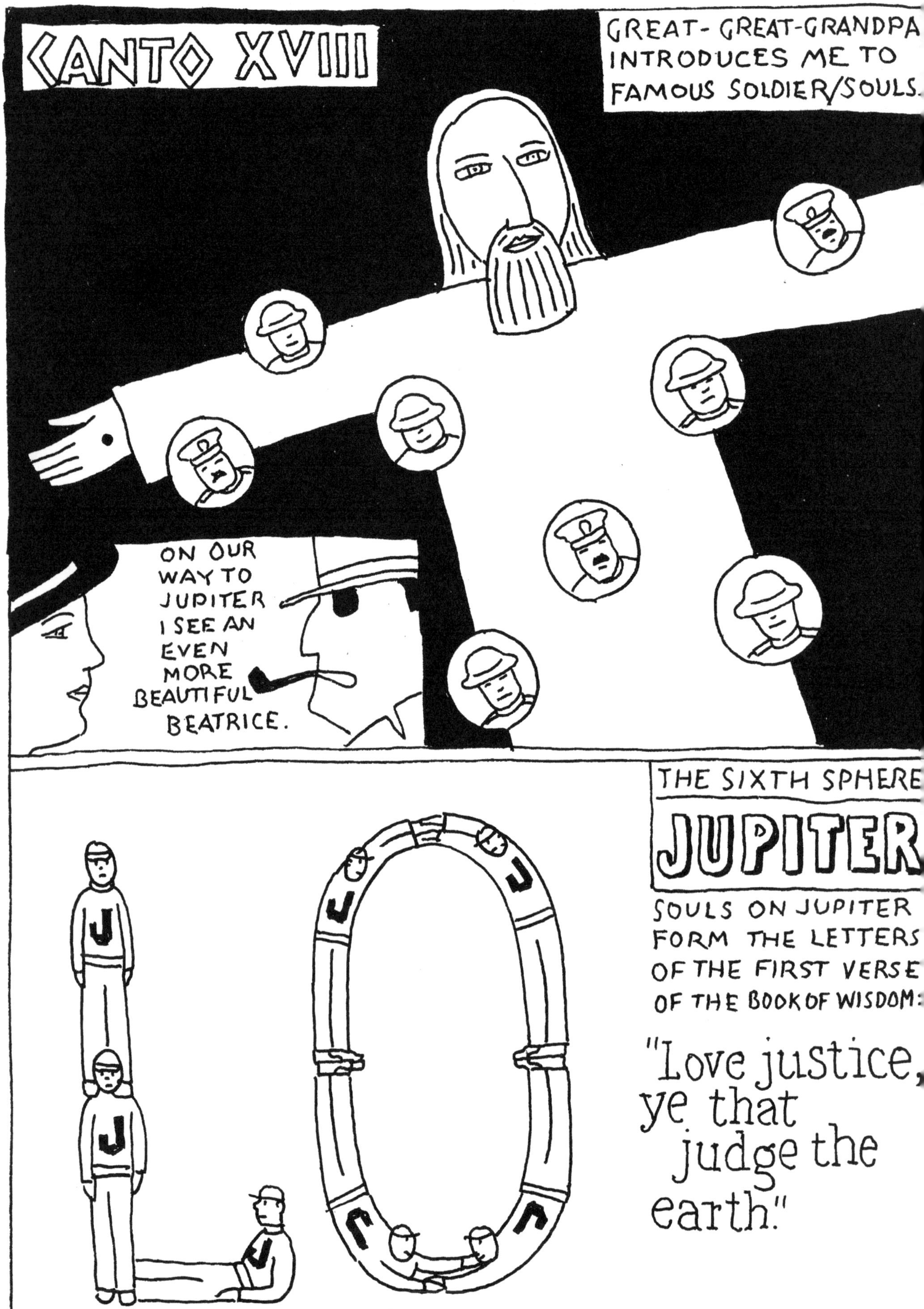
CANTO XVIII
GREAT-GREAT-GRANDPA INTRODUCES ME TO FAMOUS SOLDIER/SOULS.
ON OUR WAY TO JUPITER I SEE AN EVEN MORE BEAUTIFUL BEATRICE.
THE SIXTH SPHERE
JUPITER
SOULS ON JUPITER FORM THE LETTERS OF THE FIRST VERSE OF THE BOOK OF WISDOM:
"Love justice, ye that judge the earth."

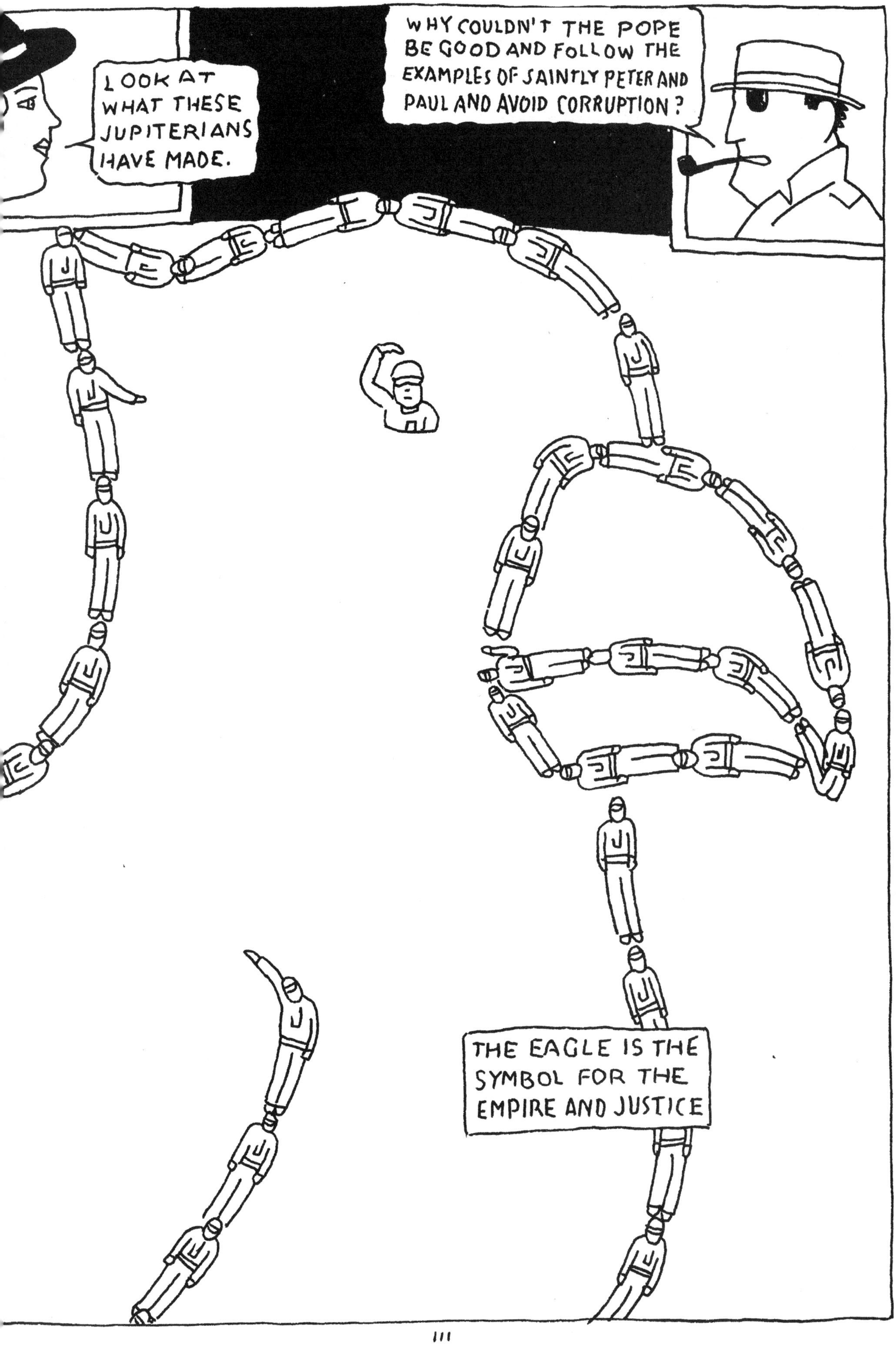
LOOK AT WHAT THESE JUPITERIANS HAVE MADE.
WHY COULDN'T THE POPE BE GOOD AND FOLLOW THE EXAMPLES OF SAINTLY PETER AND PAUL AND AVOID CORRUPTION?
THE EAGLE IS THE SYMBOL FOR THE EMPIRE AND JUSTICE

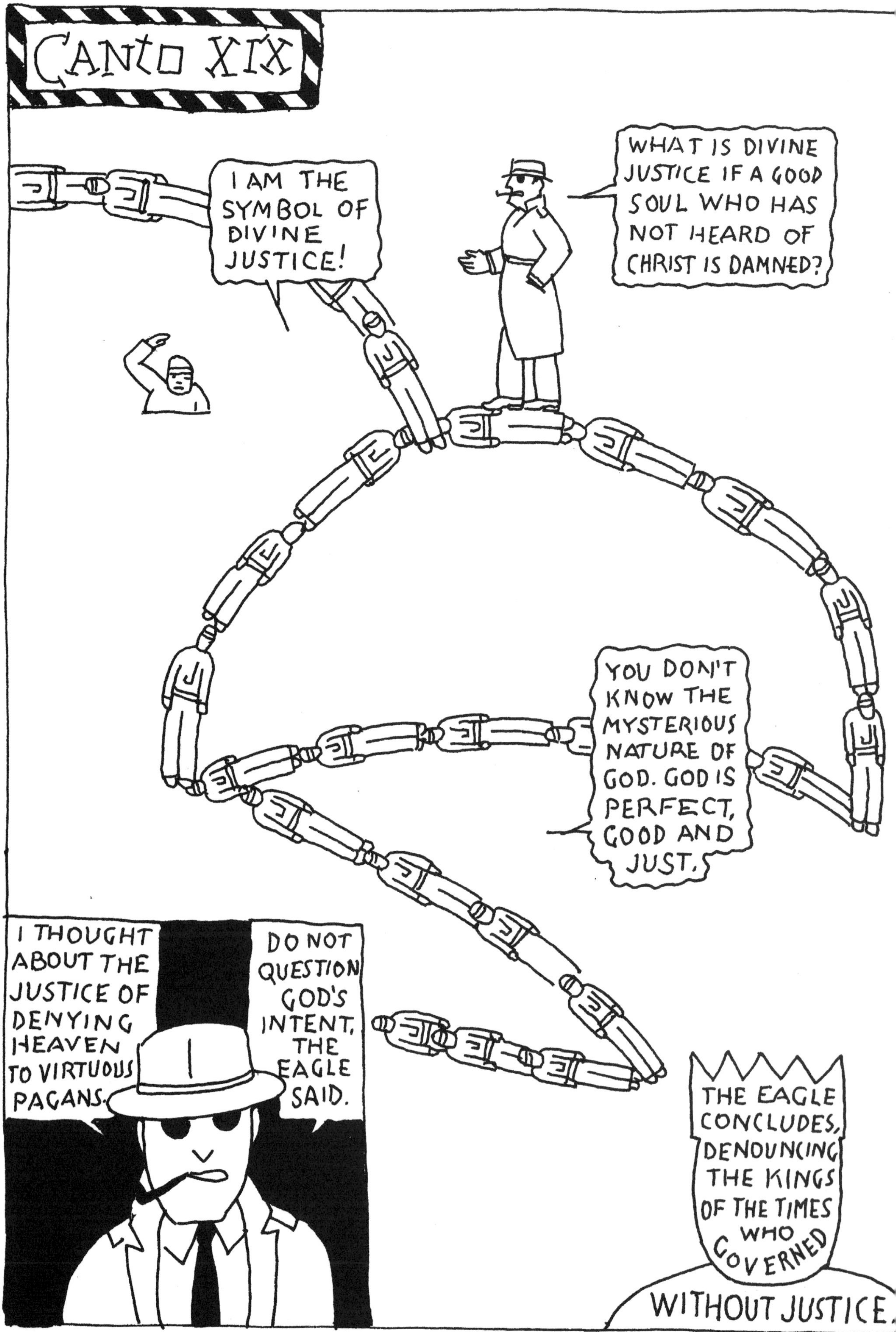
CANTO XIX
I AM THE SYMBOL OF DIVINE JUSTICE!
WHAT IS DIVINE JUSTICE IF A GOOD SOUL WHO HAS NOT HEARD OF CHRIST IS DAMNED?
YOU DON'T KNOW THE MYSTERIOUS NATURE OF GOD. GOD IS PERFECT, GOOD AND JUST.
I THOUGHT ABOUT THE JUSTICE OF DENYING HEAVEN TO VIRTUOUS PAGANS.
DO NOT QUESTION GOD'S INTENT, THE EAGLE SAID.
THE EAGLE CONCLUDES, DENOUNCING THE KINGS OF THE TIMES WHO GOVERNED WITHOUT JUSTICE.

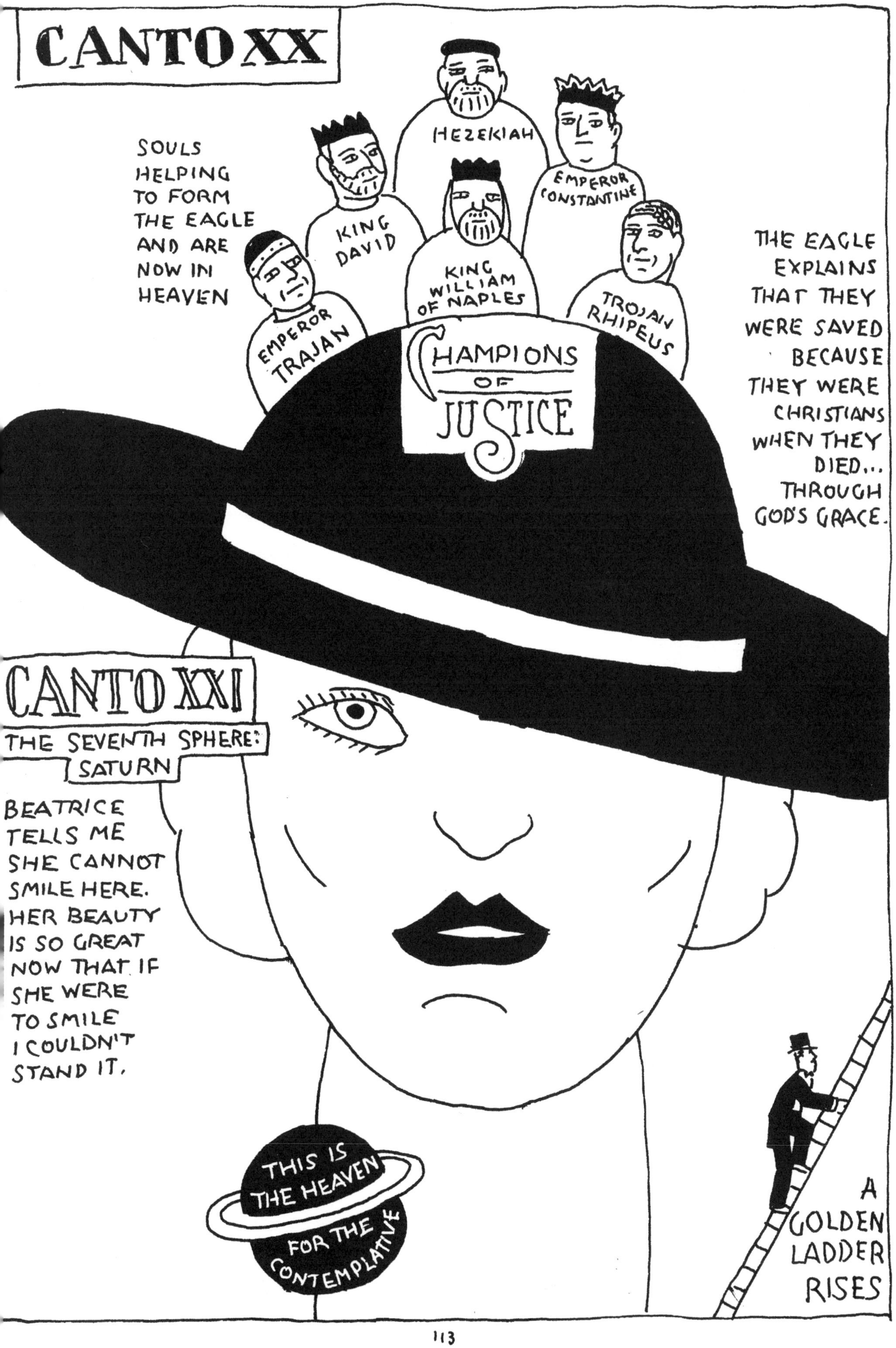
CANTO XX
SOULS HELPING TO FORM THE EAGLE AND ARE NOW IN HEAVEN
HEZEKIAH
EMPEROR CONSTANTINE
KING DAVID
KING WILLIAM OF NAPLES
EMPEROR TRAJAN
TROJAN RHIPEUS
CHAMPIONS OF JUSTICE
THE EAGLE EXPLAINS THAT THEY WERE SAVED BECAUSE THEY WERE CHRISTIANS WHEN THEY DIED... THROUGH GOD'S GRACE.
CANTO XXI
THE SEVENTH SPHERE: SATURN
BEATRICE TELLS ME SHE CANNOT SMILE HERE. HER BEAUTY IS SO GREAT NOW THAT IF SHE WERE TO SMILE I COULDN'T STAND IT.
THIS IS THE HEAVEN FOR THE CONTEMPLATIVE
A GOLDEN LADDER RISES

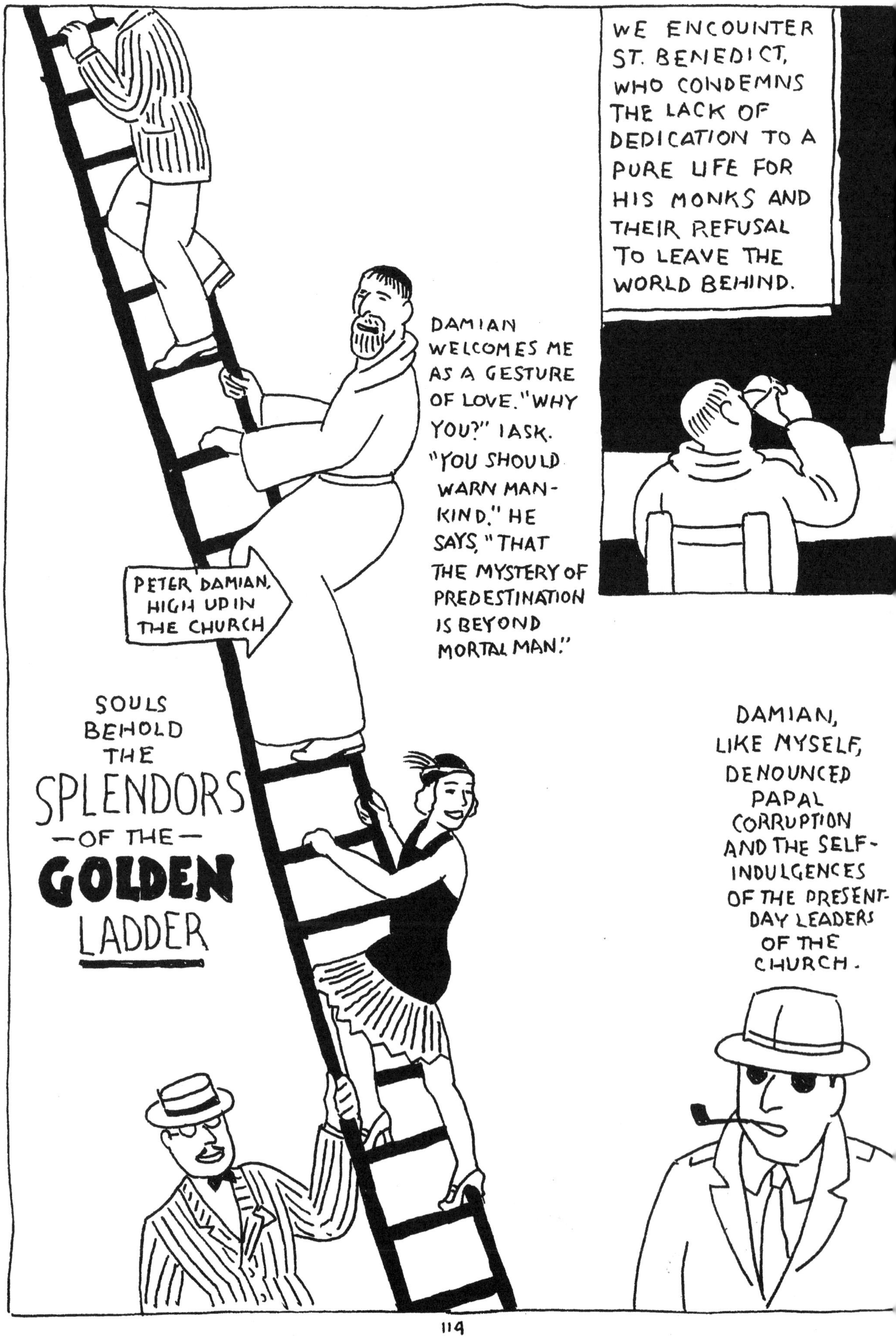
WE ENCOUNTER ST. BENEDICT, WHO CONDEMNS THE LACK OF DEDICATION TO A PURE LIFE FOR HIS MONKS AND THEIR REFUSAL TO LEAVE THE WORLD BEHIND.
DAMIAN WELCOMES ME AS A GESTURE OF LOVE. "WHY YOU?" I ASK. "YOU SHOULD WARN MAN-KIND," HE SAYS, "THAT THE MYSTERY OF PREDESTINATION IS BEYOND MORTAL MAN."
PETER DAMIAN, HIGH UP IN THE CHURCH
SOULS BEHOLD THE SPLENDORS —OF THE— GOLDEN LADDER
DAMIAN, LIKE MYSELF, DENOUNCED PAPAL CORRUPTION AND THE SELF-INDULGENCES OF THE PRESENT-DAY LEADERS OF THE CHURCH.

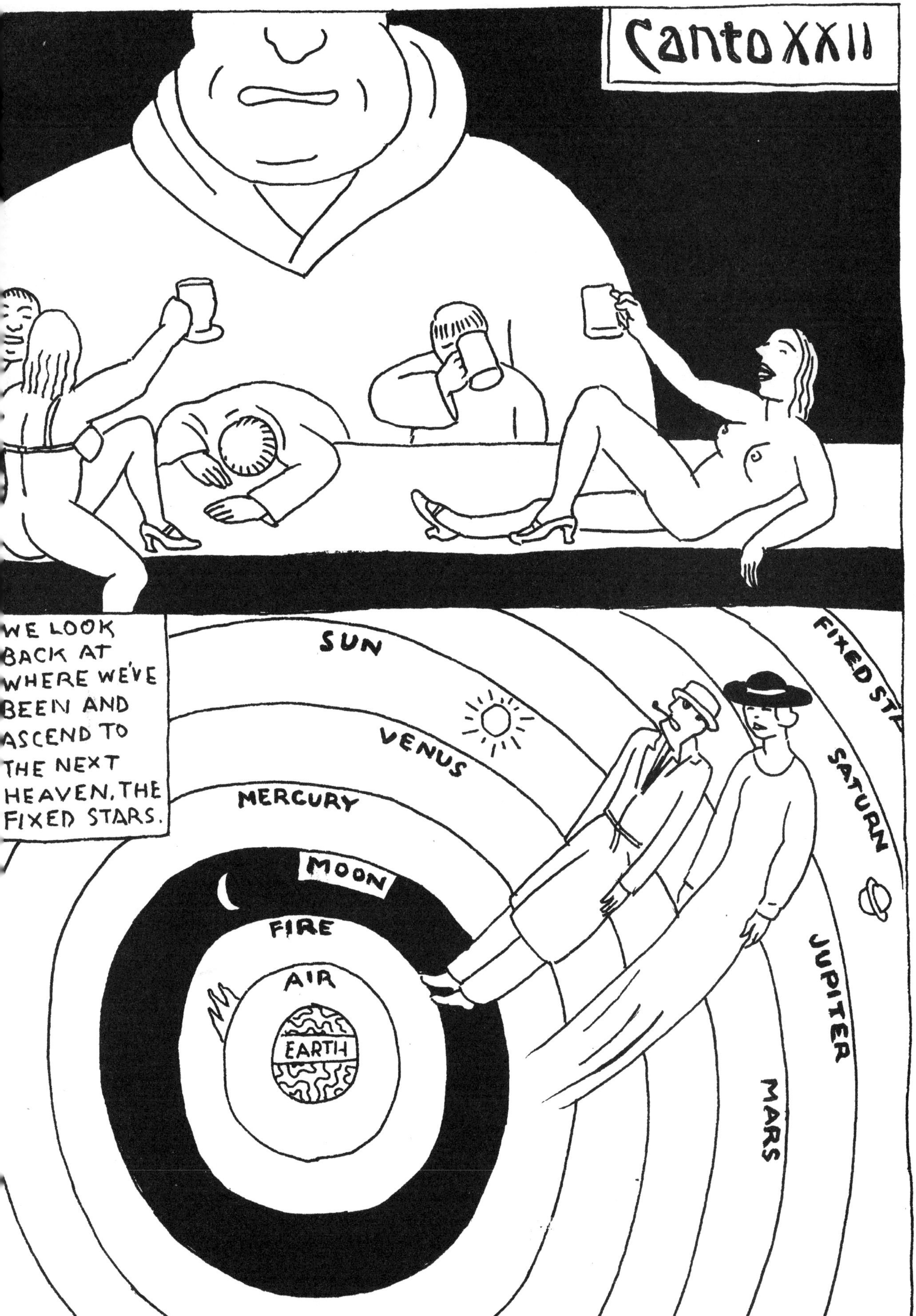
Canto XXII
WE LOOK BACK AT WHERE WE'VE BEEN AND ASCEND TO THE NEXT HEAVEN, THE FIXED STARS.
SUN
VENUS
MERCURY
MOON
FIRE
AIR
EARTH
SATURN
JUPITER
MARS

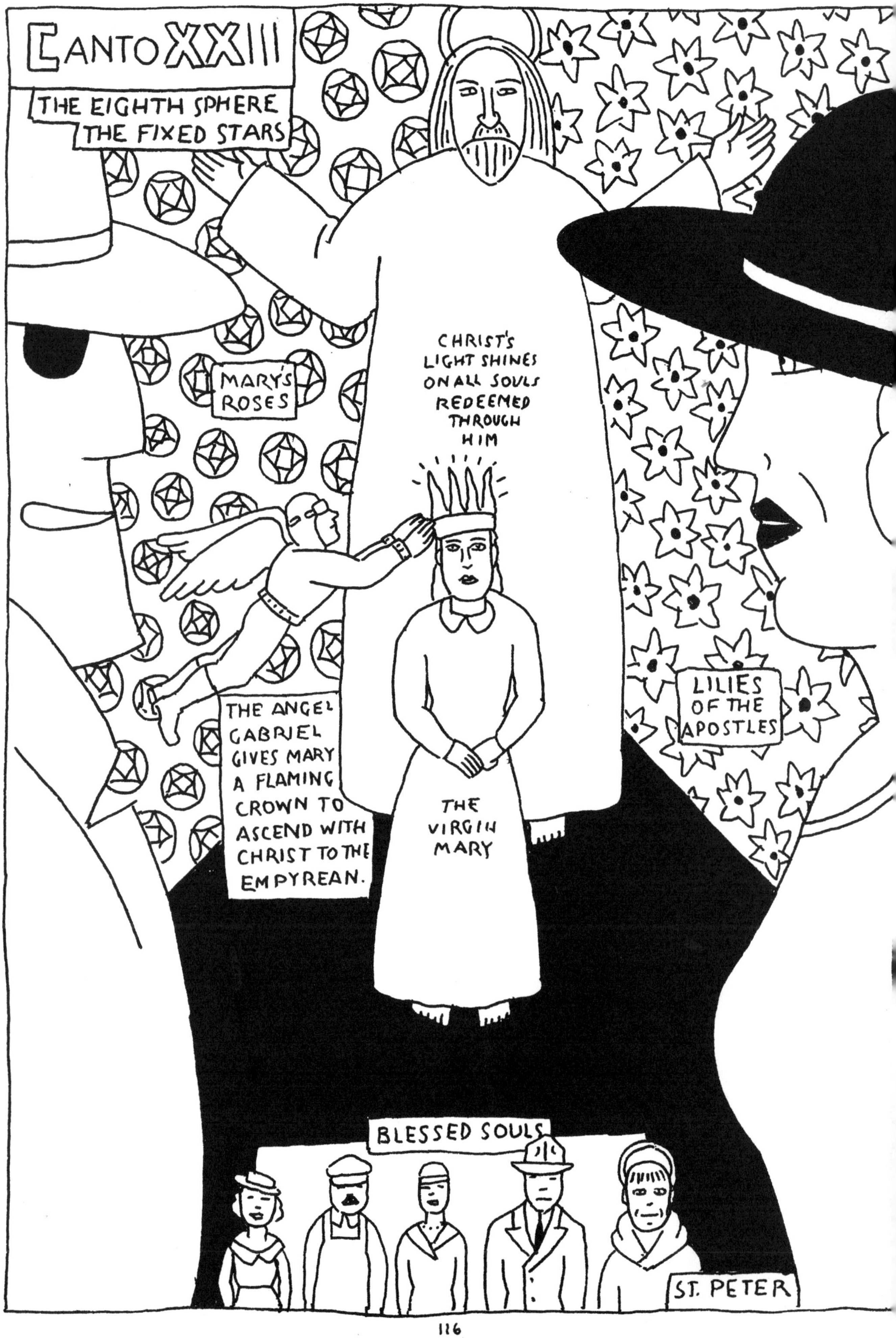

CANTO XXIII
THE EIGHTH SPHERE
THE FIXED STARS
MARY'S ROSES
CHRIST'S LIGHT SHINES ON ALL SOULS REDEEMED THROUGH HIM
LILIES OF THE APOSTLES
THE ANGEL GABRIEL GIVES MARY A FLAMING CROWN TO ASCEND WITH CHRIST TO THE EMPYREAN.
THE VIRGIN MARY
BLESSED SOULS
ST. PETER

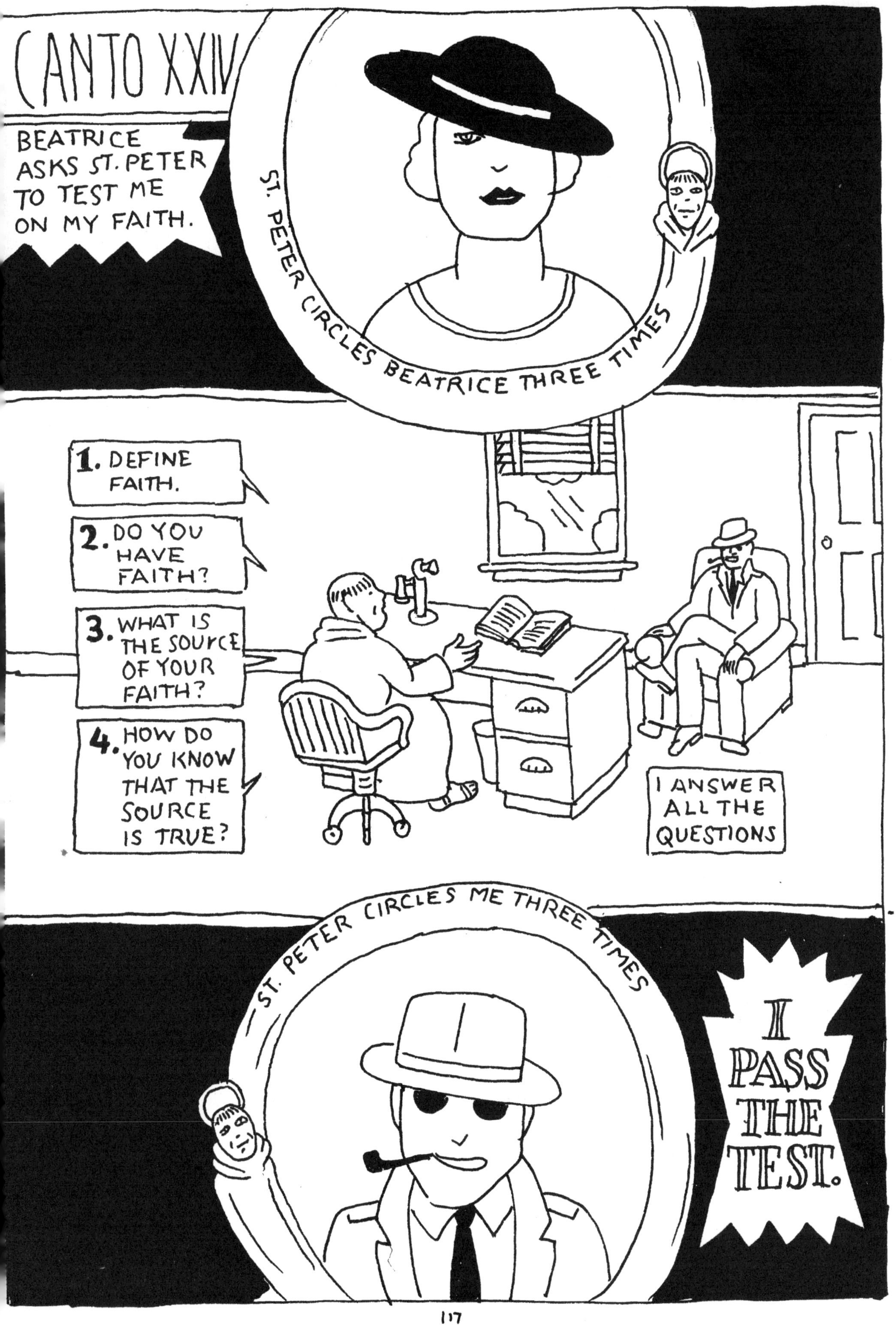

CANTO XXIV
BEATRICE ASKS ST. PETER TO TEST ME ON MY FAITH.
ST. PETER CIRCLES BEATRICE THREE TIMES
1. DEFINE FAITH.
2. DO YOU HAVE FAITH?
3. WHAT IS THE SOURCE OF YOUR FAITH?
4. HOW DO YOU KNOW THAT THE SOURCE IS TRUE?
I ANSWER ALL THE QUESTIONS
ST. PETER CIRCLES ME THREE TIMES
I PASS THE TEST.

Canto XXV

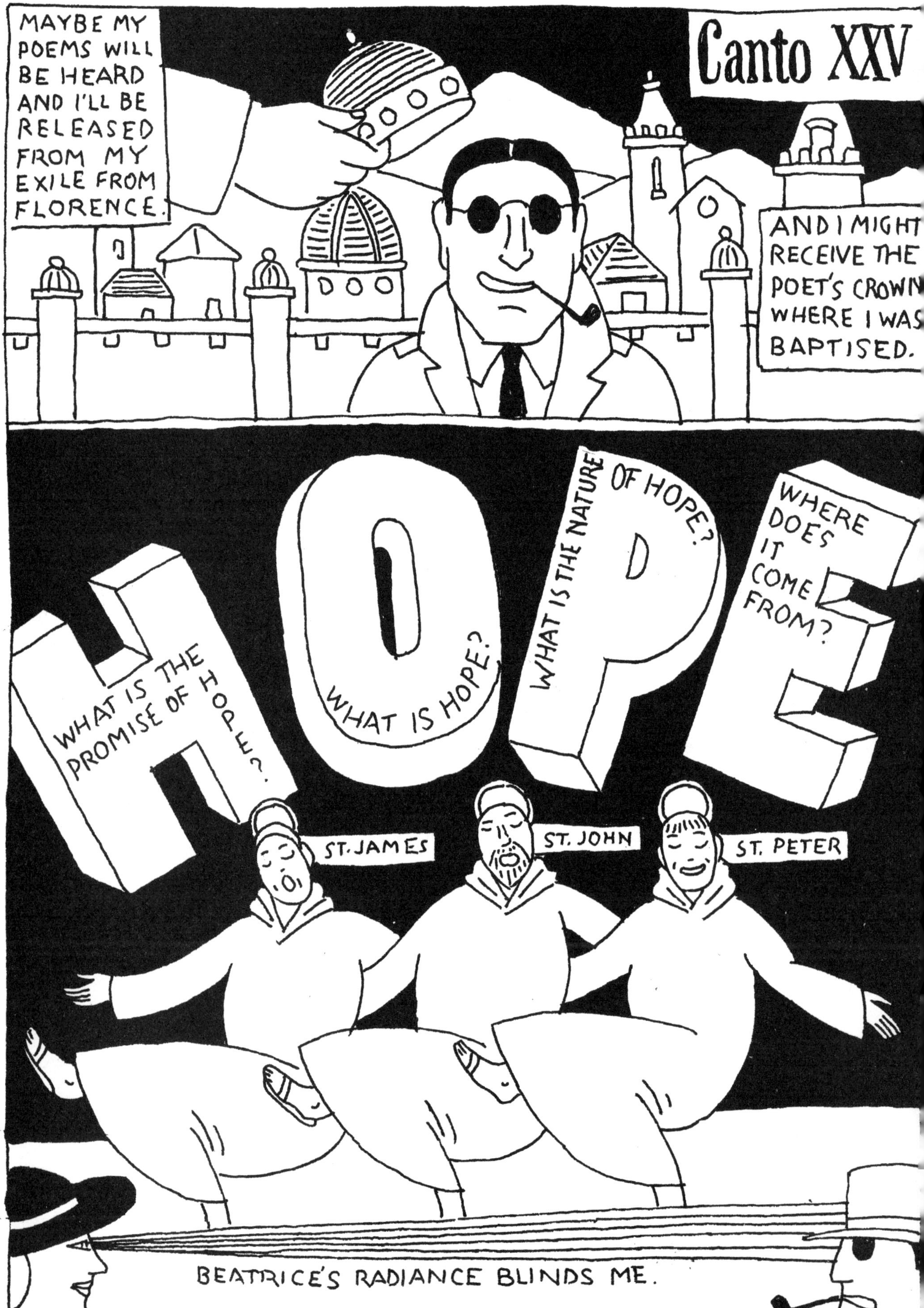
MAYBE MY POEMS WILL BE HEARD AND I'LL BE RELEASED FROM MY EXILE FROM FLORENCE.
AND I MIGHT RECEIVE THE POET'S CROWN WHERE I WAS BAPTISED.
HOPE
WHAT IS THE PROMISE OF HOPE?
WHAT IS HOPE?
WHAT IS THE NATURE OF HOPE?
WHERE DOES IT COME FROM?
ST. JAMES
ST. JOHN
ST. PETER
BEATRICE'S RADIANCE BLINDS ME.

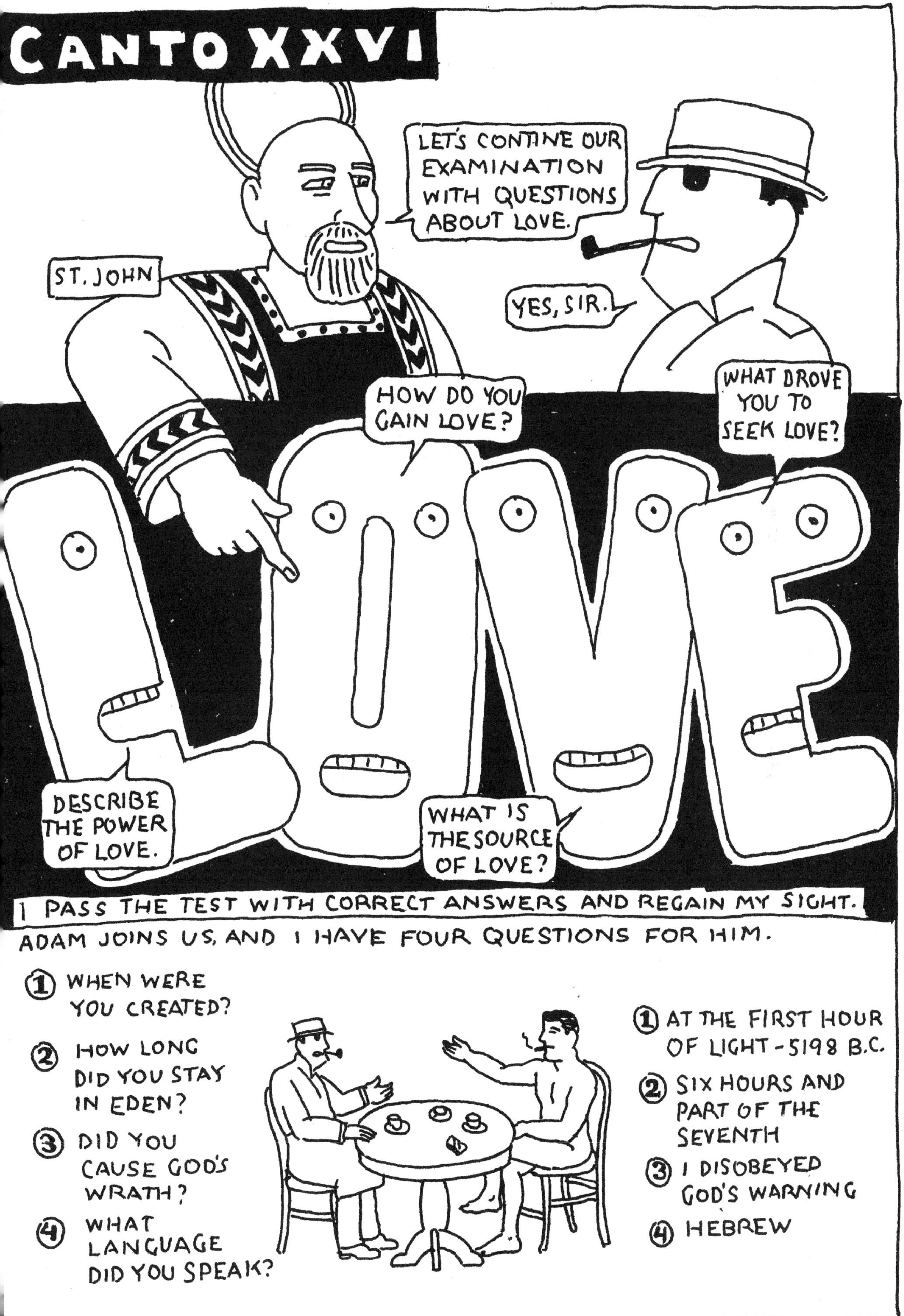
CANTO XXVI
ST. JOHN
LET'S CONTINE OUR EXAMINATION WITH QUESTIONS ABOUT LOVE.
YES, SIR.
HOW DO YOU GAIN LOVE?
WHAT DROVE YOU TO SEEK LOVE?
LOVE
DESCRIBE THE POWER OF LOVE.
WHAT IS THE SOURCE OF LOVE?
I PASS THE TEST WITH CORRECT ANSWERS AND REGAIN MY SIGHT.
ADAM JOINS US, AND I HAVE FOUR QUESTIONS FOR HIM.
① WHEN WERE YOU CREATED?
② HOW LONG DID YOU STAY IN EDEN?
③ DID YOU CAUSE GOD'S WRATH?
④ WHAT LANGUAGE DID YOU SPEAK?
① AT THE FIRST HOUR OF LIGHT - 5198 B.C.
② SIX HOURS AND PART OF THE SEVENTH
③ I DISOBEYED GOD'S WARNING
④ HEBREW

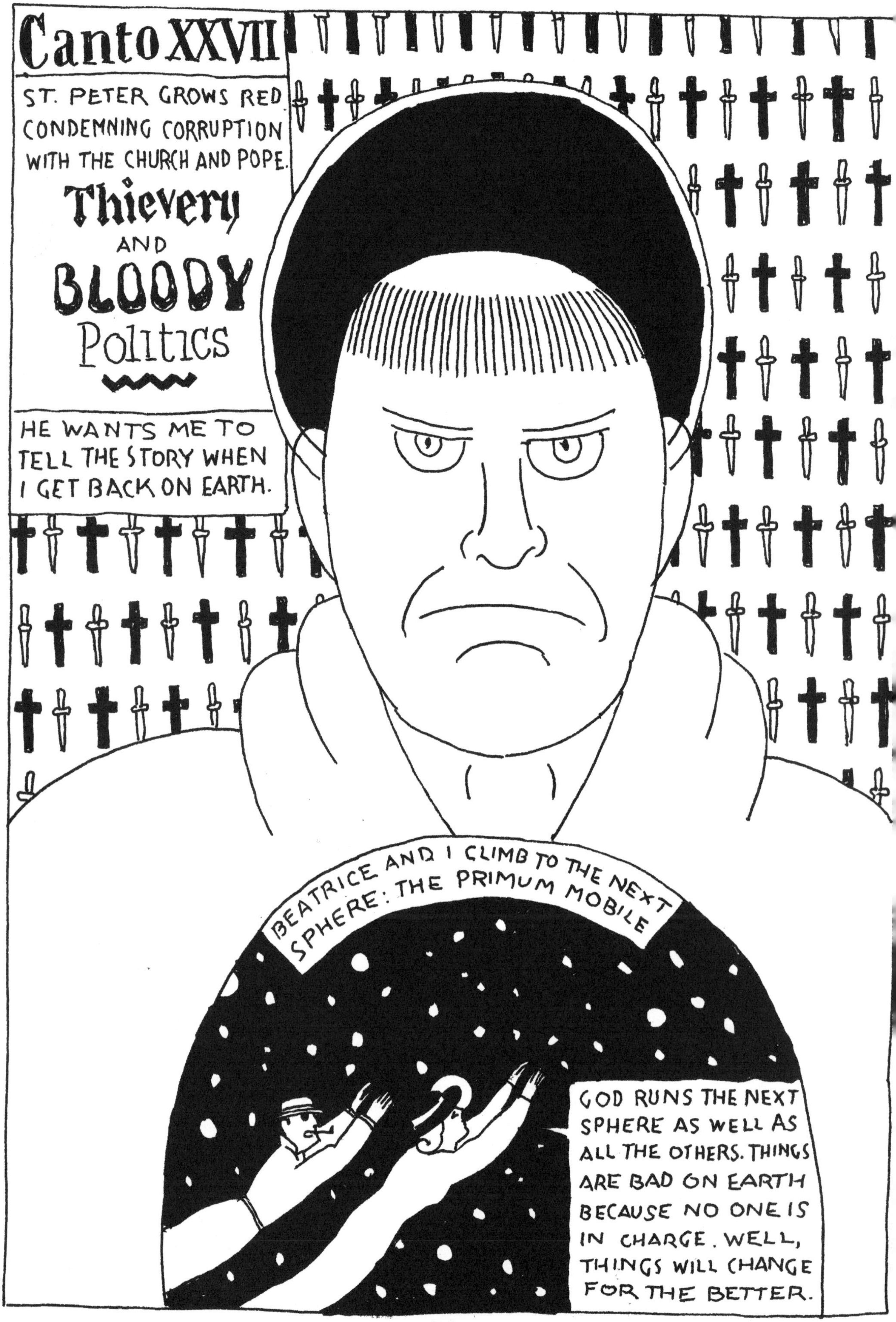
Canto XXVII
ST. PETER GROWS RED CONDEMNING CORRUPTION WITH THE CHURCH AND POPE.
Thievery AND BLOODY Politics
HE WANTS ME TO TELL THE STORY WHEN I GET BACK ON EARTH.
BEATRICE AND I CLIMB TO THE NEXT SPHERE: THE PRIMUM MOBILE
GOD RUNS THE NEXT SPHERE AS WELL AS ALL THE OTHERS. THINGS ARE BAD ON EARTH BECAUSE NO ONE IS IN CHARGE. WELL, THINGS WILL CHANGE FOR THE BETTER.

CANTO XXVIII

THE NINTH SPHERE: THE PRIMUM MOBILE

BEATRICE AND I SEE GOD AS A POINT OF LIGHT CIRCLED BY NINE GLOWING CIRCLES OF ANGELS. THE MOST POWERFUL ANGELS ARE CLOSEST TO GOD WHILE THEY REPRESENT THE SMALLEST SPHERE. BEATRICE NAMES THE HIERARCHY OF THE ANGELS.

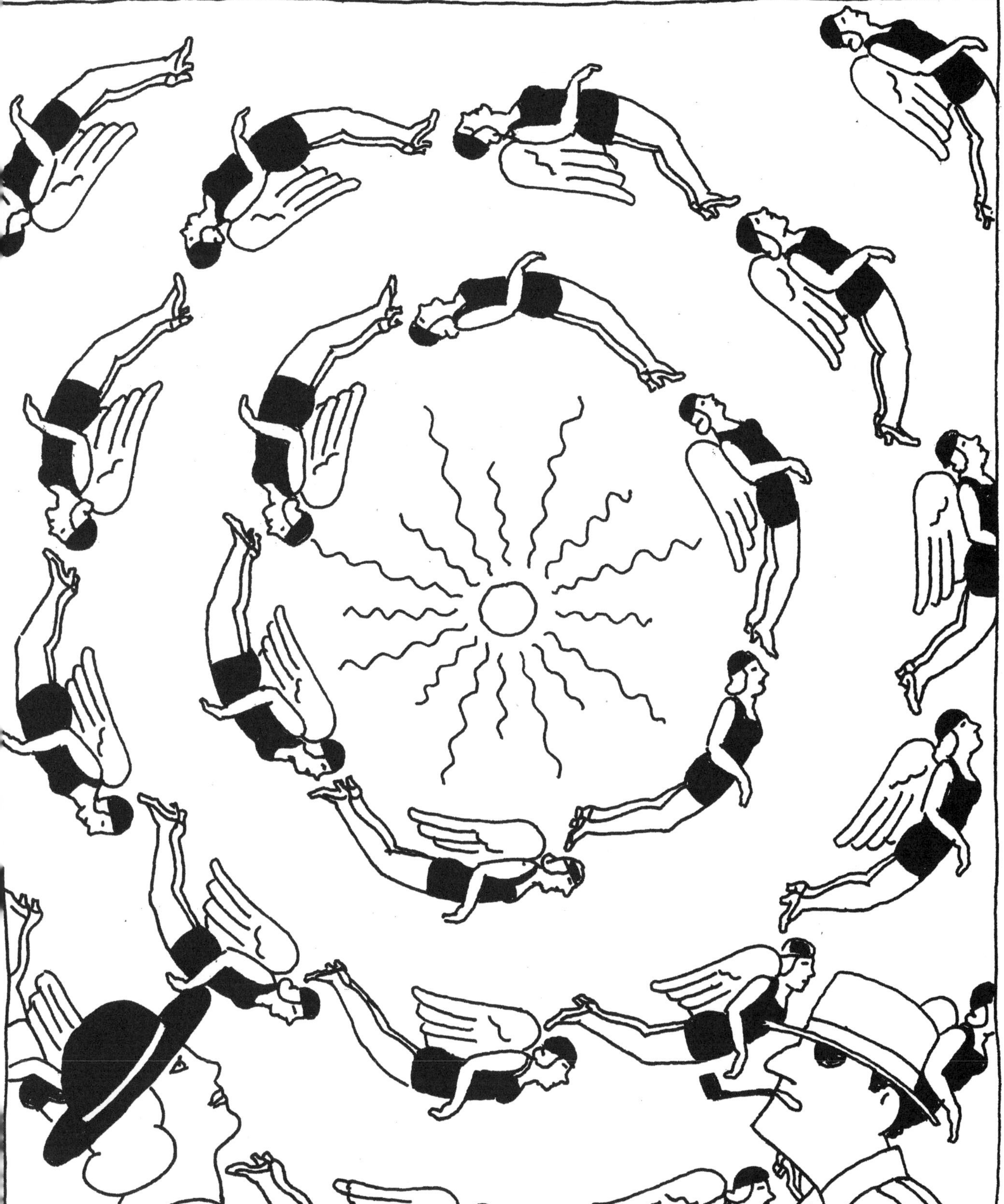

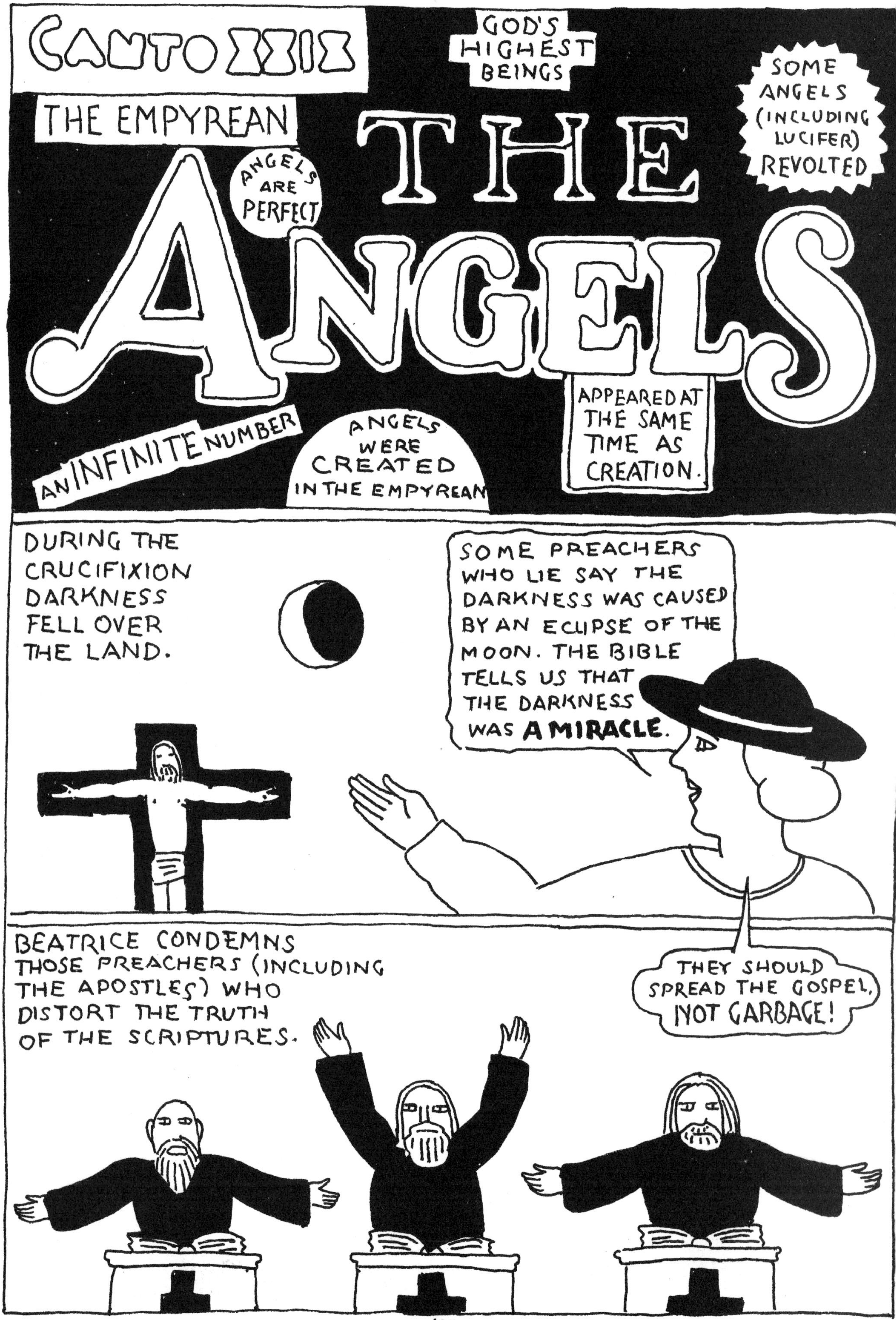
CANTO XXIX
THE EMPYREAN
GOD'S HIGHEST BEINGS
THE ANGELS
ANGELS ARE PERFECT
SOME ANGELS (INCLUDING LUCIFER) REVOLTED
AN INFINITE NUMBER
ANGELS WERE CREATED IN THE EMPYREAN
APPEARED AT THE SAME TIME AS CREATION.
DURING THE CRUCIFIXION DARKNESS FELL OVER THE LAND.
SOME PREACHERS WHO LIE SAY THE DARKNESS WAS CAUSED BY AN ECLIPSE OF THE MOON. THE BIBLE TELLS US THAT THE DARKNESS WAS **A MIRACLE**.
BEATRICE CONDEMNS THOSE PREACHERS (INCLUDING THE APOSTLES) WHO DISTORT THE TRUTH OF THE SCRIPTURES.
THEY SHOULD SPREAD THE GOSPEL, NOT GARBAGE!

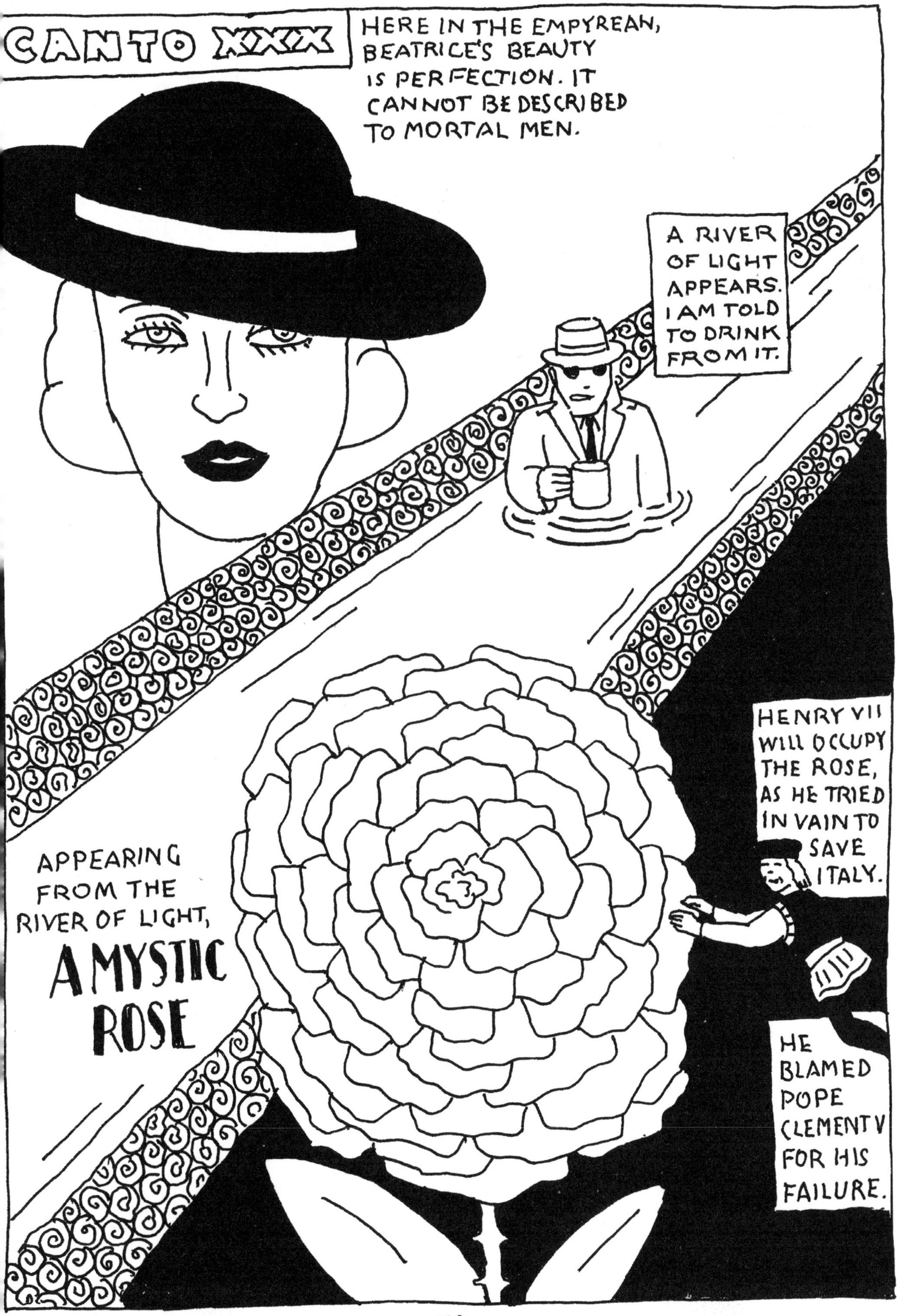

CANTO XXX
HERE IN THE EMPYREAN, BEATRICE'S BEAUTY IS PERFECTION. IT CANNOT BE DESCRIBED TO MORTAL MEN.
A RIVER OF LIGHT APPEARS. I AM TOLD TO DRINK FROM IT.
APPEARING FROM THE RIVER OF LIGHT,
A MYSTIC ROSE
HENRY VII WILL OCCUPY THE ROSE, AS HE TRIED IN VAIN TO SAVE ITALY.
HE BLAMED POPE CLEMENT V FOR HIS FAILURE.

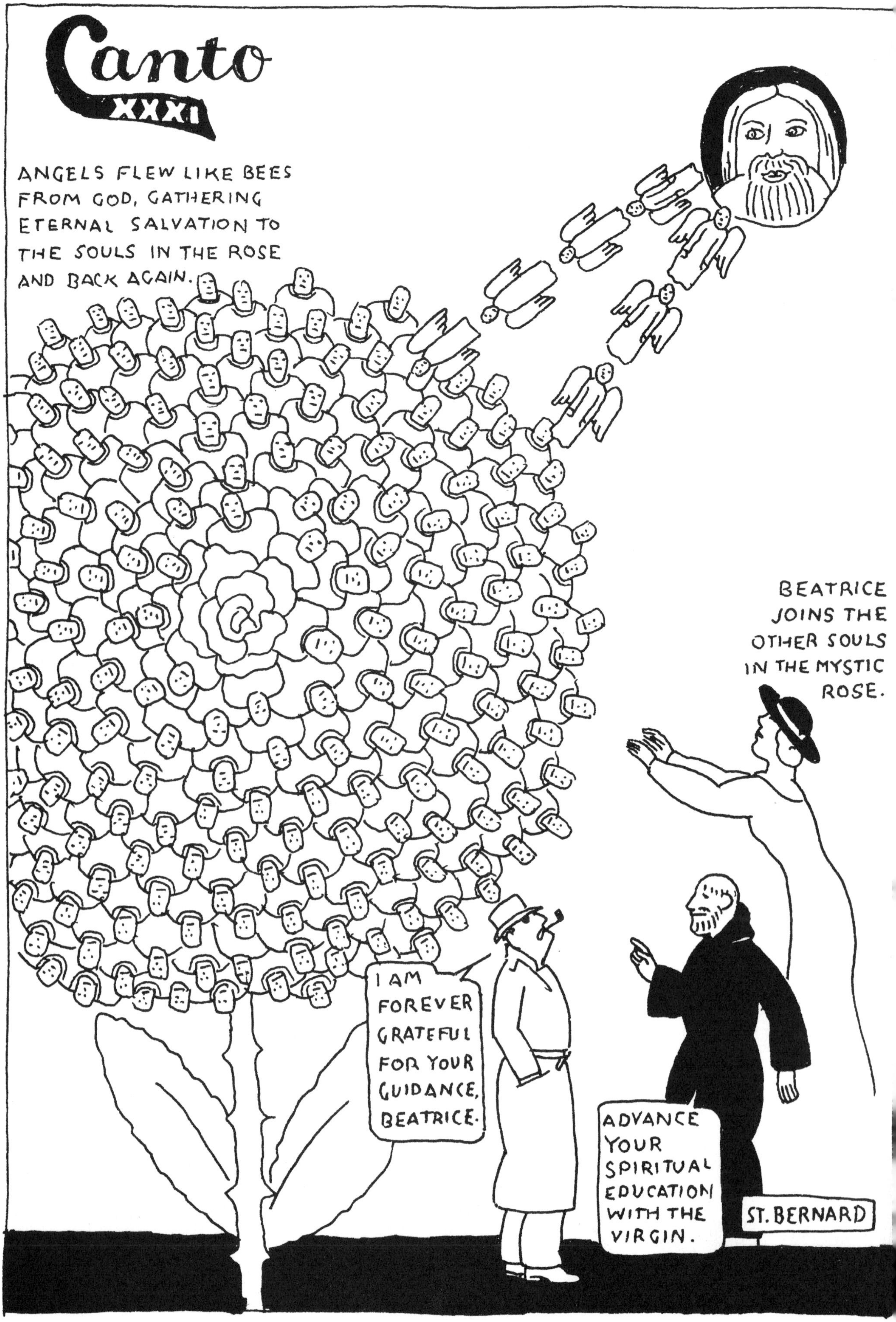
Canto XXXI
ANGELS FLEW LIKE BEES FROM GOD, GATHERING ETERNAL SALVATION TO THE SOULS IN THE ROSE AND BACK AGAIN.
BEATRICE JOINS THE OTHER SOULS IN THE MYSTIC ROSE.
I AM FOREVER GRATEFUL FOR YOUR GUIDANCE, BEATRICE.
ADVANCE YOUR SPIRITUAL EDUCATION WITH THE VIRGIN.
ST. BERNARD

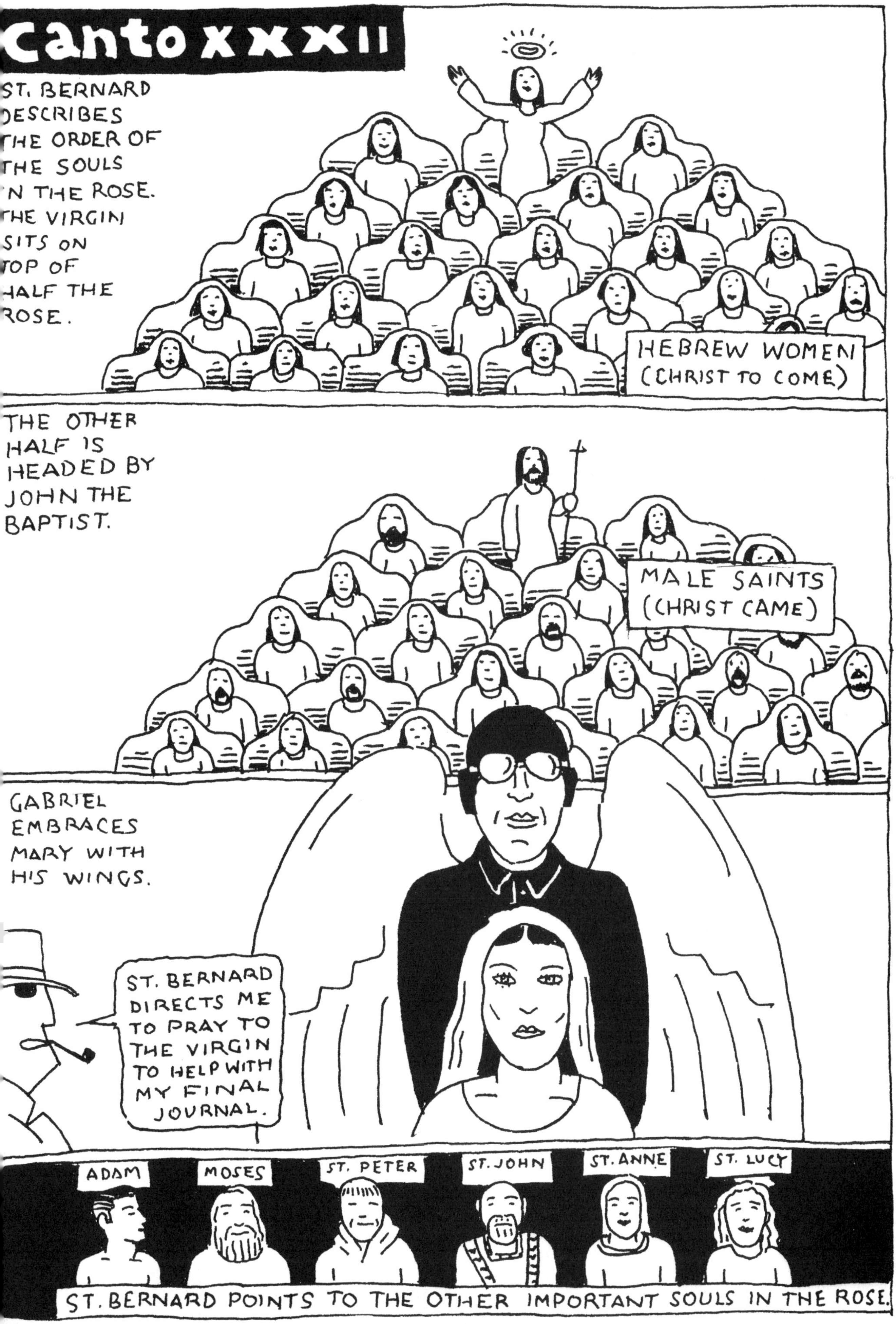

Canto XXXII
ST. BERNARD DESCRIBES THE ORDER OF THE SOULS IN THE ROSE. THE VIRGIN SITS ON TOP OF HALF THE ROSE.
HEBREW WOMEN (CHRIST TO COME)
THE OTHER HALF IS HEADED BY JOHN THE BAPTIST.
MALE SAINTS (CHRIST CAME)
GABRIEL EMBRACES MARY WITH HIS WINGS.
ST. BERNARD DIRECTS ME TO PRAY TO THE VIRGIN TO HELP WITH MY FINAL JOURNAL.
ADAM
MOSES
ST. PETER
ST. JOHN
ST. ANNE
ST. LUCY
ST. BERNARD POINTS TO THE OTHER IMPORTANT SOULS IN THE ROSE.

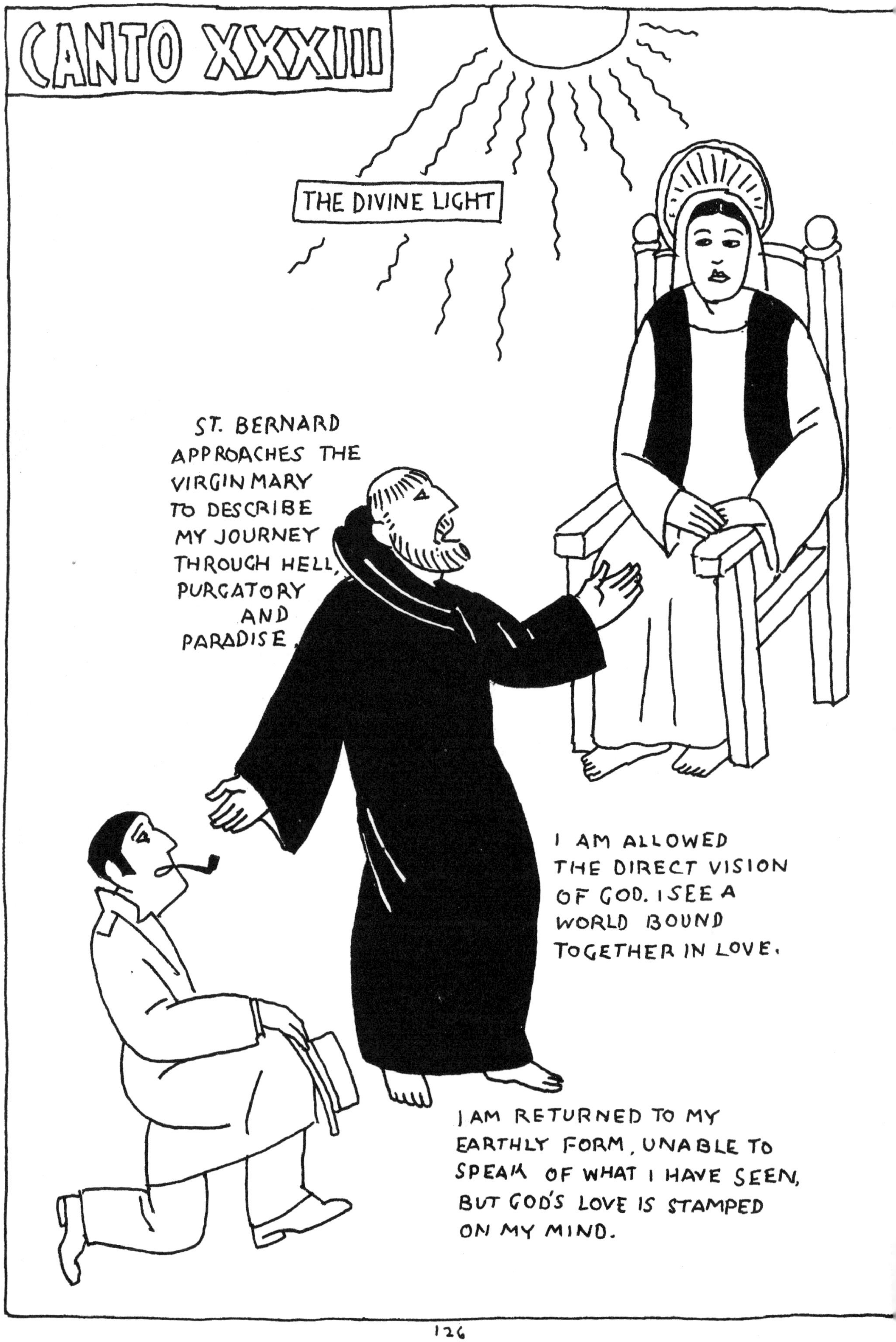
CANTO XXXIII
THE DIVINE LIGHT
ST. BERNARD APPROACHES THE VIRGIN MARY TO DESCRIBE MY JOURNEY THROUGH HELL, PURGATORY AND PARADISE.
I AM ALLOWED THE DIRECT VISION OF GOD. I SEE A WORLD BOUND TOGETHER IN LOVE.
I AM RETURNED TO MY EARTHLY FORM, UNABLE TO SPEAK OF WHAT I HAVE SEEN, BUT GOD'S LOVE IS STAMPED ON MY MIND.

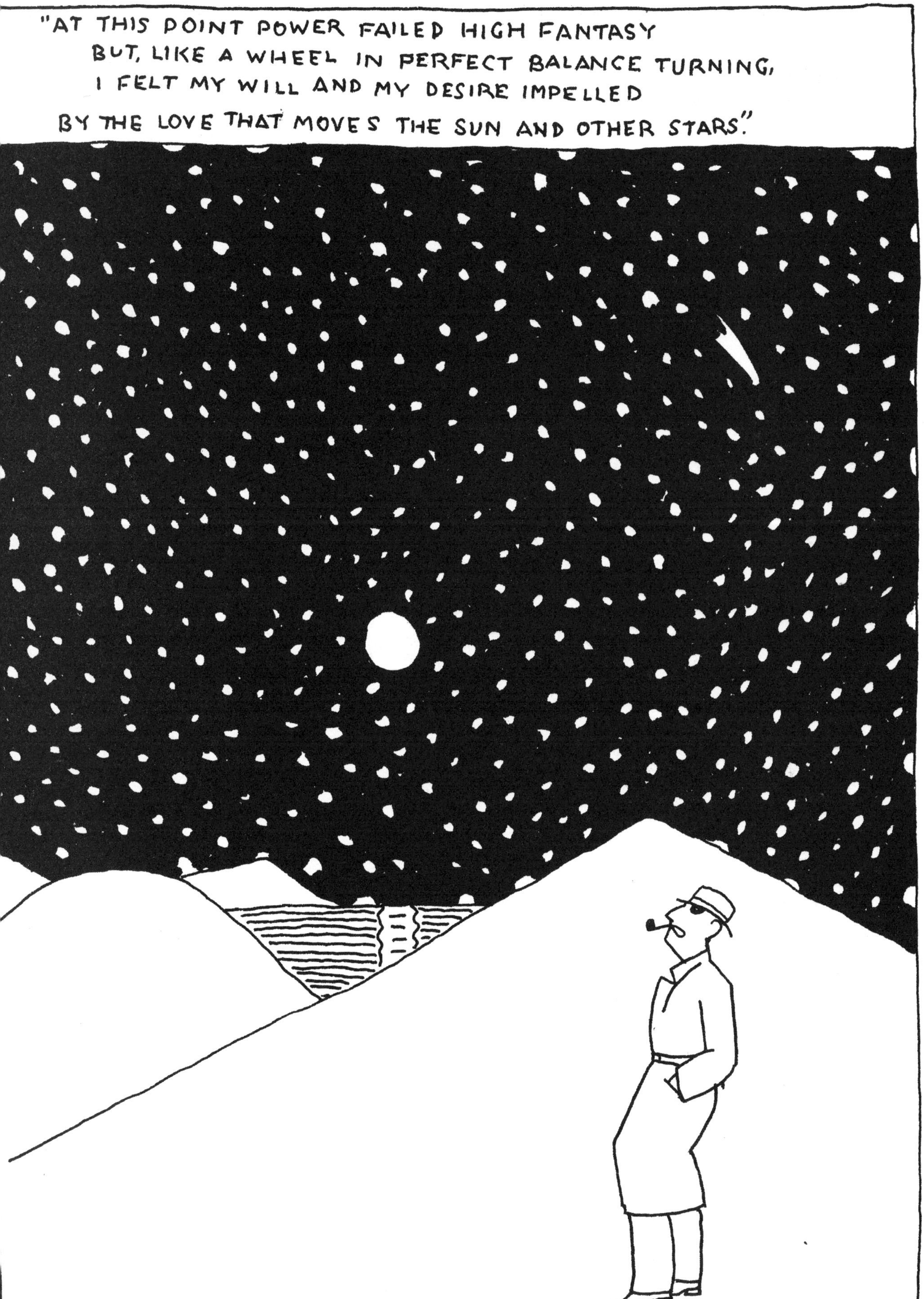
"AT THIS POINT POWER FAILED HIGH FANTASY
BUT, LIKE A WHEEL IN PERFECT BALANCE TURNING,
I FELT MY WILL AND MY DESIRE IMPELLED
BY THE LOVE THAT MOVES THE SUN AND OTHER STARS."

A NOTE ON THE AUTHOR

SEYMOUR CHWAST'S AWARD-WINNING WORK
HAS INFLUENCED TWO GENERATIONS OF
DESIGNERS AND ILLUSTRATORS.

HE COFOUNDED PUSH PIN STUDIOS, WHICH
RAPIDLY GAINED AN INTERNATIONAL REPUTATION
FOR INNOVATIVE DESIGN AND ILLUSTRATION.
PUSH PIN'S VISUAL LANGUAGE (WHICH REFERENCED
CULTURE AND LITERATURE) AROSE FROM ITS
PASSION FOR HISTORICAL DESIGN MOVEMENTS
AND HELPED REVOLUTIONIZE THE WAY PEOPLE
LOOK AT DESIGN.

CHWAST IS A RECIPIENT OF THE A.I.G.A.
MEDAL, WAS INDUCTED INTO THE ART DIRECTORS
HALL OF FAME, AND HAS AN HONORARY PhD
IN FINE ART FROM THE PARSONS SCHOOL OF
DESIGN. HIS WORK IS IN THE COLLECTION OF THE
MUSEUM OF MODERN ART, THE METROPOLITAN
MUSEUM OF ART, AND HAS BEEN COLLECTED IN
THE LEFT-HANDED DESIGNER AND SEYMOUR:
THE OBSESSIVE IMAGES OF SEYMOUR CHWAST.

HE LIVES IN NEW YORK WITH HIS WIFE,
THE GRAPHIC DESIGNER PAULA SCHER.

THIS IS HIS FIRST GRAPHIC NOVEL.

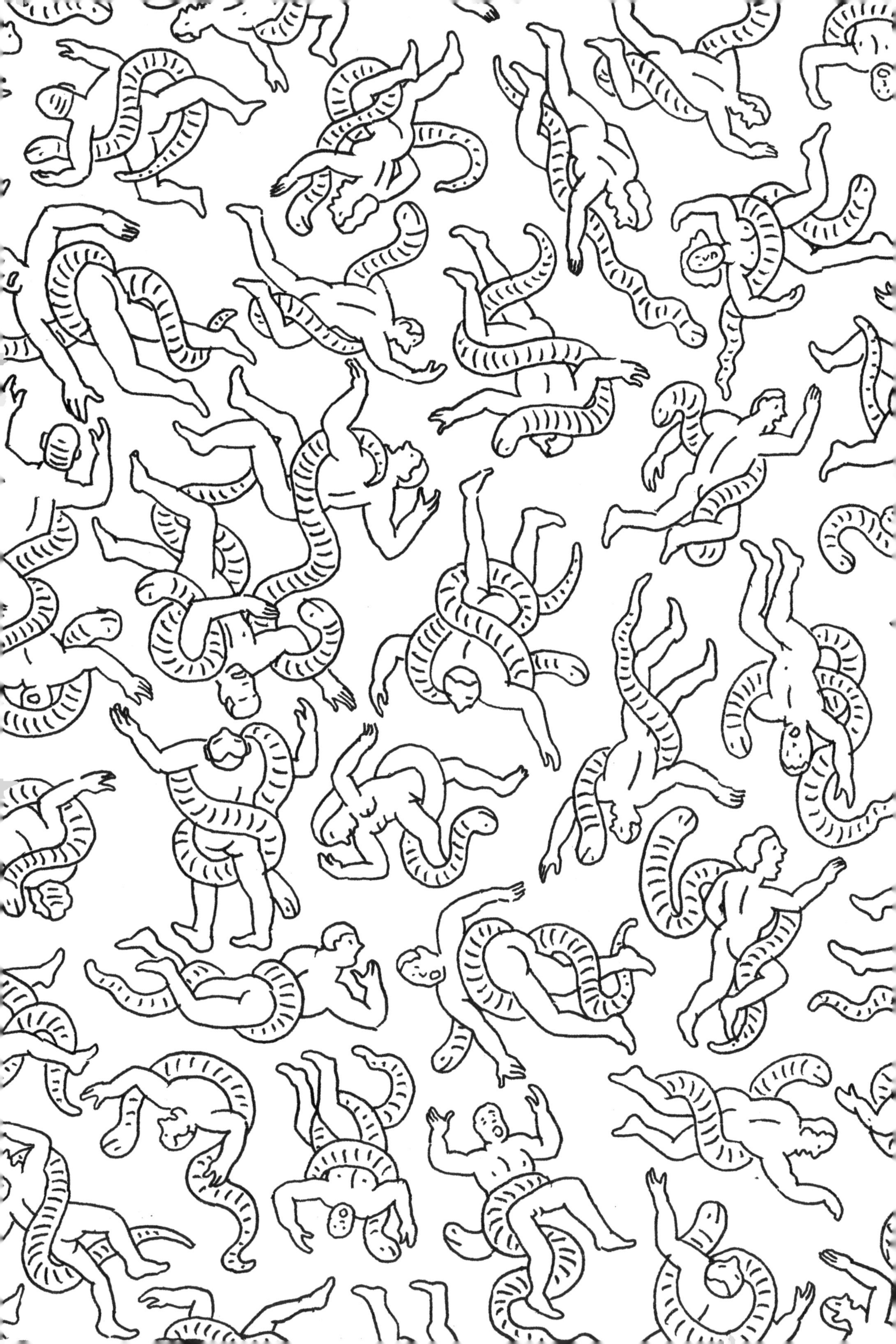

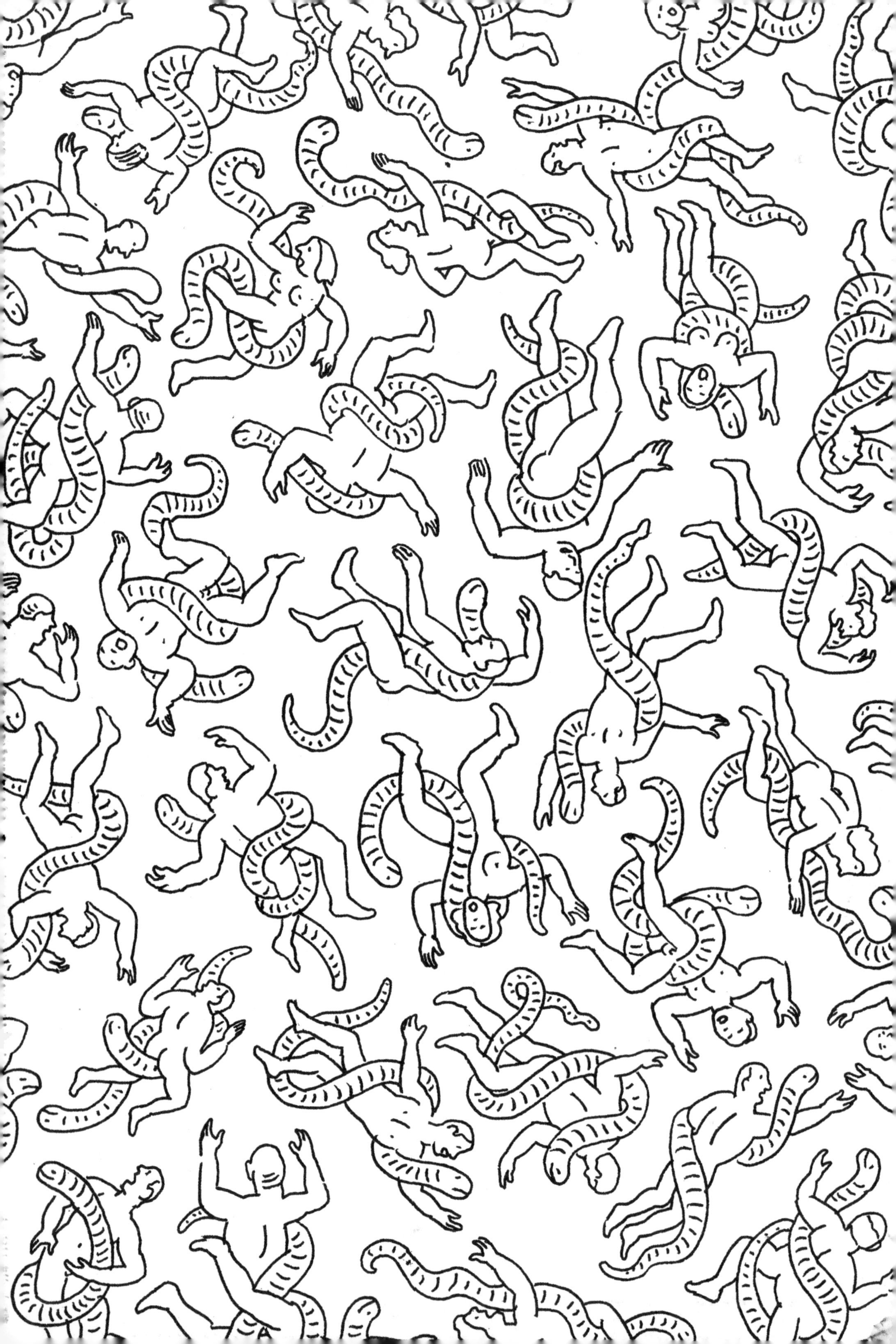